DIAGNOSIS & RELIABLE DESIGN OF DIGITAL SYSTEMS

DIGITAL SYSTEM DESIGN SERIES

ARTHUR D. FRIEDMAN, *Editor*
University of Southern California

BREUER   *Digital System Design Automation:*
Languages, Simulation & Data Base
BREUER and FRIEDMAN   *Diagnosis & Reliable Design of*
Digital Systems
VANCLEEMPUT   *Computer Aided Design of Digital Systems —*
A Bibliography
VANCLEEMPUT   *1975-76 Update Computer Aided Design of Digital*
Systems — A Bibliography
FRIEDMAN   *Logical Design of Digital Systems*
FRIEDMAN and MENON   *Theory & Design of Switching Circuits*

Also of interest
Journal of Design Automation & Fault Tolerant Computing

DIAGNOSIS &
RELIABLE DESIGN
OF DIGITAL SYSTEMS

MELVIN A. BREUER, *University of Southern California*
ARTHUR D. FRIEDMAN, *University of Southern California*

COMPUTER SCIENCE PRESS, INC.

Computer Science Press, Inc.
4566 Poe Avenue
Woodland Hills, California 91364

Library of Congress Cataloging in Publication Data

Breuer, Melvin A.
    Diagnosis & reliable design of digital systems.

    (Digital system design series)
    Includes bibliographies and index.
    1. Digital electronics.   2. Electronic
apparatus and appliances — Testing.   3. Electronic
circuit design.   I. Friedman, Arthur D., joint
author.   II. Title.   III. Series.
TK7868.D5B73   621.3815   76-19081
ISBN 0-914894-57-9

PREFACE

Since the early 1960's there has developed a great interest, both in industry and academia, in the subjects of maintenance and reliability of digital systems. The increased complexity of current systems makes this interest well justified. Costs associated with the necessity to maintain such systems represent a substantial and growing percentage of total system costs. In this book we consider many of the problems associated with diagnosing failures in digital systems, locating the source of such failures, and the related problem of design of ultra reliable systems — systems which do not fail despite the presence of physical defects (*fault tolerance*), systems which diagnose their own failures (*self checking*), and systems which are easily tested. Although many of the problems considered are *in theory* intractable, in practice most have solution procedures which are practical and effective. The book emphasizes these procedures and when available presents several procedures for each problem.

With the increased interest in this subject area courses have been developed at many universities. This book is intended as a text for such courses and can also be used for self study by the practicing engineer familiar with digital circuits and systems. The first chapter is an introduction to the subject matter and notation of the book. The next two chapters consider in detail the problems associated with efficient detection and location of failures in combinational and sequential circuits respectively. Chapter 4 considers the subject of digital simulation, the most important tool of engineers concerned with digital system maintenance. The final chapter considers the problem of designing systems which are easily testable, self checking, or fault tolerant. It emphasizes concepts rather than describing actual systems, and presents several general design procedures to achieve these goals. Each chapter contains examples as well as unsolved homework problems.

We would like to thank many of our friends and colleagues for their helpful suggestions. These include J. P. Hayes and Y. Levendel of U.S.C., N. Benowitz of Hughes Aircraft, and S. Chappell of Bell Telephone Laboratories.

Melvin A. Breuer
Arthur D. Friedman

CONTENTS

CHAPTER 3   TEST GENERATION FOR SEQUENTIAL CIRCUITS

Chapter 1

INTRODUCTION

With the increased complexity of current digital systems, reliability considerations have become increasingly important. Being physical devices, digital circuits are subject to failure. Although current technologies employed to construct digital systems are more reliable than earlier technologies, to a great extent the resulting decrease in the failure rate of individual components has been offset by the increased complexity of today's circuits. We will define a fault as any change in a system which causes it to behave differently from the original system. In digital systems, typical maintenance goals deal with the rapid detection, location, and repair of any system faults.

In many digital systems involving real-time processes, such as telephone switching networks and aircraft or spacecraft flight controls, it is desirable to continuously monitor, exercise and test the system in order to determine whether the system is performing as desired. Such monitoring may enable automatic detection of failures via periodic testing or through the use of codes and checking circuits (e.g. self-testing or self-checking circuits), or may enable continuous operation under failure conditions (i.e., *fault tolerance*) and automatic repair via switching networks. In such systems special hardware and software must be incorporated in the system to obtain these reliability objectives. In this book we will consider problems associated with testing of digital systems to detect and locate faults, as well as theoretical and practical design techniques of relevance to the development of highly reliable digital systems.

Subjects to be considered include (1) the problem of test generation (i.e., diagnostic program development) for detection and location of faults in digital circuits, (2) the use of digital simulation as a diagnostic tool for test generation and verification of the initial system design, and (3) the design of self checking and fault tolerant systems.

A problem related to that of detection of failures is that of verification of initial circuit design. Since design errors cannot reasonably be restricted to

1

as great an extent as physical circuit faults, the verification problem is much more difficult. One theoretical approach to this problem involves a form of functional testing. An example of this form of testing, called *checking sequences*, will also be considered.

In this chapter we will present the necessary background information. Section 1.1 briefly reviews the fundamental concepts of digital circuits including combinational circuits, synchronous sequential circuits and asynchronous sequential circuits. Section 1.2 discusses various types of physical faults in digital technologies and current testing procedures. The concept of logical fault models is introduced in Section 1.3 and models for the logical faults to be considered herein are developed.

1.1   DIGITAL CIRCUITS

Digital circuits are characterized by the feature that steady state circuit signals can assume only one of two values. Such circuits may be studied at the circuit level or the logic level. At the circuit level, one is interested in analysis and synthesis in terms of electrical components such as transistors, diodes, resistors, etc., as well as voltages, currents, wave shapes, etc. At the logical level the circuit is considered to consist of elements whose inputs and outputs assume only the values denoted by 0 and 1. The logical behavior of an element can be completely described by specifying the value of its output for each possible combination of input values. In this book we will be interested in logical level analysis and synthesis of digital circuits.

1.1.1   Combinational Circuits

The basic elements of combinational circuits are called *gates*. The operation of a gate can be described by specifying the value of its output for every possible combination of input values. Some common gate types and their representations are shown in Figure 1.1(a). A diode-transistor realization of a NAND gate is shown in Figure 1.1(b). As the gate name implies, the output of an AND gate is 1 if and only if all of its inputs are 1; the output of an OR gate is 1 if and only if any of its inputs are 1; and the output of an inverter is 1 if and only if its input is 0. A NAND (*Not AND*) gate has output 1 if and only if *any* of its inputs are 0 and a NOR (*Not OR*) gate has output 1 if and only if *all* of its inputs are 0.

The basic tool used in analyzing digital circuits is Boolean algebra with the operations $+$ and $\cdot$ corresponding to OR and AND, and inversion (complementation) being denoted by an overbar. If we use variable x_1 and x_2 to represent the inputs of an AND gate and z to represent its output,

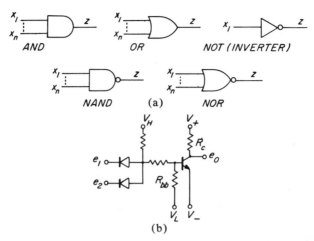

Figure 1.1 (a) Common Gate Types (b) NAND Gate Circuit

then $z = x_1 \cdot x_2$.[†] Similarly, the output of a 2-input OR gate is represented by $z = x_1 + x_2$ and the NOT gate output is represented by $z = \overline{x}$. The NAND and NOR gate outputs are represented by $z = \overline{x_1 x_2} = \overline{x}_1 + \overline{x}_2$ and $z = \overline{x_1 + x_2} = \overline{x}_1 \overline{x}_2$ respectively. It will be assumed that the reader is familiar with Boolean algebra.

Digital circuits can be classified as *combinational* or *sequential*. A combinational circuit consists of a collection of gates with no feedback loops[‡] (an *acyclic* circuit). Combinational circuits can be used to realize *combinational functions* whose present output values depend only on the present value of their input variables, and is independent of their previous values. A combinational function can be specified by a *truth table*, a Karnaugh map, or a listing of its 1-points. Figure 1.2 demonstrates these three forms for a 3-variable combinational function where the list of 1-points of Figure 1.2(c) is in cubical form with $-$'s used to indicate that the function will have the value 1 independent of the value of the corresponding variables.

Three important characteristics of a combinational logic circuit are *redundancy*, *fanout*, and *reconvergent fanout*. Redundancy refers to the concept that a circuit may function properly in the presence of certain faults.

[†]When unambiguous, product terms will be represented without the product sign(•).

[‡]A circuit is said to have feedback if there exists a path from the output of some gate G through a sequence of (zero or more) other gates terminating at the input to G.

x_1	x_2	x_3	f
0	0	0	0
0	0	1	0
0	1	0	1
0	1	1	0
1	0	0	1
1	0	1	0
1	1	0	1
1	1	1	1

(a)

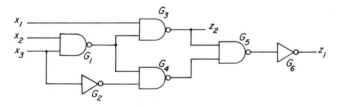

(b)

x_1	x_2	x_3
—	1	0
1	1	—
1	—	0

(c)

(d)

Figure 1.2 Forms for representing a combinational function $f(x_1,x_2,x_3)$ (a) Truth Table (b) Karnaugh map (c) Minimal covering of 1-points (d) Circuit realization

For certain classes of faults, the concept of redundancy can be shown to be equivalent to the presence of more components or lines than are actually required in order to produce the desired output function.

Fanout refers to the fact that a signal is used as an input to two or more other gates. Reconvergent fanout refers to the concept that there are two or more paths from a signal source to inputs (two or more) of the same gate. In Figure 1.3 we see that gate G_1 fans out to both G_3 and G_4, and input x_3 fans out to G_1 and G_2. There exists reconvergent fanout between G_1 and G_5 and between x_3 and G_4. Reconvergent fanout leads to problems in test generation and simulation due to the fact that a signal change at a

Figure 1.3 Circuit Demonstrating Reconvergent Fanout

source (output of a gate) can produce changes on several inputs to a gate, which, due to delays in the circuit, occur at different times.

1.1.2 Synchronous Sequential Circuits

A *sequential function* is a mapping whose output depends on both the present input as well as previous inputs. We associate with the function the concept of *memory* or *state* which represents pertinent information consource (output of a gate) can produce changes on several inputs to a gate, which, due to delays in the circuit, occur at different times.

The truth table representation used for combinational functions is inadequate for describing sequential functions. A finite state sequential function can be modeled as a *sequential machine* which receives inputs from a finite set of possible inputs, and produces outputs from a finite set of possible outputs. It has a finite number of *internal states* (or simply, states). The operation of a finite state sequential machine is as follows: if initially in some state q_i an input I_m is received, the machine goes to state q_j and produces an output z_k. The next state q_j and the output z_k are uniquely determined by the present state and input, and are only of interest at the discrete instants of time defined by an input sequence.

A *finite state* sequential machine can be represented by a *state table* which has a row corresponding to every internal state of the machine and a column corresponding to every possible input. The entry in row q_i and column I_m represents the next state and the output produced if I_m is applied when the machine is in state q_i. This entry will be denoted by $N(q_i,I_m)$, $Z(q_i,I_m)$. N and Z are called the *next state* and *output functions* of the machine.

An example of a state table is shown in Figure 1.4. This machine has four internal states labeled 1, 2, 3, 4, and has a binary input x with possible

	x	
	0	1
1	2,1	3,0
2	2,1	4,0
3	1,0	4,0
4	3,1	3,0

$N(q,I), Z(q,I)$

Figure 1.4 Example State Table

values $x = 0$ and $x = 1$, and a binary output z with possible values $z = 0$ and $z = 1$. The state table can be used to determine the output sequence generated by the application of any input sequence for any initial state. Thus the entry in row 1 and column 0 specifies that the input $x = 0$ applied to initial state 1 causes the machine to go to state 2 and generate an output $z = 1$. Similarly, starting in initial state 1, the input sequence 010 causes the machine to pass through the state sequence 243 and generate the output sequence 101.

In representing a sequential function in this way there is an inherent assumption of *synchronization* which is not explicitly represented by the state table. The inputs are synchronized in time with some timing sequence, $t(1), t(2), \ldots, t(n)$. At time $t(1)$ the input is sampled, the next state is entered and the next output is produced. At $t(2)$ this situation is repeated, etc.

In a circuit realization of a sequential function the inherent concept of synchronization is explicitly implemented by using an additional input, usually called a *clock* line (or simply clock). The occurrence of an event, such as $t(1)$, is represented to the circuit by some type of a signal transition on this line, usually referred to as a clock pulse. Since the sequential circuit must store or remember its state between events on the clock line, a bistable memory element, called a clocked flip-flop, is required. A clocked flip-flop can only change state upon receiving a clock pulse. These clock pulses are assumed to occur in synchronization with the input thus resulting in the discrete behavior defined for a sequential function.

A synchronous sequential circuit can be schematically represented as shown in Figure 1.5.

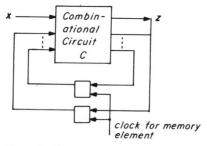

Figure 1.5 Canonical Form for a Synchronous Sequential Circuit

Flip-flops are usually represented as having two outputs, y and $\bar{y}$, and the two stable states ($y = 0$, $\bar{y} = 1$) and ($y = 1$, $\bar{y} = 0$). Several different types of flip-flops will be used in this book. The *SR* flip-flop consists of a latch made up of two cross-connected NAND gates,* and input clocking (Figure 1.6). The flip-flop becomes set ($y = 1$, $\bar{y} = 0$) if the input excitations (at the time of a clock pulse) are $S = 1$, $R = 0$ and becomes reset ($y = 0$, $\bar{y} = 1$) if $R = 1$, $S = 0$. If $S = R = 0$, the flip-flop remains stable in its present state and hence exhibits memory. The input condition $S = R = 1$ is prohibited (indicated by the unspecified entries in the state table), since this excitation would cause both outputs to be 0. Also if the inputs are changed from $S = R = 1$ to $S = R = 0$, the next state is unpredictable, since it will depend on the exact order in which y and $\bar{y}$ change.

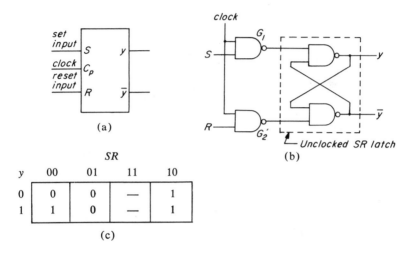

		SR			
y		00	01	11	10
0		0	0	—	1
1		1	0	—	1

(c)

Figure 1.6 Three representations for a SR Flip-Flop (a) Functional representation (b) Circuit representation (c) State table

Note that the circuit realization of a flip-flop element consists of basic gate elements, but contains feedback, and hence is not a combinational circuit. The feedback is necessary in order for the element to have memory.

The *characteristic equation* of a flip-flop specifies the next state (Y) of the element as a function of its present state y and the input excitations. For an SR flip-flop, utilizing the fact that $S = R = 1$ is a prohibited input, the characteristic equation is $Y = S + \bar{R}y$. Other commonly utilized flip-flops are shown in Figure 1.7.

The JK flip-flop operates identically to the SR flip-flop (where J corresponds to S and K to R), except for the fact that the input $J = K = 1$ is

*A latch consisting of cross-connected NOR gates behaves in a similar manner.

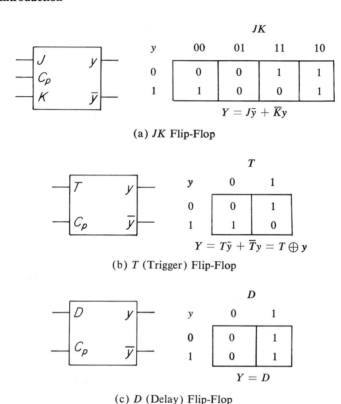

(a) JK Flip-Flop

(b) T (Trigger) Flip-Flop

(c) D (Delay) Flip-Flop

Figure 1.7   Three Types of Flip-Flops

permitted and results in the device changing state, i.e., if the present state is $y = 1, \bar{y} = 0$ the state becomes $y = 0, \bar{y} = 1$ and vice versa. The T flip-flop operates like a JK flip-flop if inputs J and K are always identical. If $T = 0$, the device remains in its present state, and if $T = 1$ the device changes state. The D flip-flop behaves like an SR flip-flop under the restrictions $S = \bar{R}$. The state of this device is always equal to the previous·value of its input excitation D.

1.1.3   Asynchronous Sequential Circuits

Sequential circuits can also be designed without clocks. Such circuits are commonly called *asynchronous*. An asynchronous sequential circuit can be schematically represented as shown in Figure 1.8. Note that there may exist some feedback paths which do not contain memory elements. Some memory elements may be clocked while others are unclocked. The absence of a synchronizing clock signal in every feedback path creates many problems which require the use of special design procedures to solve.

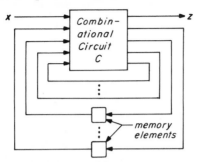

Figure 1.8   Canonical Form for an Asynchronous Circuit

The behavior of an asynchronous sequential circuit can be defined by a *flow table* which is very similar to the synchronous machine state table. Due to the absence of clock pulses, inputs and outputs are assumed to be level signals, rather than pulse signals,* and transitions may involve a sequence of state changes, due to a signal input change to I_j, until a stable configuration is reached, denoted by the condition $N(q_i, I_j) = q_i$. Such stable configurations are circled in the flow table. Figure 1.9 shows a flow table for an asynchronous machine.

$x_1 x_2$

	00	01	11	10	y_1	y_2	y_3
1	①,0	5 ,1	2 ,0	①,0	0	0	0
2	1 ,0	②,0	②,0	5 ,1	0	1	1
3	③,1	2 ,0	4 ,0	③,0	1	1	1
4	3 ,1	5 ,1	④,0	④,0	1	0	0
5	3 ,1	⑤,1	4 ,0	⑤,1	1	0	1

Figure 1.9   Asynchronous Machine Flow Table and Corresponding State Assignment

---

*In synchronous circuits inputs can effectively be treated as pulses since memory elements can only change state during a clock pulse.

Here, we see that if the circuit is in stable state 1 under input $x_1 = x_2$ $= 0$, denoted by $(1,00)$ and the input x_2 changes to 1, the circuit should go to stable state 5, and the total state/input configuration is denoted by $(5,01)$. In the circuit realization corresponding to a flow table, the internal states are realized by signal values on the feedback lines. In Figure 1.9 we have indicated the coding for signals y_1, y_2, y_3, used to represent the five states of this table.

Hazards and Races

One of the most common causes of circuit malfunction is due to circuit delays. Delay is an inherent property of all circuit elements and interconnections. There are several types of delay which may be present in a circuit, and they will be dealt with in more detail in Chapter 4. In this section we will consider only *pure delay* elements, i.e. elements whose output value at time t is equal to its input value at time $(t - \Delta)$.

In combinational circuits one form of malfunction caused by delays associated with elements is referred to as a *hazard*. Consider the combinational circuit of Figure 1.10(a) and assume that gates G_1, G_2, and G_3 have delays Δ_1, Δ_2, Δ_3 associated with them.

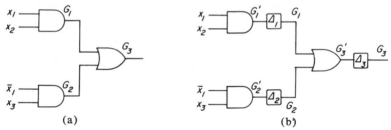

(a)   (b)

Figure 1.10   Simple Model for Gate Delays

We represent these delays as shown in Figure 1.10(b), where G_1', G_2', and G_3' are assumed to have 0-delay.

Suppose that the inputs at some time t are $x_1 = x_2 = x_3 = 1$ and at time $t_0 > t$, x_1 changes to 0. Ideally, the output of the circuit should be 1 both before and after the change. However, if $\Delta_1 < \Delta_2$, even by a very small amount ϵ, the output may contain a 0-pulse as shown in Figure 1.11 (which illustrates the signals x_1, G_1, G_2, and G_3 as functions of time).

We see that due to delays a combinational circuit may produce a transient error or spike. This is called a *hazard*.* Such an error, if applied

---

*A hazard indicates the *possibility* of a pulse being produced. However under actual delay conditions it is possible that no pulse will be produced. Hence this represents a worst case analysis.

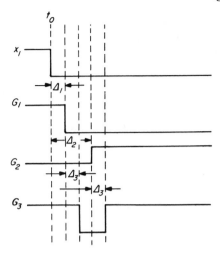

Figure 1.11   Generation of a Hazard at the Output of G_3

to the input of a flip-flop, may result in a permanent incorrect state. In synchronous circuits this possibility is eliminated by ensuring that no clock pulse occurs until the combinational circuit stabilizes. Thus transient excitations will be masked and will not affect the operation of the circuit.

In asynchronous circuits hazards cannot be masked in this way and they must be eliminated by proper design, or the circuit must be designed to operate properly in spite of the presence of transients caused by hazards.

Several different types of hazards can be defined. *Static hazards* involve signals which should remain stable. Thus a *static 0-hazard* produces a 1-pulse in a stable 0 signal, and a *static 1-hazard* produces a 0-pulse in a stable 1 signal. *Dynamic hazards* are hazards associated with signals which are supposed to change value. Thus a *dynamic 1-hazard* is the presence of the sequence $0 \rightarrow 1 \rightarrow 0 \rightarrow 1$ in a signal which was supposed to change from 0 to 1, and a *dynamic 0-hazard* is the presence of the sequence $1 \rightarrow 0 \rightarrow 1 \rightarrow 0$ in a signal which was supposed to change from 1 to 0. That is, the signal changes value three or more times when it is supposed to change value only once. By proper design it is possible to eliminate all hazards in a combinational circuit caused by the change of a *single* input variable. Thus the circuit of Figure 1.10(a) can be redesigned as shown in Figure 1.12 and all transitions involving single input variable changes are free of hazards. However it may be impossible to eliminate all hazards caused by the change of *several* input variables. For the function f shown in the Karnaugh map of Figure 1.13, there will be a static hazard associ-

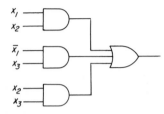

Figure 1.12   Hazard Free Realization

ated with the transition $(x_1,x_2,x_3) = (0,0,0) \rightarrow (0,1,1)$ in any circuit realizing f. Such hazards which cannot be eliminated are called *function hazards*, while those which can be eliminated are called *logic hazards*.

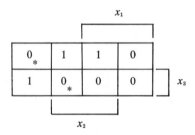

Figure 1.13   Combinational Function f Having a Function Hazard

Due to the absence of clock pulses, signals which are intended to change concurrently cannot be assumed to change in synchronism. The concurrent change of several signals is called a *race*. For a race condition, the behavior of the circuit may depend on the actual order in which the signals change. For this reason asynchronous circuits are usually restricted to transitions produced by changing a single binary input variable. State assignments* must also be restricted to ensure proper behavior. As an example, consider the state assignment shown in Figure 1.9. For the transition $(2,01) \rightarrow (1,00)$ both y_2 and y_3 change during the transition, thus creating a race condition. If y_2 changes first the state variable set assumes value $(0,0,1)$, while if y_3 changes first the state variable set assumes value $(0,1,0)$. Since neither of

---

*Each state of an asynchronous machine corresponds to a unique assignment of signal values on the feedback lines of the circuit. This assignment is called the *state assignment*.

these codings have been assigned to any other state it is possible to design the circuit so that for both of these possibilities the transition is successfully completed. Such a race condition is called a *noncritical race*. For the transition $(2,11) \rightarrow (5,10)$ both y_1 and y_2 change. If y_1 changes first the state variable set assumes value $(1,1,1)$. However this value has been assigned to state 3. For this case the transition to state 5 may not be successfully completed. In this case the race is called a *critical race*.

The concepts of hazards and races are intimately related. Referring to Figure 1.8, a critical race defines a multiple input change to the state variable combinational circuit excitation logic C, which causes a function hazard in C. A noncritical race defines a multiple input change which does not cause a function hazard in C.

The delay associated with gates and lines is called *stray delay* and it is (conservatively) assumed that this delay may vary greatly from element to element. Due to the variance in stray delay associated with different circuit elements, it is possible for the change of an input variable x_1 to cause a state variable y_j to change value, and for some gates within C to sense the y_j change before they sense the x_i change. In effect a race between x_i and y_j occurs which may cause a malfunction. Such a race may be "fixed" by inserting a delay element in the feedback loop corresponding to y_j. The inserted delay element is assumed to have much greater delay than any of the stray delays in C. The necessity for such delays can be ascertained from the flow table and is referred to as an *essential hazard*. The reader who is interested in more detailed information on asynchronous circuit properties is referred to [6].

Complex Flip-Flops

In order to ensure against incorrect circuit operation due either to stray delays in the circuit, especially on the clock line, or due to variances in the width of the clock pulse, flip-flops more complex than those previously discussed are often used. One such device is called a *master-slave flip-flop* and essentially consists of two flip-flops connected in series with complementary enabling signals. Figure 1.14 shows the functional representation and circuit diagram for an SR master-slave flip-flop having preset (P) and clear (C) signals. S and R are said to be clocked inputs. When the clock is high ($C_P = 1$) the first (master) latch is enabled and takes a value dependent on the logic values of S and R. When the clock changes to $C_P = 0$, the master is disabled and hence remains stable and the contents of the master is gated to the second (slave) latch, at which time the outputs may change.

In Figure 1.14(b) the heavy lines indicate the additional connections required to implement the asynchronous preset (P) and clear (C) inputs. Applying a 0 to either of these inputs will set or reset the flip-flop, independent of R, S, and C_P.

A JK master-slave flip-flop can be obtained from an RS flip-flop by connecting the output $\bar{y}$ to the input of G_1, and the output y to the input of G_2, as shown by the dotted connections in Figure 1.14(b).

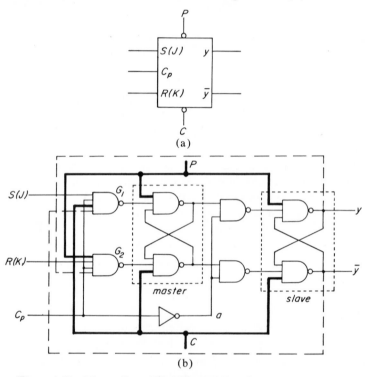

Figure 1.14   Master-Slave Flip-Flops (a) Functional representation (b) Circuit diagram

If we consider the clocked SR master-slave flip-flop without preset and clear inputs to be a 3-input 2-output device, then it becomes a rather complex asynchronous circuit. If hazards or multiple input changes occur at its input leads, then indeterminant operation is likely. Under fault conditions the operation of such a flip-flop is even more complex. Note that a single internal fault can cause incorrect operation of either the master or the slave, or both, and that both outputs may appear to be incorrect.

1.2 PHYSICAL FAULTS AND TESTING

In this section we will discuss the basic concepts relevant to faults and tests, and describe some types of faults which occur in different technologies, such as integrated circuits, and types of testing procedures which are used for detecting and locating these faults.

In its most general sense testing consists of applying a sequence of inputs to a circuit, observing the output sequence, and comparing it with a precomputed "expected" output sequence. Any discrepancy is said to constitute an error, the cause of which is said to be a *physical fault*. Faults can be classified as *logical* or *parametric*. A logical fault is one which causes the logic function of a circuit element (or elements) or an input signal to be changed to some other function. A typical logical fault which is frequently considered is for some circuit signal to become fixed at a constant value, say logical one, in which case the signal is said to be stuck-at-one (*s-a-1*), or logical zero, in which case the signal is stuck-at-zero (*s-a-0*). For example, for a two-input *OR* gate with inputs x_1 and x_2, a *s-a-0* fault on the x_1 input causes the logic function of the OR gate to change from $x_1 + x_2$ to x_2. Many faults such as shorts and opens* can be modeled as logical faults. Parametric faults frequently alter the magnitude of a circuit parameter causing a change in some factor such as circuit speed, current, or voltage. Such faults cannot be treated as logical faults. In the circuit of Figure 1.1(b) an open diode corresponds to an input *s-a-1* and a short across the transistor corresponds to the output *s-a-0*.

Testing must be done throughout the life of a system, since faults may occur or be introduced into a circuit during manufacturing, assembly, storage and service. During each of these periods, the nature of the faults introduced and consequently the type of testing which must be performed is different. During manufacturing typical faults which may exist are open bonds, open interconnections, bulk shorts, shorts due to scratches, shorts through dielectric, pin shorts, cracks, etc. Hence a newly manufactured circuit may contain multiple faults, some permanent (i.e., always being present) and some intermittent (i.e., the fault is, or appears to be present at some times, but not at others), such as the shorting of two leads due to mechanical or voltage stressing. Some of these faults can be modeled as logical faults, while others cannot. Faults may also be introduced during assembly and testing. In addition, faulty elements may not be discovered until after assembly. During storage new faults may occur in a circuit due to factors such as temperature, humidity, leakage of sealed elements, and

---

*In some technologies, such as CMOS, an open circuit may cause unpredictable circuit operation, and thus cannot be modeled as a permanent fault.

aging. These factors usually cause parametric rather than logical faults in a circuit. Finally, in service, these same factors occur as well as others caused by heat dissipation, vibration, and voltage and current stress. It appears that as a circuit ages, the occurrence of intermittent faults increases. One cause for this problem is in the deterioration of contacts with time.

Failures are frequently not random but are the result of an imperfect manufacturing process. Hence the accurate determination of the location and cause of such failures is important so that the manufacturing process can be perfected.

Three types of testing, *DC (static or functional), AC (dynamic or parametric) and clock-rate testing*, are usually performed on circuits and element devices. In *DC testing* the elements are exercised by applying binary input patterns and analyzing the corresponding steady state outputs to determine correct functional behavior. *Parametric testing* verifies the time-related behavior of the element and involves the measurement of actual voltage and current levels. *Clock rate-testing* is similar to DC functional testing but is performed at frequencies near the maximum device rate. It is used to speed up the testing of complex devices for which parametric testing is impractical and for dynamic devices whose stored information must be refreshed during operation, such as MOS memories. Parametric tests are usually constructed manually. In this book we will restrict ourselves to the generation of DC functional tests.

Tests are applied to the circuit (unit) under test (UUT) using *automatic test equipment (ATE)*. In one class of such systems, binary patterns are applied to the UUT and also to a reference unit realizing the same function as the UUT, and the outputs are compared. In more sophisticated computer controlled testing systems, test programs are automatically translated to the appropriate input stimuli and the output signals are automatically interpreted and processed by the computer. A typical configuration for such a test system is shown in Figure 1.15. Here X is the applied test stimuli, and Z' is the observed response from the UUT. The processor compares Z' with Z, which is the known good response from the UUT. Based upon this information the ATE can determine whether or not the UUT is faulty (fault detection), and if so, where is the site of the fault (fault location). Often, more accurate fault location information can only be obtained by probing signals internal to the UUT. Sophisticated ATE would instruct the test operator, via the display, as to exactly which signals should be probed. The central problem in test generation is creating the input X and computing the normal response Z and the responses due to each fault of interest such that fault detection and location can be efficiently carried out.

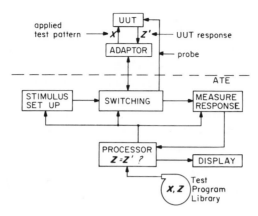

Figure 1.15   Stored Program Automatic Test Equipment (ATE) System Configuration

The generation of test patterns to be applied by the digital tester to the unit under test is an important and difficult problem which will be considered in great detail in Chapters 2 and 3. Such test patterns are sometimes computer generated. Figure 1.16 shows a block diagram for a typical *automatic test pattern generation (ATPG) system.* The inputs to the system are a description of the circuit for which test patterns are to be generated,

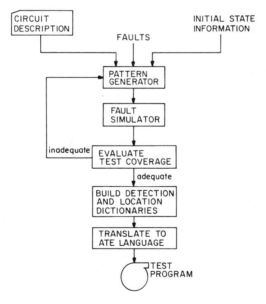

Figure 1.16   ATPG System

including the faults to be tested, and initial state information. Test patterns are then generated, simulated, and the circuit response is analyzed to produce *dictionaries* which specify circuit response to tests under various fault conditions in a format which is easily utilized for repair. This is repeated for each test pattern until the pattern generation is concluded.

Many characteristics of ATE may influence the properties of the test patterns to be generated. For example, *input skew*, i.e., slight variations in the order of application of input signals to the circuit can represent a serious problem. For example, for the circuit of Figure 1.17 assume that the flip-flop outputs become 1 only if the clock pulse becomes 1 when the input is 1. If y_1 is initially 0, and B and C change simultaneously, then $F = 0$. However, if B changes before C, F could be 1.

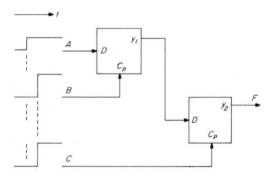

Figure 1.17   Potential Error due to Skew in the Clock Time

In many systems involving real-time processes the diagnostic program is stored within the system itself, and is periodically applied and interpreted by the system. In such systems, faults within the special hardware and software utilized to apply and interpret tests must also be considered in developing the diagnostic program.

1.3 LOGICAL FAULT MODELS

In this section we shall present definitions of tests for logical faults and develop logical fault models for the most common faults which occur in current technologies. By modeling physical faults as logical faults, the problem of fault analysis becomes a logical problem which is frequently technology independent in the sense that the same fault model is applicable to many technologies. In addition, tests derived for logical faults may be useful for physical faults whose effect on circuit behavior is incompletely understood or too complex to be analyzed [8].

For a combinational circuit which realizes the function $f(x_1,x_2, \ldots,x_n)$, a logical fault α changes the function realized to $f_\alpha(x_1,x_2, \ldots,x_n)$. An input $(x_1,x_2, \ldots,x_n) = (a_1,a_2, \ldots,a_n) = \mathbf{a}$, $a_i = 0$ or 1, will be said to *detect* the fault α if $f(\mathbf{a}) = 1$ and $f_\alpha(\mathbf{a}) = 0$ or vice versa. The inputs which detect α are those inputs for which the Boolean expression

$$f \cdot \bar{f}_\alpha + \bar{f} \cdot f_\alpha = f \oplus f_\alpha$$

has the value 1. A set of inputs which detect all possible (detectable) faults is called a *complete detection test set*. An input $\mathbf{b} = (b_1,b_2, \ldots,b_n)$ distinguishes a fault α from another fault β, if $f_\alpha(\mathbf{b}) \neq f_\beta(\mathbf{b})$. The inputs which distinguish these faults are those for which the Boolean expression $f_\alpha \cdot \bar{f}_\beta + \bar{f}_\alpha \cdot f_\beta = f_\alpha \oplus f_\beta$ has the value 1. A set of tests which distinguish all pairs of possible faults is said to be a *complete location test set*.

If all possible logical faults are considered, then f_α may be any of the $2^{2^n} - 1$ combinational functions of n variables other than $f(x_1,x_2, \ldots,x_n)$. It is easily shown that to test for all such possible faults it is necessary to apply all 2^n inputs as tests and observe and compare the outputs with f. Even such *exhaustive testing* is only adequate under the assumption that the fault is permanent rather than intermittent. Furthermore it must be assumed that if a fault does exist, then that fault was present when the test which detects that fault was applied. This implies that the fault must be present at the commencement of testing if it exists at the conclusion of testing.

In developing a logical fault model it is necessary to specify the effect of the fault on the logical behavior of circuit elements, the number of such faults which it is assumed may be present simultaneously, and the variation of such faults with respect to time. An intermittent fault will only be detected if an appropriate test is applied to the circuit during a period when the fault occurs [1, 10]. For such a fault it cannot be assumed that the fault will be present when the test for it is applied. Hence it is not sufficient to apply tests for them only once as is done for permanent faults. One approach to this problem is to apply tests for these faults repeatedly, the number of times being determined by a decision rule which is based on the probabilities of fault occurrence and fault appearance. Unfortunately the statistical data on probability of fault occurrence which is required by these models is usually not available. Thus the logical fault model utilized is usually restricted to permanent faults, although intermittent faults are prevalent in many technologies.

Exhaustive testing is only feasible for very small circuits. For this reason we wish to restrict the class of faults to be considered. The most frequent restrictions, which we shall also adopt, is to only consider faults for which some signals are or appear to be stuck at a logical constant of 0 or 1. In many technologies this model corresponds to the most common types of physical faults, namely shorts and opens.

The stuck fault model assumes that an input signal or an input or output of a circuit element is faulty. Such a fault on an element input may model an open-circuited gate rather than a stuck signal value. A signal which fans out to two gates may appear normal at one gate and faulty at the other. For the circuit of Figure 1.18, the fault x_2 s-a-1 results in permanent 1 signals on both a and b and the output z becomes $x_1 + x_3$. However the fault in which the input lead a to G_1 is open-circuited can be modelled by assuming the signal a is permanently 1 but the signal b still corresponds to x_2. Thus for the fault a s-a-1 the output z becomes $x_1 + x_2x_3$, and similarly for the fault b s-a-1 the output z becomes $x_1x_2 + x_3$.

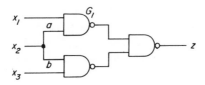

Figure 1.18

For a circuit with a total of k input signals and element inputs and outputs, if we restrict the class of stuck type fault to those involving only one of these k signals there are a total of $2k$ such single faults to consider. However if several of these k signals may be simultaneously faulty there are a total of $3^k - 1$ such multiple faults to consider. For this reason the single fault assumption is frequently incorporated in the logical fault model. If the model is to be realistic, this assumption can only be justified if multiple faults do not occur in practice, or, if when they do occur, they can always be detected and located by the same tests which detect and locate single faults. However faults which occur during circuit manufacture frequently affect several parts of the circuit and consequently can be more closely modelled as multiple stuck faults than as single stuck faults. Furthermore in order for multiple faults not to occur after the circuit is in operation, it is necessary to assume that all single faults will be detected and repaired before a second fault can (i.e. is statistically likely to) occur. There exist circuits for which single fault test sets do not detect all multiple faults as we shall show in Chapter 2. In practice it seems that single fault test sets are relatively good for the *detection* of multiple faults, but are not as good for the *location* of multiple faults [9]. Thus multiple fault models should also be considered. However, because of the great number of such faults, the single fault assumption is frequently utilized. Although we will restrict ourselves primarily to this latter model, we will also present results for multiple stuck type faults. We will also present some test generation procedures which can be used to derive tests for other logical faults which correspond to some types of shorts in certain technologies. One such fault is the shorted diode (shorted emitter) fault in diode-resistor (or diode transistor) logic [3]. For this fault the output of the faulty gate is unaffected but the input connected to the faulty diode and all fan-out leads from the input are forced to a value dependent on the output of the faulty gate. For example, in Figure 1.19, assuming positive logic (i.e. logical 1 is represented by a higher voltage than logical 0), if the input diode of G_1 connected to a is shorted and $x_1 = 0$, then $z_1 = 0$ and a and b are forced to 0 independent of the value of x_2. If $x_1 = 1$ then a and b take the value assumed by x_2. Thus although the fault is associated with gate G_1, the output z_1 is unchanged by the fault while the output function z_2 becomes $x_1 x_2 x_3$.

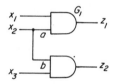

Figure 1.19

Shorted diode faults can also induce oscillations in combinational circuits. Consider the circuit of Figure 1.20(a) and the shorted diode fault on a. If $x_1 = x_2 = 1$ then $b = 0$ and because of the fault, a and hence x_2 become 0 causing b to become 1 and a and x_2 to revert to 1. In effect the circuit reduces to that shown in Figure 1.20(b).

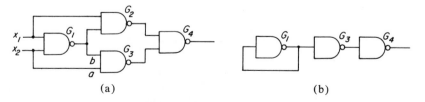

(a)   (b)

Figure 1.20   Example of a short causing oscillation

Another category of faults which we shall consider is the fault in which two wires become shorted. In certain technologies, this *bridge* fault may result in the affected signals being ANDed or ORed. Thus in the circuit of Figure 1.19 the *OR bridge* fault between x_1 and x_2 may cause the circuit outputs to become $z_1 = x_1 + x_2$ (instead of $x_1 x_2$) and $z_2 = (x_1 + x_2)x_3$ (instead of $x_2 x_3$). A bridge fault can also create a feedback loop, and thus convert a combinational circuit to a sequential circuit.

In general the faults of interest depend on the technology. Although for the most part we shall limit our consideration to stuck-type and short-type faults, many of the techniques presented may be applied to other logical fault models. In some technologies faults occur for which it is difficult to formulate logical models. A random access memory (RAM) is a set of independently addressable binary storage registers. RAM's have been constructed from magnetic cores and semiconductor technologies. For these circuits there exist a class of faults, called *pattern sensitive faults*, in which the result of reading or writing in some register R is affected by the contents of the other registers of the RAM. A frequently used approach for testing such faults is functional in nature and is based upon treating the RAM as a "black box" (with little use made of circuit information), and applying test patterns which tend to "exercise" the functional model (i.e., cause it to pass through many configurations and cause many signal transitions).

REFERENCES

[1] Breuer, M. A., "Testing for intermittent faults in digital circuits," *IEEE Transactions on Computers*, vol. C-22, pp. 241–246, March 1973.

[2] Brown, J. R., "Pattern sensitivity in MOS memories," in *Testing to Integrate Semiconductor Memories into Computer Mainframes*, Digest of Symposium, Cherry Hill, New Jersey, October 1972.

[3] Chang, H. Y., "A method for digitally simulating shorting input diode failures," *Bell System Technical Journal*, vol. 48, pp. 1957–1966, 1969.

[4] Friedman, A. D., "Diagnosis of short-circuit faults in combinational circuits," *IEEE Transactions on Computers*, vol. C-23, pp. 746–752, July 1974.

[5] Friedman, A. D., *Logical Design of Digital Systems*, Computer Science Press, Woodland Hills, California, 1975.

[6] Friedman, A. D. and P. R. Menon, *Theory and Design of Switching Circuits*, Computer Science Press, Woodland Hills, California, 1975.

[7] Hayes, J. P., "Detection of pattern sensitive faults in random access memories," *IEEE Transactions on Computers*, vol. C-24, pp. 150–157, February 1975.

[8] Hayes, J. P., "Modeling Faults in Digital Logic Circuits," Symposium on Rational Fault Analysis, Texas Tech University, Lubbock, Texas, August 19–20, 1974.

[9] Henckels, L., private communication.

[10] Kamal, S. and Ç. V. Page, "Intermittent faults: a model and a detection procedure," *IEEE Transactions on Computers*, vol. C-23, pp. 713–719, July 1974.

[11] Lambert, H. R., "Characteristics of faults in MOS arrays," *Proceedings Spring Joint Computer Conference*, pp. 403–410, 1969.

[12] Mei, K. C. Y., "Bridging and stuck-at-faults," *IEEE Transactions on Computers*, vol. C-23, pp. 720–727, July 1974.

[13] Millman, J. and H. Taub, *Pulse, Digital, and Switching Waveforms*, McGraw-Hill Book Company, New York, New York, 1965.

PROBLEMS

1.1 a) If possible find a circuit which has some fault which is *undetectable* (i.e., there are no tests which detect the fault).

b) If possible find a circuit which has two faults' α and β which are indistinguishable (i.e., $f_\alpha = f_\beta$).

1.2 Is it possible to have a combinational circuit C with some signal S and test T such that T detects both S s-a-1 and S s-a-0? Give an example or prove it impossible.

1.3 For the circuit of Figure 1.21 and the following faults find the circuit output.

a) Shorted diode on a.

b) AND bridge between inputs to gate G_1

c) The multiple fault: x_3 s-a-1, x_2 s-a-0

1.4 In the circuit of Figure 1.21 which if any of the following tests detect the fault x_1 s-a-0?

a) (0,1,1,1)

b) (1,1,1,1)

c) (1,1,0,1)

d) (1,0,1,0)

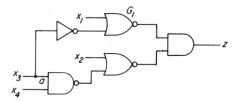

Figure 1.21 Problems 1.3, 1.4, and 1.5.

1.5 For the circuit of Figure 1.21 find a Boolean expression for the set of all tests which detect the fault.

a) x_3 s-a-0
b) x_2 s-a-0
c) x_2 s-a-1

1.6 For the circuit of Figure 1.22(a) and (b) find a Boolean expression for the set of all tests which distinguish the following pairs of faults.

a) x_1 s-a-0 and x_3 s-a-1
b) x_2 s-a-1 and x_3 s-a-0
c) x_1 s-a-0 and x_3 s-a-0

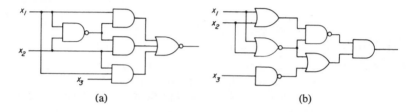

(a)   (b)

Figure 1.22

1.7 Construct a flow table for an *SR* master-slave clocked flip-flop, considering it to be an asynchronous 3-input, 2-output device. Consider only single input changes.

1.8 Determine a list of some of the possible hazard and race conditions which can adversely affect an *SR* master-slave clocked flip-flop, assuming multiple input changes may occur.

1.9 Consider the *JK* master-slave flip-flop shown in Figure 1.14.

a) Assume the master and slave are both in the reset state and $C_p = 1$ (master enabled). Show that the input $(J,K) = (1,0)$ sets the master, and if this input is followed by $(J,K) = (0,1)$ the master is not reset. How should this information be used in the operation of this device? Compare this situation with that for the SR flip-flop.

b) Study the operation of this device under the fault conditions *a* s-a-1 and *a* s-a-0.

c) What influence does the stuck at faults at output *y* have on output $\bar{y}$?

CHAPTER 2

TEST GENERATION FOR COMBINATIONAL CIRCUITS

Many algorithms have been proposed for generating tests for digital circuits. In this chapter we will present several of these algorithms. Some of these procedures make use of an algebraic description (equation) of the circuit under consideration. Others directly utilize the gate level circuit topology and functional description. In this chapter we will restrict our attention to test generation for combinational circuits.

First we will present a simple example. For the circuit of Figure 2.1 and the fault α corresponding to A s-a-1, $f = AB + BC$ and $f_\alpha = B + BC = B$. The set of tests which detect this fault are defined by the logical expression

$$f \oplus f_\alpha = (AB + BC) \oplus B = \overline{A}B\overline{C}.$$

The input combination $(0,1,0)$ which makes the term $\overline{A}B\overline{C}$ equal to 1 is thus the only test for this fault. Figure 2.1 shows the various signal values

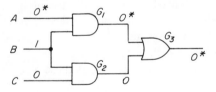

Figure 2.1

for the normal circuit and given input. Those signals which have the opposite value when the fault α is present are denoted with an asterisk. Notice that the asterisks constitute a path from the site of the fault to the output. The test is said to *sensitize* this path and, in addition to detecting the fault A s-a-1, all stuck faults along this sensitized path which are stuck at the value opposite to that in the normal circuit are detected by this test. In this example these faults are G_1 s-a-1 and G_2 s-a-1. Faults other than those on the path shown, such as C s-a-1, are also detected by this test. The concept of sensitizing a path or sensitizing the output to the value of a particular signal is central to all test generation procedures.

The problem of generating tests to detect faults can be readily solved in an exhaustive manner by analysis of the responses of the normal and faulty circuit for each fault and every possible input. Consequently the primary considerations in evaluation of test generation algorithms are the speed or computational complexity of the algorithm (i.e., the growth in number of operations required as a function of the size of the circuit) and to a lesser extent the minimality of the set of tests which is generated.

An important question is: Does there exist a test generation algorithm which, for an arbitrary combinational circuit, can compute a test for any detectable fault in p^r operations where p is the total number of gates and primary inputs in the circuit and r is a finite constant? If for some finite r such an algorithm existed, the problem would be said to be *polynomially complete*. Ibarra and Sahni [17] have shown that the problem of determining whether a given fault in a combinational circuit is testable is polynomially complete if and only if such difficult combinatoric problems as the *traveling salesman problem* are polynomially complete. At present, it is not known whether or not this famous problem is polynomial complete. Hence it seems very unlikely that highly efficient test generation algorithms can be developed for general circuits. This result also suggests that in the future, maintenance requirements may dictate the use of special canonical circuit realizations. We shall consider several such design procedures in Chapter 5. Though test generation is a difficult problem, there do exist several test generation algorithms which are of practical use for moderate size digital circuits. We shall now consider several of these algorithms.

2.1 BOOLEAN DIFFERENCE

Consider a combinational circuit C which realizes the function $f(x_1, x_2, \ldots, x_n)$. If we denote by α the fault in which input x_i is s-a-0, the function realized by the faulty circuit is

$$f_\alpha(x_1, x_2, \ldots, x_n) = f(x_1, x_2, \ldots, x_{i-1}, 0, x_{i+1}, \ldots, x_n).$$

We will represent this function as $f_i(0)$. Similarly if x_i is s-a-1 the function realized by the faulty circuit is

$$f_i(1) \equiv f(x_1, x_2, \ldots, x_{i-1}, 1, x_{i+1}, \ldots, x_n).$$

The set of tests which detect the fault α corresponds to the 1-points of the function

$$T = f(\mathbf{x}) \cdot \overline{f}_\alpha(\mathbf{x}) + \overline{f}(\mathbf{x}) \cdot f_\alpha(\mathbf{x})*$$
$$= f(\mathbf{x}) \oplus f_\alpha(\mathbf{x})$$
$$= (\overline{x}_i \cdot f_i(0) + x_i \cdot f_i(1)) \oplus f_i(0)$$
$$= x_i \cdot f_i(1) \cdot \overline{f}_i(0) + x_i \cdot \overline{f}_i(1) \cdot f_i(0)$$
$$= x_i \cdot (f_i(1) \oplus f_i(0)).$$

The factor $f_i(1) \oplus f_i(0)$, which is referred to as the *Boolean difference of f with respect to x_i*, is denoted by $\dfrac{df}{dx_i}$ and represents all conditions (associated with the variables in $\mathbf{x}$ excluding x_i) under which the value of f is sensitive to the value of x_i alone. Thus $x_i \cdot \dfrac{df}{dx_i}$ represents the *set of all tests* for the fault x_i *s-a-0* since x_i applies the opposite signal value on the faulty input and the factor $\dfrac{df}{dx_i}$ ensures that this erroneous signal affects the value of f. Similarly the set of all tests which detect x_i *s-a-1* is defined by the Boolean expression $\overline{x}_i \cdot \dfrac{df}{dx_i}$.

Example 2.1: The output of the circuit of Figure 2.2 is defined by the Boolean expression $f = (x_2 + x_3) x_1 + \overline{x}_1 x_4$.

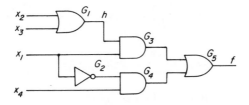

Figure 2.2

---

*The notation x is used to represent the variable vector $(x_1, x_2, \ldots, x_n)$ and $\mathbf{x}_i$ is used to represent a specific binary value of such a vector.

The set of tests which detect the fault x_1 s-a-0 is defined by the Boolean expression $x_1 \dfrac{df}{dx_1}$ where

$$\frac{df}{dx_1} = f(0,x_2,x_3,x_4) \oplus f(1,x_2,x_3,x_4)$$

$$= x_4 \oplus (x_2 + x_3)$$

$$= \bar{x}_2\bar{x}_3x_4 + x_2\bar{x}_4 + x_3\bar{x}_4.$$

Thus the set of all tests which detect this fault is defined by the Boolean expression $T = x_1(\bar{x}_2\bar{x}_3x_4 + x_2\bar{x}_4 + x_3\bar{x}_4)$. An input combination $\mathbf{x}_i$ detects this fault if and only if $T(\mathbf{x}_i) = 1$. The set of tests which detect x_4 s-a-1 is defined by the Boolean expression

$$\bar{x}_4 \cdot \frac{df}{dx_4} = \bar{x}_4(x_1(x_2 + x_3) \oplus (x_1(x_2 + x_3) + \bar{x}_1))$$

$$= \bar{x}_1\bar{x}_4. \qquad \square$$

For large circuits a great amount of algebraic manipulation may be required in order to determine $\dfrac{df}{dx_i}$. This problem can be facilitated through the use of certain identities which express the Boolean difference of the product, sum, complement, etc. of a pair of functions, in terms of the Boolean differences of the component functions. In their general form these identities are as follows:

$$\frac{d\bar{f}(\mathbf{x})}{dx_i} = \frac{df(\mathbf{x})}{dx_i} \tag{1}$$

$$\frac{d[f(\mathbf{x}) \cdot g(\mathbf{x})]}{dx_i} = f(\mathbf{x}) \cdot \frac{dg(\mathbf{x})}{dx_i} \oplus g(\mathbf{x}) \cdot \frac{df(\mathbf{x})}{dx_i} \oplus \frac{df(\mathbf{x})}{dx_i} \cdot \frac{dg(\mathbf{x})}{dx_i} \tag{2}$$

$$\frac{d[f(\mathbf{x}) + g(\mathbf{x})]}{dx_i} = \bar{f}(\mathbf{x}) \cdot \frac{dg(\mathbf{x})}{dx_i} \oplus \bar{g}(\mathbf{x}) \cdot \frac{df(\mathbf{x})}{dx_i} \oplus \frac{df(\mathbf{x})}{dx_i} \cdot \frac{dg(\mathbf{x})}{dx_i} \tag{3}$$

$$\frac{d[f(\mathbf{x}) \oplus g(\mathbf{x})]}{dx_i} = \frac{df(\mathbf{x})}{dx_i} \oplus \frac{dg(\mathbf{x})}{dx_i}. \tag{4}$$

These identities can be proven using the basic laws of Boolean algebra. The proofs of (1) and (4) are trivial and are left as an exercise. The proof of (2) is as follows: For notational convenience we denote $f(x_1, x_2, \ldots, x_{i-1}, a, x_{i+1}, \ldots, x_n)$ as $f_i(a)$ for $a = 0, 1$, and use similar notation for g. Starting with the right hand side of the equation we obtain

$$f(\mathbf{x}) \cdot \frac{dg(\mathbf{x})}{dx_i} \oplus g(\mathbf{x}) \cdot \frac{df(\mathbf{x})}{dx_i} \oplus \frac{df(\mathbf{x})}{dx_i} \cdot \frac{dg(\mathbf{x})}{dx_i}$$

$$= f(\mathbf{x}) \cdot (g_i(0) \oplus g_i(1)) \oplus g(\mathbf{x}) \cdot (f_i(0) \oplus f_i(1))$$
$$\oplus (f_i(0) \oplus f_i(1)) \cdot (g_i(0) \oplus g_i(1))$$

$$= f(\mathbf{x}) \cdot (g_i(0) \oplus g_i(1)) .$$

Substituting $x_i f_i(1) \oplus \overline{x}_i f_i(0)$ for $f(\mathbf{x})$* and factoring we obtain

$$(f_i(1) \cdot g_i(0) \oplus f_i(0) \cdot g_i(1))(x_i \oplus \overline{x}_i \oplus 1)$$
$$\oplus f_i(1) \cdot g_i(1) \cdot (x_i \oplus x_i \oplus 1)$$
$$\oplus f_i(0) \cdot g_i(0)(\overline{x}_i \oplus \overline{x}_i \oplus 1)$$
$$= f_i(1)g_i(1) \oplus f_i(0)g_i(0)$$
$$= \frac{d(f(\mathbf{x}) \cdot g(\mathbf{x}))}{dx_i} .$$

The proof of (3) follows directly from (1) and (2) since

$$\frac{d(f(\mathbf{x}) + g(\mathbf{x}))}{dx_i} = \frac{d(\overline{f}(\mathbf{x}) \cdot \overline{g}(\mathbf{x}))}{dx_i} .$$

These identities are especially useful, and easy to apply, in the degenerate case when one of the component functions is independent of the variable x_i, since if $g(\mathbf{x})$ is independent of x_i then $\frac{dg(\mathbf{x})}{dx_i} = 0$. In this case the AND and OR relations simplify as follows, where $g(\mathbf{x})$ is independent of x_i:

$$\frac{d(f(\mathbf{x}) \cdot g(\mathbf{x}))}{dx_i} = g(\mathbf{x}) \frac{df(\mathbf{x})}{dx_i} \qquad (2')$$

$$\frac{d(f(\mathbf{x}) + g(\mathbf{x}))}{dx_i} = \overline{g}(\mathbf{x}) \frac{df(\mathbf{x})}{dx_i} . \qquad (3')$$

---

*This substitution is an extension of Shannon's Law, $f(\mathbf{x}) = \overline{x}_i \cdot f_i(0) + x_i \cdot f_i(1)$.

Referring to Figure 2.3 we see that these identities simply state that to sensitize the output h of an AND gate to an input x_i of $f(\mathbf{x})$, requires the other AND gate input $g(\mathbf{x})$ to be 1 (Figure 2.3(a)) and to sensitize the output j of an OR gate to an input x_i of $f(\mathbf{x})$, requires the other OR gate input $g(\mathbf{x})$ to be 0 (Figure 2.3(b)).

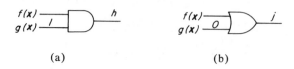

(a)   (b)

Figure 2.3

The Boolean difference can also be used to derive tests for stuck at faults on signals which are internal to the circuit.

Theorem 2.1:   Let C be a circuit which realizes the function $f(\mathbf{x})$ and let h be an internal signal of C. Then h can be expressed as a function of the inputs $h(\mathbf{x})$, and f can be expressed as a function f' of $\mathbf{x}$ and h (by considering h as an input). Then the set of all tests which detect the fault h s-a-0 is defined by the Boolean expression

$$h(\mathbf{x}) \cdot \frac{df'(\mathbf{x},h)}{dh}$$

and the set of all tests which detect the fault h s-a-1 is defined by the Boolean expression

$$\overline{h(\mathbf{x})} \cdot \frac{df'(\mathbf{x},h)}{dh}$$

where $f'(\mathbf{x},h) = f(\mathbf{x})$.

Proof: Exercise.   □

Example 2.2:   For the circuit of Figure 2.4, consider the fault h s-a-0, where h is the output of G_1. The output $f = (x_2 + x_3) x_1 + \overline{x}_1 x_4$ can be expressed as a function of h and $\mathbf{x}$, $f' = hx_1 + \overline{x}_1 x_4$ and h can be expressed as a function of $\mathbf{x}$, $h = x_2 + x_3$. Then

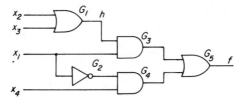

Figure 2.4

$$\frac{df'(x_1,x_4,h)}{dh} = f'(x_1,x_4,0) \oplus f'(x_1,x_4,1)$$

$$= \overline{x}_1 x_4 \oplus (x_1 + \overline{x}_1 x_4)$$

$$= x_1.$$

Alternatively $\dfrac{df'}{dh}$ can be computed as $\dfrac{d(f_1 + f_2)}{dh}$. where $f_1 = hx_1$ and $f_2 = \overline{x}_1 x_4$. From (3'), $\dfrac{d(f_1 + f_2)}{dh} = f_2 \cdot \dfrac{df_1}{dh}$

$$= (x_1 + x_4) \cdot x_1$$

$$= x_1.$$

The set of all tests which detect h s-a-0 is defined by the Boolean expression

$$h \frac{df}{dh} = (x_2 + x_3)x_1$$

and the set of all tests which detect h s-a-1 is defined by the Boolean expression

$$\overline{h} \frac{df}{dh} = (\overline{x}_2 \overline{x}_3)x_1. \qquad \square$$

In addition to the previous specified identities, the *simple chain rule* expressed in the following Lemma greatly simplifies the computation of Boolean differences for complex circuits.

Lemma 2.1 *(Simple Chain Rule):*   For a circuit C (see Figure 2.5) which realizes the combinational function $G = g(x,y)$, if $G = g(f(x),y)$, where x and y have no variables in common, then $\dfrac{dG}{dx_i} = \dfrac{dG}{df} \cdot \dfrac{df}{dx_i}$.

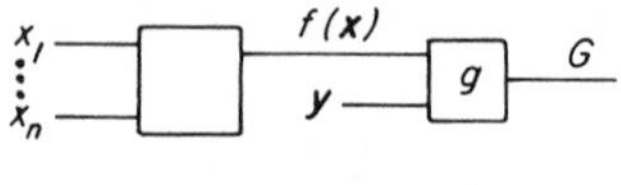

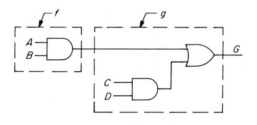

Figure 2.5

Proof: Exercise   □

Example 2.3:   For the circuit of Figure 2.6, $f = AB$, $g = f + CD$, $\dfrac{dg}{df} = (\overline{C} + \overline{D})$ and hence $\dfrac{dG}{dA} = \dfrac{dg}{df} \cdot \dfrac{df}{dA} = (\overline{C} + \overline{D}) \cdot B$.   □

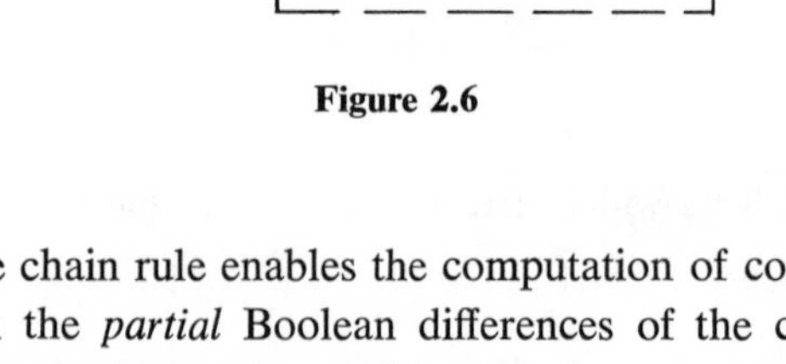

Figure 2.6

   The use of the chain rule enables the computation of composite Boolean differences from the *partial* Boolean differences of the component functions. If each circuit element is considered to be a separate subcircuit the method becomes very similar to a path sensitization procedure which will be considered in Section 2.3. A more general formulation of the chain rule, which is applicable to more complex circuits, has been derived by Chang, Reed, and Banes [6]. For a combinational circuit which realizes $F = f(g_1, g_2, \ldots, g_m)$ where $g_i = g_i(x_1, x_2, \ldots, x_n)$, $1 \le i \le m$, we have

$$\frac{dF}{dx_i} = \frac{dF}{dg_1} \cdot \frac{dg_1}{dx_i} \oplus \frac{dF}{dg_2} \cdot \frac{dg_2}{dx_i} \oplus \ldots \oplus \frac{dF}{dg_m} \cdot \frac{dg_m}{dx_i}$$

$$\oplus \frac{d^2F}{dg_1 dg_2} \cdot \frac{dg_1}{dx_i} \cdot \frac{dg_2}{dx_i} \oplus \frac{d^2F}{dg_1 dg_3} \cdot \frac{dg_1}{dx_i} \cdot \frac{dg_3}{dx_i} \oplus \ldots$$

$$\oplus \frac{d^mF}{dg_1 dg_2 \ldots dg_m} \cdot \frac{dg_1}{dx_i} \cdot \frac{dg_2}{dx_i} \cdot \ldots \cdot \frac{dg_m}{dx_i}$$

where

$$\frac{d^2F}{dg_i dg_j} = \frac{d}{dg_i}\left[\frac{dF}{dg_j}\right]$$

and

$$\frac{d^iF}{dg_1 dg_2 \ldots dg_i} = \frac{d}{dg_1}\left[\frac{d^{i-1}F}{dg_2 dg_3 \ldots dg_i}\right].$$

This formula is closely related to the concept of simultaneous sensitization of several paths when there is more than one path from x_i to the output. This concept will be explained in Section 2.3.

Example 2.4: Consider the circuit of Figure 2.7.

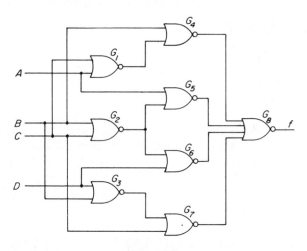

Figure 2.7

A test for the fault G_2 s-a-0 is defined by $G_2 \dfrac{df}{dG_2}$. We can compute $\dfrac{df}{dG_2}$ using the general formulation of the chain rule as follows:

$$\frac{df}{dG_2} = \frac{df}{dG_5} \cdot \frac{dG_5}{dG_2} \oplus \frac{df}{dG_6} \cdot \frac{dG_6}{dG_2} \oplus \frac{d^2f}{dG_5 dG_6} \cdot \frac{dG_5}{dG_2} \cdot \frac{dG_6}{dG_2}$$

$$G_5 = \overline{G_2 + A}$$

$$\frac{dG_5}{dG_2} = \overline{A}$$

$$G_6 = \overline{G_2 + D}$$

$$\frac{dG_6}{dG_2} = \overline{D}$$

$$f = \overline{G_4 + G_5 + G_6 + G_7}$$

$$\frac{d^2f}{dG_5 dG_6} = \overline{G_4} \cdot \overline{G_7} = (B + \overline{A}\,\overline{C})(C + \overline{B}\,\overline{D}) = BC + \overline{A}\,\overline{B}\,\overline{C}\,\overline{D}$$

$$\frac{df}{dG_5} = \overline{G_4}\,\overline{G_6}\,\overline{G_7} = (B + \overline{A}\,\overline{C})(\overline{B}\,\overline{C} + D)(C + \overline{B}\,\overline{D}) = BCD \cdot + \overline{A}\,\overline{B}\,\overline{C}\,\overline{D}$$

$$\frac{df}{dG_6} = \overline{G_4}\,\overline{G_5}\,\overline{G_7} = (B + \overline{A}\,\overline{C})(\overline{B}\,\overline{C} + A)(C + \overline{B}\,\overline{D}) = ABC + \overline{A}\,\overline{B}\,\overline{C}\,\overline{D}$$

$$\frac{df}{dG_2} = (BCD + \overline{A}\,\overline{B}\,\overline{C}\,\overline{D})A \oplus (ABC + \overline{A}\,\overline{B}\,\overline{C}\,\overline{D})\overline{D} \oplus (BC + \overline{A}\,\overline{B}\,\overline{C}\,\overline{D})\overline{A}\,\overline{D}$$

$$= \overline{A}\,\overline{B}\,\overline{C}\,\overline{D} + \overline{A}BCD \oplus ABC\overline{D} \oplus \overline{A}BC\overline{D}$$

$$= \overline{A}\,\overline{B}\,\overline{C}\,\overline{D} + \overline{A}BC + BC\overline{D}$$

$$G_2 \frac{df}{dG_2} = \overline{B}\,\overline{C} \quad \frac{df}{dG_2} = \overline{A}\,\overline{B}\,\overline{C}\,\overline{D}. \qquad \square$$

The definition of Boolean difference can be generalized to enable test generation for multiple faults as we shall show in Section 2.8.1.

The Boolean difference approach to test generation has the advantage of deriving *all* tests which detect a given fault, but it is limited to stuck type faults. Furthermore, for large circuits, time and memory requirements for generation of the circuit equations may be excessive.

2.2   OTHER ALGEBRAIC TEST GENERATION PROCEDURES

The Boolean difference procedure generates equations for the fault free circuit and manipulates these equations to generate tests. It is also possible to generate equations which specify both the normal and faulty behavior of a circuit. These are called *line condition* equations and are denoted by P.

Associate with line ℓ three binary variables defined as follows:

$$\ell_n = 1 \quad \text{if and only if } \ell \text{ is normal}$$

$$\ell_1 = 1 \quad \text{if and only if } \ell \text{ is } s\text{-}a\text{-}1$$

$$\ell_0 = 1 \quad \text{if and only if } \ell \text{ is } s\text{-}a\text{-}0.$$

Then the value of a line a connected to a primary input x_i is expressed by the expression

$$P_a = x_i a_n + a_1.$$

This expression can be used to determine the value of line a in both the normal and faulty circuits. Similarly the complement expression is given by

$$\overline{P}_a = \overline{x}_i a_n + a_0.$$

These expressions can be used to determine the value of line a in both the normal and faulty circuits. This can be generalized to derive similar equations for gates (as shown in Figure 2.8) and circuits.

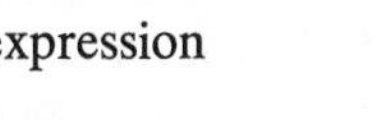

$$P_a = x_1 a_n + a_1$$
$$P_b = x_2 b_n + b_1$$
$$P_c = \overline{(P_a \cdot P_b)} c_n + c_1 \, .$$
$$= \overline{(x_1 a_n + a_1)(x_2 b_n + b_1)} \, c_n + c_1$$

Figure 2.8

If the line condition expression for a circuit is P, by substituting $a_{in} = 1$, $a_{i1} = a_{i0} = 0$ for all i we derive a Boolean expression P_n for the behavior of the normal circuit. Similarly the behavior P_b of the faulty circuit for any single or multiple stuck type fault can be derived by substituting $a_{in} = 1$, $a_{i1} = a_{i0} = 0$ for those signals a_i which are fault-free; $a_{jn} = a_{j0} = 0$, $a_{j1} = 1$ for those signals a_j which are s-a-1; and $a_{kn} = a_{k1} = 0$, $a_{k0} = 1$ for those signals which are s-a-0. From the two expressions, P_n and P_b, the set of all tests which detect the fault can be derived. For large circuits the equations become unwieldy and consequently this procedure, due to Poage [22], is of more theoretic than practical significance.

Several other equation approaches which are modifications of Poages method have been developed. These include the equivalent normal procedure of Armstrong [2], the cause-effect equation of Bossen and Hong [5], and the SPOOF procedure due to Clegg [8].

2.3 PATH SENSITIZATION AND THE D-ALGORITHM

The test generation procedures considered in the previous sections can be characterized as algebraic or functional in that they utilize circuit equations to generate tests. We will now consider a test generation procedure which utilizes the topological gate level description of a circuit, and the concepts of path sensitization and signal propagation.

The basic principles involved in path sensitization and signal propagation are relatively simple. In order for an input x_i to detect a fault a s-a-j, $j = 0,1$ the input x_i must cause the signal a in the normal (fault-free) circuit to take the value $\bar{j}$. Thus, for the circuit of Figure 2.2 (repeated as Figure 2.9), to detect the fault G_1 s-a-1, an input x_i must be such that $G_1(x_i) = 0$. For this circuit this implies that $x_2 = x_3 = 0$, denoted by the expression $\bar{x}_2\bar{x}_3$.

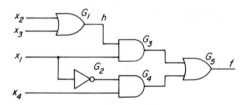

Figure 2.9

This condition is necessary but not sufficient to detect the fault. The effect of the fault, i.e., the error signal, must then be propagated along some path from its site or origin to an output. For this circuit, there is only one output, f, and only one path from G_1 to f, namely through G_3 and G_5. In order to propagate the fault through G_3 the input x_1 must be 1, since if x_1 is 0, the output of G_3 is 0 independent of the value of G_1. To propagate the fault through G_5, G_4 must be 0, since if G_4 is 1, the output f is 1 independent of the value of G_3 and hence G_1. In order for G_4 to be 0 either $x_1 = 1$ or $x_4 = 0$, $(x_1 + \bar{x}_4)$. Combining all these conditions we obtain the Boolean expression $x_4(\bar{x}_2\bar{x}_3)(x_1 + \bar{x}_4) = x_1\bar{x}_2\bar{x}_3$ which is the same result as obtained in Example 2.2.

Thus the path sensitization procedure can be described as follows:

Procedure 2.1 *(Path Sensitization):* To generate a test to detect a fault in a combinational circuit:

(1) Specify inputs so as to generate the appropriate value (0 for *s-a*-1 and 1 for *s-a*-0 faults) at the site of the fault.
(2) Select a path from the site of the fault to an output and specify additional signal values to propagate the fault signal along this path to the output *(error propagation)*.
(3) Specify input values so as to produce the signal values specified in (2) *(line justification)*. □

The rules for error propagation through individual gate elements are simply derived and are summarized in the table of Figure 2.10.

Type of Gate	Restrictions on other gate inputs
AND	All must be 1
OR	All must be 0
NAND	All must be 1
NOR	All must be 0
INVERTER (NOT)	None

Figure 2.10   Rules for Error Propagation

For the previously considered circuit and fault there was a unique excitation which could be applied to generate the appropriate signal value at the site of the fault, a unique path from the site of the fault to an output, and a unique input specification required to propagate the error signal along this path. However in general there may be several possible choices for each of these.

Example 2.5:   For the circuit of Figure 2.11 consider the fault a s-a-1. To generate the opposite value (0) at the output of G_1 requires $A = B = C = 1$. We now have a choice of propagating the faulty signal to an output via a path through G_5 or through G_6. To propagate through G_5 requires the output of G_2 to be 1 which implies $A = D = 0$. But this contradicts the previous requirements. To propagate through G_6 requires the output of $G_4 = 1$ which implies $C = 1$, $E = 0$. This generates the test $ABC\overline{E}$. Thus we see that there may exist a choice of paths for fault propagation.

For the fault a s-a-0 there is a choice of excitations to produce $G_1 = 1$. If we specify $A = 0$ or $B = 0$ we can propagate through G_5 or G_6. If we specify $C = 0$ we can only propagate through G_5.

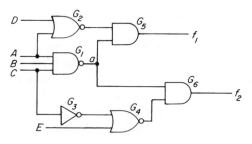

Figure 2.11

A choice may also exist with respect to line justification. Consider the fault E s-a-1 in the circuit of Figure 2.12. To detect this fault we must set $E = 0$. The condition $C = D = 1$ is required to propagate through G_1 and

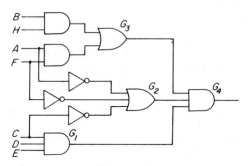

Figure 2.12

$G_2 = G_3 = 1$ is required to propagate the error signal through G_4. The condition $G_3 = 1$ can be justified if $A = F = 1$ or $B = H = 1$. However, if $A = F = 1$, since C has already been specified as 1, $G_2 = 0$ which leads to an inconsistency. Therefore we must justify $G_3 = 1$ by $B = H = 1$. The condition $G_2 = 1$ can then be justified by $A = 0$ or $F = 0$, leading to the two tests $\bar{A}BCD\bar{E}H$ and $BCD\bar{E}\bar{F}H$.   □

In general, it may be necessary to consider several alternatives in path propagation, line justification, and choice of excitations to produce the opposite value at the site of the fault. Now let us consider the circuit of Figure 2.13 and the fault a s-a-0. To generate the value 1 at the output of G_1 requires the input $A = B = 1$. To propagate the error along path G_3G_6

requires $C = 1$ and $G_2 = G_4 = G_5 = 1$. In order for G_4 to be 1, $E = 0$ or $G_1 = 0$, which implies $A = 0$ or $B = 0$. Since these latter conditions are

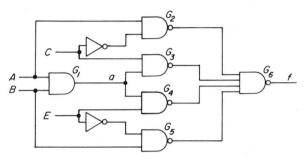

Figure 2.13

inconsistent with previous input specifications we specify $E = 0$. However with $E = 0$ and $B = 1$, $G_5 = 0$ leading to an inconsistency. Similarly propagation along path G_4G_6 requires $E = 1$, and $G_2 = G_3 = G_5 = 1$ must be justified, requiring $C = 1$ (to justify $G_2 = 1$). However, $A = B = C = 1$ implies $G_3 = 0$. This inconsistency seems to imply that the fault cannot be detected (i.e., there exists no test which detects the fault). However, if we attempt to generate a test using the Boolean difference we obtain the following:

$$f = A\overline{C} + G_1C + G_1E + B\overline{E}$$

$$\frac{df}{dG_1} = (A\overline{C} + B\overline{E}) \oplus (A\overline{C} + C + E + B\overline{E}) = C(\overline{B} + E) + E(\overline{A} + C)$$

$$G_1 = AB.$$

The set of tests which detects G_1 s-a-0 is defined by the Boolean expression

$$G_1\frac{df}{dG_1} = AB(C(\overline{B} + E) + E(\overline{A} + C)) = ABCE.$$

In Figure 2.14 we analyze the behavior of both the normal and faulty circuits for this input using the symbol 0/1 to represent a signal which has the value 0 in the normal circuit and 1 in the faulty circuit, and 1/0 to represent a signal which has the value 1 in the normal circuit and 0 in the faulty circuit. The symbols 0 and 1 are used for signals in which both the normal and faulty circuits have the value 0 and 1 respectively.* From this figure we see that the effect of the fault has been propagated simultaneously along two paths. Since our algorithm only attempted single path sensitization, this test was not derived. In order to ensure the generation of a test when one exists, we must exhaustively consider propagation along all multiple paths. (Note that in the generalized formulation of the Boolean

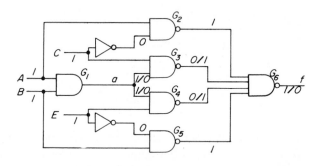

Figure 2.14

difference chain rule, there exists a term corresponding to the simultaneous sensitization of all multiple paths).

To facilitate the multiple path sensitization process we introduce the symbol D to represent a signal which has the value 1 in the normal circuit and 0 in the faulty circuit, and $\overline{D}$ to represent a signal which has the value 0 in the normal circuit and 1 in the faulty circuit. For example the output of 2-input AND and OR gates, each of whose inputs can take on the four composite values $\{0,1,D,\overline{D}\}$ is defined by the tables of Figure 2.15(a) and (b) respectively. Note that $D + \overline{D} = 1$, $D \cdot \overline{D} = 0$, $D \cdot D = D + D = D$, and $\overline{D} \cdot \overline{D} = \overline{D} + \overline{D} = \overline{D}$. Thus D behaves in accordance with the rules of Boolean algebra for a Boolean variable.

The path sensitization procedure can be formalized in terms of a *cubical algebra* to enable automatic (computer) generation of tests. This also facilitates test generation for more complex fault models and for fault propagation through complex logic elements. We shall define three types of cubes (line values specified in positional notation).

---

*These signal values are called *composite* values since they represent signal values in both the normal and faulty circuits simultaneously.

AND

	0	1	D	$\bar{D}$
0	0	0	0	0
1	0	1	D	$\bar{D}$
D	0	D	D	0
$\bar{D}$	0	$\bar{D}$	0	$\bar{D}$

OR

	0	1	D	$\bar{D}$
0	0	1	D	$\bar{D}$
1	1	1	1	1
D	D	1	D	1
$\bar{D}$	$\bar{D}$	1	1	$\bar{D}$

(a)   (b)

Figure 2.15

(1) For a circuit element E which realizes the combinational function f, the *primitive* cubes (pc) of f are a typical representation of the prime implicants of f and $\bar{f}$. These cubes concisely represent the logical behavior of E.

Consider a logic element E, shown in Figure 2.16(a), which realizes the combinational function f shown in Figure 2.16(b). The prime implicants of f are $\bar{x}_1\bar{x}_3$ and x_2, and the prime implicants of $\bar{f}$ are $\bar{x}_2 x_3$ and $x_1 \bar{x}_2$.

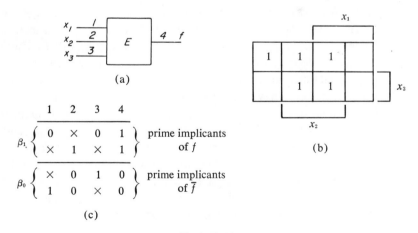

(a)

	1	2	3	4	
β_1	0	×	0	1	prime implicants
	×	1	×	1	of f
β_0	×	0	1	0	prime implicants
	1	0	×	0	of $\bar{f}$

(c)

Figure 2.16

---

*The term *primitive* is used to denote minimal input conditions required to produce a desired output.

The line labeling of Figure 2.16(a) indicates that line x_i is associated with position i of each cube and f is associated with position 4. The cubes describing the prime implicants of f (β_1) and $\bar{f}$ (β_0) are shown in Figure 2.16(c). The first cube of β_1, 0×01, represents the prime implicant $\bar{x}_1\bar{x}_3$ of f. In general a 0 in an input position denotes the complement of the corresponding variable and a 1 represents the corresponding variable. An $\times$ indicates that the output value is independent of the value of the corresponding variable.

An important concept in cubical algebra is the *intersection of two cubes* α_i, β_j. This process determines how the two circuit conditions specified by α_i and β_j can be simultaneously satisfied. If the intersection of α_i and β_j does not exist, i.e., the two conditions assign different values to the same line, then the cubes α_i and β_j are said to be inconsistent. The *intersection*, $\alpha_i \cap \beta_j$, of two cubes α_i, β_j is defined to be the value of the two cubes in each position in which they have identical values, and if one cube is unspecified ($\times$) for some position the intersection has the value of the other cube in that position. If the two cubes α_i, β_j have specified but unequal values in some position, the intersection does not exist ($\alpha_i \cap \beta_j = \phi$). Thus if $\delta = 0\times10$, $\epsilon = \times110$, and $\gamma = 1\times1\times$, then $\delta \cap \epsilon = 0110$, $\epsilon \cap \gamma = 1110$, and $\delta \cap \gamma = \phi$.

(2) A *primitive D-cube of a logic fault (pdcf)* α in a logic element E specifies the minimal input conditions which must be applied to E in order to produce an error signal (D or $\bar{D}$) at the output of E. These input conditions can be determined from the primitive cubes of f, the normal function realized by E, and f_α, the function realized by the faulty circuit as follows: An input condition produces a faulty output $D(\bar{D})$ if it is contained in a prime implicant of $f(\bar{f})$ and also contained in a prime implicant of $\bar{f}_\alpha(f_\alpha)$. We denote the set of prime implicants of $f(\bar{f})$ as $\beta_1(\beta_0)$ and the prime implicants of $f_\alpha(\bar{f}_\alpha)$ as $\alpha_1(\alpha_0)$. The primitive D-cubes of the fault which result in output $\bar{D}$ can be obtained by intersecting the inputs of each cube in α_1 with those for each cube in β_0. The primitive D-cubes of a fault α resulting in output D can be obtained by intersecting cubes in α_0 and β_1.

For the logic element defined in Figure 2.16 and the faulty function f_α defined in Figure 2.17(a),(b), the primitive D cubes of the fault are shown in Figure 2.17(c).

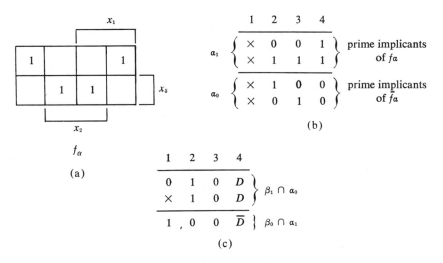

Figure 2.17

The first cube is derived by intersecting the first cubes of β_1 and α_0. The second cube is derived from the intersection of the second cube of β_1 and the first of α_0. The third cube is derived from the intersection of the first cube of α_1 and the second cube of β_0. Note that the first cube is a special case of the second cube and hence may be eliminated since it does not define *minimal* input conditions to produce an error. The second cube specifies that if the second and third inputs are set to 1 and 0 respectively the output of the logic element E will have the value D in the composite circuit.

For output stuck-at-faults the primitive D-cubes of the fault for an element E can be easily generated from the primitive cubes of E. If the output is s-a-0 the output coordinate of every cube in β_1 is changed to a D, and if the output is s-a-1, the output coordinate of every cube in β_0 is changed to a $\overline{D}$. The resulting cubes are the desired *pdcf*'s.

Primitive D-cubes of a fault may also be produced for logic blocks with several outputs as illustrated in the following example.

Example 2.6:   Consider the circuit of Figure 2.18(a) and the input bridge fault which creates the AND of the shorted signals. Part (b) of the figure specifies the primitive cubes of the normal and faulty circuit. The primitive D cubes of the fault result from the intersection of an α cube and β cube which differ in at least one output. In this case the two D-cubes result from

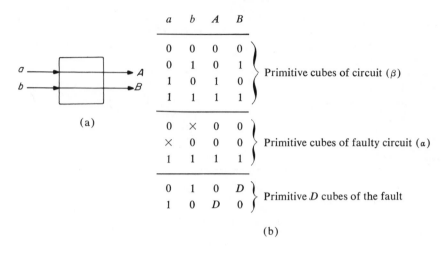

(a)

a	b	A	B
0	0	0	0
0	1	0	1
1	0	1	0
1	1	1	1

Primitive cubes of circuit (β)

0	×	0	0
×	0	0	0
1	1	1	1

Primitive cubes of faulty circuit (α)

0	1	0	D
1	0	D	0

Primitive D cubes of the fault

(b)

Figure 2.18

the intersection of the normal cube 0101 with the faulty cube ×000 and from the intersection of 1010 with 0×00.   □

(3) The *propagation D-cubes of a logic element E* specify minimal input conditions to the logic element which are required to propagate an error signal on an input(or inputs) to the output of that element. Let the logical behavior of E be defined by two sets of primitive cubes β_0 and β_1 which result in 0 and 1 outputs from E respectively. In order to propagate an error on an input line r, the other inputs must be defined so that if $r = 0$ the resulting cube is in β_0, and if $r = 1$ the resulting cube is in β_1, or vice versa. Such cubes can be derived by either (1) intersecting cubes in β_0 with $r = 0$ and β_1 with $r = 1$ (ignoring the rth position), resulting in $\bar{D}$ or D on both r and the output, or by (2) intersecting cubes in β_0 with $r = 1$ and β_1 with $r = 0$, resulting in D on r and $\bar{D}$ on the output or $\bar{D}$ on r and D on the output. Note that propagation D-cubes always occur in pairs which differ only in that all D components have complementary values.

Consider the propagation of an error on line 1 through the logic element defined in Figure 2.16. The propagation D-cubes can be derived from the primitive cubes of Figure 2.16(c) by intersecting cubes in β_0 for which line 1 has the value 1 with those cubes in β_1 for which line 1 has the value 0. This results in the following propagation D-cubes:

1	2	3	4
D	0	0	$\overline{D}$
$\overline{D}$	0	0	D

There are no cubes in β_0 for which line 1 has the value 0. Propagation D-cubes for multiple input faults can be similarly derived as illustrated in the following example.

Example 2.7:   Consider the propagation of error signals $\overline{D}$ and D on input lines 1 and 2 respectively for the logic element of Figure 2.16. Intersecting the cubes of β_0 with 0 or $\times$ and 1 or $\times$ in positions 1 and 2 with cubes in β_1 with 1 or $\times$ in position 1 and 0 or $\times$ in position 2 we obtain the following propagation D-cube from the intersection of the second cube in β_1 with the second cube in β_0.

1	2	3	4
$\overline{D}$	D	0	D

Note that the intersected cubes must not be differently specified in any of the positions corresponding to nonfaulty lines.   □

Figure 2.19 shows the primitive cubes, primitive D-cubes of all stuck faults, and propagation D-cubes for a 3-input NAND gate with input lines

1	2	3	4			1	2	3	4	Fault		1	2	3	4
0	$\times$	$\times$	1			0	$\times$	$\times$	D	4 s-a-0		D	1	1	$\overline{D}$
$\times$	0	$\times$	1	β_1		$\times$	0	$\times$	D	4 s-a-0		1	D	1	$\overline{D}$
$\times$	$\times$	0	1			$\times$	$\times$	0	D	4 s-a-0		1	1	D	$\overline{D}$
1	1	1	0	β_0		1	1	1	$\overline{D}$	4 s-a-1		D	D	1	$\overline{D}$
						$\overline{D}$	1	1	D	1 s-a-1		D	1	D	$\overline{D}$
	(a)					1	$\overline{D}$	1	D	2 s-a-1		1	D	D	$\overline{D}$
						1	1	$\overline{D}$	D	3 s-a-1		D	D	D	$\overline{D}$
							(b)						(c)		

Figure 2.19   (a) Primitive cubes (b) Primitive D-cubes of faults (c) Propagation D-cubes for NAND gate

1, 2, 3 and output line 4. Additional propagation D-cubes can be obtained by complementing the D's and $\overline{D}$'s in the cubes shown.

Having defined *primitive cubes, primitive D-cubes of a fault,* and *propagation D-cubes* we can now specify a test generation procedure which can be shown to be algorithmic in the sense that it will derive a test for any logical fault, if such a test exists. [24]

Procedure 2.2 *(D-Algorithm—Generation of a test for a logic fault):*

(1) Select a primitive D-cube of the fault under consideration. This produces the error signal D or $\overline{D}$ at the site of the fault. (Usually a choice exists. The initial choice is arbitrary but it may be necessary during the execution of the algorithm to return and consider another possible choice. This is called *backtrack*. Backtrack may have to be iterated until all choices have been considered.)

(2) *Implication:* In the execution of (1), some gate inputs or outputs may be specified so as to uniquely *imply* values on other signals in the circuit. The *Implication* procedure traces such signal determination both forwards and backwards through the circuit. Implication proceeds as follows: Whenever a previously unspecified signal value becomes specified, all the elements associated with this signal are placed on a list B and processed one at a time (and removed). For each element processed, based upon the previously specified inputs and outputs, it is determined if new line values of 0, 1 are implied.* These implied line values can be determined by intersecting the *test cube (tc)* (which specifies all previously determined signal values of the circuit) with the primitive cubes for this circuit element. If the line associated with the output of an element E is specified in the test cube, and only one primitive cube C_p of E has the same specified value on this line, C_p is intersected with the test cube. Similarly if *all* the specified inputs of some primitive cube C_p' of E' are identical to the values associated with these lines in the test cube, C_p' is intersected with the test cube. If any line values are implied, they are specified in the test cube and the associated gate indices are placed on the list B. When a line a is assigned a value due to implications from its inputs (forward implication), then all gates having a as an input are placed on B. If a is assigned a value due to the backward implication on element E, then the gate whose output is a is placed

---

*Here we have only determined signal values implied by inputs of 0 or 1. It is also possible to have signal values implied by inputs of D or $\overline{D}$. For example, for a 2-input NAND with inputs 1 and D the output is implied to be $\overline{D}$. For basic gate elements (AND, OR, NOT, NAND, NOR) implication of D's and $\overline{D}$'s is simply determined. For example, for an AND element the output is implied to be $D(\overline{D})$ if and only if some input(s) are $D(\overline{D})$ and all other inputs are 1. Similarly the output is implied to be 0 if one input value is D and another input value is $\overline{D}$. For general complex elements the determination of implication of D and $\overline{D}$ inputs is much more complex. Since implication only affects the *efficiency* of execution of this procedure, we will not consider this problem in detail (See Problem 2.17).

onto list B along with all gates having a as an input, except for element E itself.

An *inconsistency* occurs when the value 0(1) is implied on a line l which has previously been specified to the complementary value 1(0). If an inconsistency occurs, backtrack to the last point a choice existed, reset all lines to their value at this point and begin again with the next choice.

(3) *D-Drive.* The *D-frontier* consists of the set of all elements whose output values are unspecified but whose input has some signal D or $\overline{D}$. (An associated list A *consists of all of the elements in the D-*frontier.) D-drive selects an element in A and attempts to propagate the D or $\overline{D}$ on the inputs of the associated element to an output of the element. This is accomplished by intersecting the current circuit test cube tc describing the circuit signal values with a propagation D-cube of the selected element of A, resulting in a new test cube. (For this intersection to exist all D's $(\overline{D}$'s) of the propagation D-cube must correspond to D's $(\overline{D}$'s) or unspecified entries of the test cube tc. If such intersection is impossible a new element in A is selected. If intersection cannot be accomplished for any element in A, backtrack to the last point at which a choice existed, resetting all lines to their values at that point, and begin with the next choice.

(4) *Implication of D-drive:* Perform implication for the new test cube derived in (3).

(5) Repeat (3) and (4) until the faulty signal has been propagated to an output.

(6) *Line justification (Consistency).* Execution of (1)–(5) may result in specifying the output value of an element E but leaving the inputs to the element unspecified. The inputs to such elements are now specified to produce the specified output value by intersection of the test cube with the primitive cubes of the element. The test cube may be intersected with any primitive cube of the element E which has no specified signal values which differ from those of the test cube. Implication is then performed on the new test cube and the process is repeated until all specified element outputs have been justified. Backtracking may again be required.   □

The flowchart of the *D*-algorithm is shown in Figure 2.20. The boxes indicated with *** represent operations involving possible exhaustive consideration of several choices.

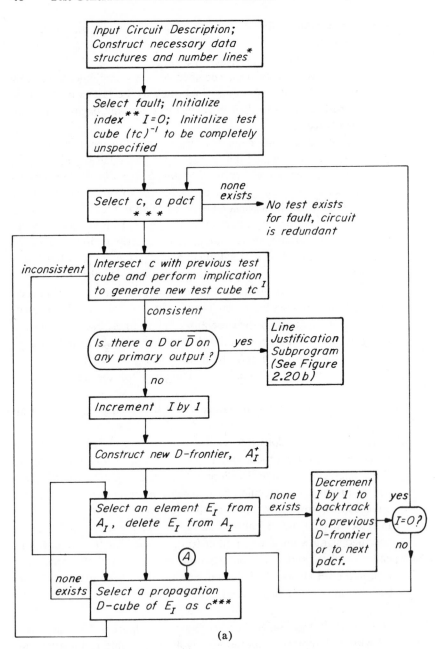

(a)

Figure 2.20   D-algorithm Flowchart

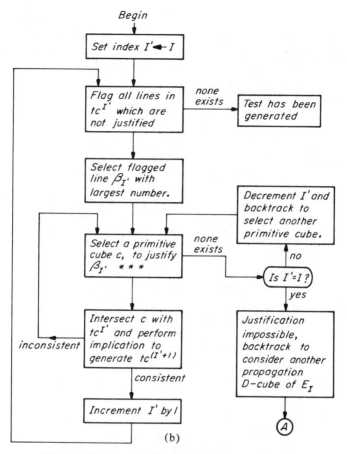

Figure 2.20 Line Justification Subprogram Flowchart

---

*Lines are numbered (assigned integer values) in such a way that the number associated with the output of a gate is larger than the number associated with any of the input lines of that gate. This is done to facilitate line justification.

**The index I is used to keep track of the different test cubes and D-frontiers generated during execution and to enable backtracking.

***Indicates sequential consideration of a set of possible choices which can be represented as a list or stack but typically are generated dynamically.

†The new D-frontier A_{I+1} can be constructed from the previous D-frontier A_I as follows: if we have just propagated through a_I, then

$$A_{I+1} = A_I - a_I \cup \{\text{all elements fed by } a_I \text{ which have unspecified outputs}\}.$$

This is only valid if implication of D and $\overline{D}$ values is not performed.

Example 2.8: For the circuit of Figure 2.21(a) and the fault G_1 s-a-0, the table of Figure 2.21(b) lists the primitive D-cube of the fault and the primitive cubes of gates G_2, G_3, G_4, G_5, G_6. Checking implication we determine that the primitive D-cube of the fault does not imply any other circuit signal values since only G_2 has a primitive cube with line 1 or 2 specified to value

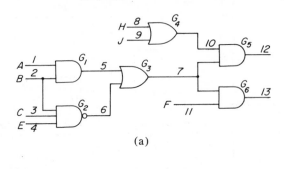

(a)

	1	2	3	4	5	6	7	8	9	10	11	12	13
Primitive D-cube of fault	1	1			D								
Primitive cubes of G_2		0	×	×		1							
		×	0	×		1							
		×	×	0		1							
		1	1	1		0							
Primitive cubes of G_3					1	×	1						
					×	1	1						
					0	0	0						
Primitive cubes of G_5							×			0		0	
							0			×		0	
							1			1		1	
Primitive cubes of G_6							0				×		0
							×				0		0
							1				1		1
Primitive cubes of G_4								1	×	1			
								×	1	1			
								0	0	0			

(b)

Figure 2.21

1 and that cube also has on lines 3 and 4 signals specified to value 1. At this stage the D-frontier, A_1, consists only of gate G_3. The relevent propagation D-cube of G_3 is shown in Figure 2.22 (row 2), and row 4 of this table shows the test cube after the D-drive through G_3.

	1	2	3	4	5	6	7	8	9	10	11	12	13
Initial test cube tc^0	1	1			D								
Propagation D-cube of G_3					D	0	D						
Test cube after D-drive through G_3 tc^1	1	1			D	0	D						
Test cube after implication	1	1	1	1	D	0	D						
Propagation D-cube of G_5							D			1		D	
Test cube after D-drive through G_5 tc^2	1	1	1	1	D	0	D			1		D	

Figure 2.22

Performing implication at this stage results in specifying lines 4 and 5 to have value 1 since line 6 has value 0. At this stage the D-frontier is $A_2 = \{G_5, G_6\}$. The relevant propagation D-cube of G_5 and the test cube after the D-drive through G_5 are shown in Figure 2.22, rows 5 and 6. Line justification of the 1 signal in position 10 results in the specification of line 8 (or 9) to have value 1.   □

Note that backtracking may be required in line justification. If line justification leads to an inconsistency, we backtrack and consider the next alternative in the current D-frontier A_I. After exhausting all alternatives in this set we would backtrack to the previous D-frontier A_{I-1} and perhaps eventually to consideration of another primitive D-cube of the fault.

As previously mentioned the D-algorithm can be shown to be algorithmic. The proof is too complex to be included here, but it hinges on the fact that all possible choices of single and multiple path sensitizations are considered. During the execution of the D-algorithm, there are frequently many subproblems to be solved. For example, the D-frontier usually consists of many elements, and a choice of which element to D-drive through next must be made. Also, due to the propagation of D's, many lines are set to 0's and 1's. These values must be justified. Again a choice exists as to which order to justify lines, and whether or not line justification should be interspersed with D-drive. The order in which these various subproblems are selected can have a significant impact on the execution time of the program. Some effort has been carried out in the area of preprocessing a circuit so that data can be generated to aid in selecting an efficient ordering for solving these subproblems [26]. However, the effectiveness of these techniques has not yet been proven, and more work on this important problem is required.

The execution of the D-algorithm (Procedure 2.2) can be represented by a tree structure. Each node represents as subproblem. In selecting one subproblem to process, new subproblems are generated. If an inconsistency occurs, part of this computation tree is pruned, and another subproblem is selected for processing. Hence the computation tree dynamically grows and contracts.

Consider the circuit of Figure 2.23 and the fault e s-a-0. We first select the $pdcf$ $b = 1$, $c = 1$ which results in $e = D$. We now have a choice of

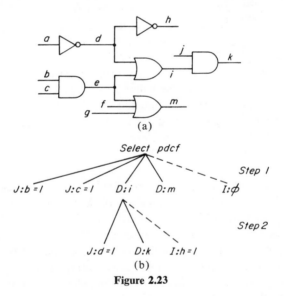

Figure 2.23

several subproblems to solve which can be represented by the tree of Figure 2.23(b), where J refers to line justification, D to D-Drive and I to implication. Implications are not considered to be problems, and are indicated by "dotted" branches in the tree. The node $J:b = 1$ refers to the problem of justifying the value 1 on line b. If we select the problem $D:i$, i.e., D drive to line i, then we produce two new problems and the implication $I:h = 1$. Assume we next try to solve the problem $D:k$, but find that it leads to an inconsistency. Since this node emanates from the node $D:i$, we return to that node and reset all line values generated by processing this node, namely we set a,d,h,k to $\times$, hence the need for the implication entries in the tree. We then remove the node $D:i$ from step 1 of the computation tree, and consider another alternative on that level.

2.4 CRITICAL PATH TEST GENERATION

The test generation techniques we have considered so far are fault oriented in that they attempt to derive tests for specific faults. Alternatively one might wish to derive tests which detect many faults (independent of which they are). Such a technique could be used in conjunction with a fault-oriented test generation procedure to reduce the total number of faults which would have to be considered by the latter. One test generation procedure which is fault independent is *random test generation*. This will be considered in the next chapter. In this section we will consider a procedure called *critical path generation*, which is similar to the technique used in the LASAR (*Logic Automated Stimulus And Response*) system [31], and is intended to detect stuck type faults. It is based on the observation that half of the stuck type faults along a sensitized path are detected by a test. Therefore it would seem desirable to generate tests which produce long sensitized paths. Such a test is produced using the concept of *sensitized cubes*. Starting from the output, whose value is defined as 0 or 1, a path is traced backwards toward the input. At each logic element, if the output value has been specified, the element input values are specified in such a way that the value of one or more of these inputs is *critical* (i.e., if the value of the critical input changes, the value of the element output will change). For example, if G is a NAND gate with inputs x_1,x_2, and the output of G is 1, the input $x_1 = 0$, $x_2 = 1$ has x_1 as a critical input and $x_1 = 1$, $x_2 = 0$ has x_2 as a critical input. The input $x_1 = 0, x_2 = 0$ has no critical inputs. If $G = 0$ the input $x_1 = x_2 = 1$ has both inputs critical. In essence, the critical path generation algorithm attempts to drive critical inputs of logic elements back to the primary inputs of the circuit by defining *single* sensitized paths.

Example 2.9:   Consider the circuit of Figure 2.24. Initially set $g = 0$. To define critical inputs to G_3 we set $e = 0$, $f = 1$ or $e = 1$, $f = 0$. Considering the first alternative, if $e = 0$, then $A = B = 1$ and G_1 has both inputs critical. The sensitized path has been driven back to the inputs. The condition $f = 1$ requires $C = D = 0$. Thus the test $(1,1,0,0)$ has been gener-

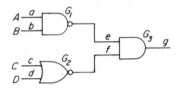

Figure 2.24

ated. Considering the second alternative the critical signal $f = 0$ is driven back through G_2 by specifying $C = 0$, $D = 1$, or $C = 1$, $D = 0$. The condition $e = 1$ is justified by $A = 0$ or $B = 0$. (Since $e = 1$ is not a critical signal no purpose is served in defining A or B as critical signals). Additional tests can be generated by initially defining the output $g = 1$. This implies $e = f = 1$ with both signals critical. The critical signal $e = 1$ can be driven back by specifying $A = 0$, $B = 1$ or $A = 1$, $B = 0$. The critical signal $f = 1$ requires $C = D = 0$. Thus the two tests $(0,1,0,0)$ and $(1,0,0,0)$ are generated.   □

The Critical Path Test Generation algorithm for combinational circuits is thus as follows:

Procedure 2.3 *(Critical Path Test Generation):*
   (1) Select an output line. Define it as a critical 0 and drive this critical value back towards the inputs using sensitizing cubes. Whenever a choice exists, select one alternative and backtrack later to consider all possibilities. For each choice made, all implications of that choice are carried out, and all critical lines generated are marked. When all critical lines have been driven back, all non-critical lines are justified using primitive cubes. If a critical line cannot be driven back via a sensitizing cube because of an inconsistency, backtrack and use a primitive cube.
   (2) Repeat for the output line initialized as a critical 1.
   (3) Repeat 1,2 for the rest of the output lines.   □

This algorithm may fail to find tests for faults which require multiple path sensitization. To save computation time we can refrain from considering all possibilities whenever a choice exists. Instead we can adopt the principle of simulating each test after it has been generated and only defining a critical $0(1)$ on a given signal s if no test for s s-a-$1(0)$ has previously been generated. This improves computation time and results in fewer generated test patterns but may fail to find tests for some faults.

Example 2.10:   Consider the circuit of Figure 2.25.

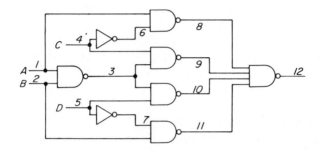

Figure 2.25

The table of Figure 2.26 shows the computation for the critical path test derivation procedure for this circuit.

	row	1	2	3	4	5	6	7	8	9	10	11	12
	1												0^c
	2								1^c	1^c	1^c	1^c	0^c
	3	0^c					1		1^c	1^c	1^c	1^c	0^c
(Implication)	4	0^c	0^c	1	0^c	0^c	1	1	1^c	1^c	1^c	1^c	0^c
	5	1					0^c		1^c	1^c	1^c	1^c	0^c
(Implication)	6	1	1	0^c	1	1	0^c	0^c	1^c	1^c	1^c	1^c	0^c
	7								0^c	1	1	1	1^c
	8	1^c	0		0^c	0	1^c		0^c	1	1	1	1^c

Figure 2.26

Starting with a critical 0 (denoted as 0^c) on line 12 implies critical 1's on lines 8, 9, 10 11 (second row of table of Figure 2.26). We now have a choice as to which of these critical 1's to drive backwards and we elect to drive back line 8, and select the sensitized cube having 0 on line 1 and 1 on line 6 (third row of table). This implies the value 0 on lines 2, 4, 5 and the value 1 on lines 3 and 7 and results in the critical values indicated by c's in the fourth row of the table of Figure 2.26. We then backtrack to our last choice and justify line 8 by the other sensitized cube having a 0 on line 6 and a 1 on line 1 (rows 5 and 6 of Figure 2.26). At this stage we would ordinarily backtrack to consider backward drive on lines 9, 10, 11. However in the course of the backward drive on line 8 critical values have already been generated along these paths. We next begin with a critical 1 on line 12 and justify it with a critical 0 on line 8 and 1's on lines 9, 10, 11 (row 7). The critical 0 on line 8 implies critical 1's on lines 1 and 6 and a critical 0 on line 4. No more sensitized paths can be generated and the 1's on lines 10 and 11 are justified by 0's on lines 2 and 5. We would next backtrack to consider a critical 0 on lines 9, 10, 11 respectively.   □

In the previous example note that the test for line 3 s-a-1 ($A = B = C = D = 1$), which requires multiple path sensitization (see Figure 2.11), is generated. However, if all NAND gates in the circuit are changed to NOR gates, a test for the s-a-0 fault on the corresponding line in the resulting circuit ($A = B = C = D = 0$) would not be generated by this procedure.

In general at some step in the procedure many lines may be critical. All of these critical signals are processed (driven backwards) in turn. For a multi-output circuit, each output line in turn is set to a critical value which is then driven backwards.

The critical path procedure is similar to the line justification procedure in the D-algorithm, except in the former we first attempt to justify a signal using sensitized cubes whereas the latter does not distinguish sensitized cubes from other primitive cubes.

2.5   FAULT EQUIVALENCE, DOMINANCE, COLLAPSING

In a combinational circuit C which realizes a function f the set of tests which *detect* a fault α is defined by the logical equation $T_\alpha = f \oplus f_\alpha$, and the set of tests which detect a fault β is defined by $T_\beta = f \oplus f_\beta$. The set of tests which *distinguish* α and β is defined by $f_\alpha \oplus f_\beta$. If $f_\alpha = f_\beta$ there is no test which distinguishes α and β. Such faults are said to be *equivalent*. (If a circuit C realizes a set of functions $\{f_1, f_2, \ldots, f_r\}$, α is equivalent to β if $f_{i_\alpha} = f_{i_\beta}$ for all i, $1 \le i \le r$). If a set of faults are equivalent, any test which detects one of them will detect all of them and no test will distinguish among them. Hence in test generation it is only necessary to explicitly consider one fault from each set of equivalent faults.

For any n-input gate there are $2(n + 1)$ single stuck type faults which can be defined. For an AND gate all s-a-0 faults are equivalent as are all s-a-1 faults on an OR gate. Similarly for a NAND (NOR) gate the set of all inputs s-a-0 (s-a-1) and the output s-a-1 (s-a-0) are equivalent. Thus only $n + 2$ faults need be considered for an n-input gate. This reduction process is called *equivalence fault collapsing*.

For fault detection tests an additional test reduction concept can be employed to reduce the number of faults which must be considered. A fault α *dominates* a fault β if for the set of tests T_α which detect α, and the set of tests T_β which detect β, $T_\beta \subset T_\alpha$. (For circuits realizing a set of functions $\{f_1, f_2, \ldots, f_r\}$, if T_{α_i} and T_{β_i} are the set of tests which detect α at f_i and β at f_i respectively, then α dominates β if and only if $\underset{i}{\cup} T_{\beta_i} \subset \underset{i}{\cup} T_{\alpha_i}$. If α dominates β then any test which detects β will also detect α. Therefore for generation of fault detection tests it is unnecessary to consider α. The consequent fault reduction is called *dominance fault collapsing*. Note that α and β may be distinguishable and for fault location test generation both must be considered.

For an AND gate, the output s-a-1 fault dominates any input to that gate s-a-1, and for an OR gate, the output s-a-0 fault dominates any input to that gate s-a-0. Similarly for NAND (NOR) gates the output s-a-1 (s-a-0) fault dominates any input s-a-0 (s-a-1) fault. Thus using both dominance and equivalence fault collapsing only $n + 1$ faults on any n-input gate need be considered. The set of $n + 1$ faults for each gate type is shown in the table of Figure 2.27. These concepts also enable us to prove some theorems which greatly simplify the fault collapsing process.

AND (NAND) gate	$(1) - (n)$: each input s-a-1 $(n + 1)$: any input s-a-0
OR (NOR) gate	$(1) - (n)$: each input s-a-0 $(n + 1)$: any input s-a-1

Figure 2.27 The Set of $n + 1$ Basic Faults Associated With Each Gate Type

Theorem 2.2: In a fanout free combinational circuit C, any set of tests which detects all stuck faults on primary inputs will detect all stuck faults.

Proof: Assume a set of tests T detects all stuck faults on primary inputs of C but does not detect all internal faults. Then there must be some gate G

in C such that T detects all faults on the inputs of G but does not detect some output fault. Assume G is an AND gate. Then the output of G s-a-0 is equivalent to any input s-a-0 and the output s-a-1 dominates any input s-a-1. Therefore if all input faults of G are detected both output faults will also be detected. A similar proof holds if G is an OR, NAND, or NOR gate.   □

Theorem 2.3:   In a combinational circuit any test which detects all single (multiple) stuck faults on all primary inputs and all branches of fanout* points detects all single (multiple) faults. The set of primary inputs and branches of fanout points are called the *checkpoints* of the circuit.

Proof: For single faults the proof is similar to that of Theorem 2.2. The proof for multiple faults follows from the fact that if line i is a predecessor of line j (i.e., there is a connected path from i to j) then any multiple fault of the form (i_a,j_b), $a,b = 0$ or 1** dominates the single fault j_0 or j_1. Thus any multiple stuck fault can be reduced to a set of stuck faults, no one of which is a predecessor of any other. Each of these dominates a single stuck fault on some checkpoint and hence the multiple fault dominates a multiple stuck checkpoint fault.   □

When considering multiple faults, input faults on lines which fanout can be ignored since they are equivalent to faults on the fanout branches.

These theorems can be used to obtain an initial collapsing of the set of faults which can then be further improved by using the concepts of equivalence and dominance as illustrated in the following example.

Example 2.11:   The circuit of Figure 2.28 has 24 single stuck faults. Using

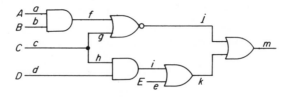

Figure 2.28

---

*If a line a fans out into k signals, those k signals are the branches of the fanout point a.

**The fault i s-a-0 (i s-a-1) is denoted by i_0 (i_1).

Theorem 2.3, this set of faults can be collapsed to 10 input faults plus 4 faults on branches of fanout points $\{g_0(g \ s\text{-}a\text{-}0), g_1, k_0, h_1\}$. This set of fourteen faults can then be further collapsed. Since A $s\text{-}a\text{-}0$ is equivalent to B $s\text{-}a\text{-}0$, we can delete the latter. The fault g_1 is equivalent to f_1 which dominates A $s\text{-}a\text{-}1$. Therefore, g_1 can be eliminated. Since h_0 is equivalent to D $s\text{-}a\text{-}0$, the latter can be eliminated. Finally E $s\text{-}a\text{-}1$ is equivalent to i_1 which dominates h_1. Therefore E $s\text{-}a\text{-}1$ can be eliminated. The original set of 24 faults has thus been reduced to 10. The faults c_0, c_1 can be eliminated for multiple fault detection.   □

Of course this simple method of fault collapsing may fail to discover some equivalent faults in a circuit such as c $s\text{-}a\text{-}1$ and d $s\text{-}a\text{-}1$ in the circuit of Figure 2.29. However determination of equivalent faults which are not

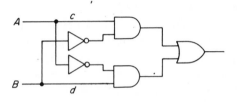

Figure 2.29

structurally related (in the manner specified in Theorem 2.3) would require a prohibitive amount of computation.

2.6 TEST REDUCTION AND MINIMIZATION

In general a test derived for a fault may have certain variables unspecified. If two such tests T_i and T_j do not specify any input variable to have opposite values then we can define a single test $T_{ij} = T_i \cap T_j$ which detects all faults detected by T_i and T_j. This technique can be iterated to reduce the number of tests required to detect all faults.

The problem of finding a *minimal* set of tests to detect all faults can be formulated as a *covering problem*. For each fault we determine all tests which detect that fault. A *test table* is then formed containing a row for each test, a column for each fault and the entry in row t_i and column f_j is 1 if and only if test t_i detects fault f_j. The problem is then to select a minimal set of rows which contain at least one 1 in each column. This problem can be formulated as an integer linear program and other solution techniques exist for small tables. For a circuit with n inputs and k signal lines the test table will have 2^n rows (all input combinations are tests for some fault) and $2k$ columns (for single stuck fault detection). This procedure is of course only feasible for very small tables. Many papers consider the problem of generating minimal (or near minimal) sets of fault detection tests. However none of these procedures are computationally feasible for large circuits and the minimality of the test set does not seem to be of great practical significance.

2.7   REDUNDANT CIRCUITS

In a circuit which realizes a function f, if for a given fault α $f_\alpha = f$, then there is no test which detects α (i.e., $f_\alpha \oplus f = 0$) and α is said to be *undetectable*. Such a circuit is said to be *redundant* with respect to the fault α. A circuit which is redundant with respect to a stuck type fault can be simplified by removing a gate or gate input. For instance, suppose that a s-a-1 fault on an input of an AND gate G is not detectable. Then the function is not changed by placing a permanent 1 signal on that lead. However an n-input AND with a permanent 1 signal is logically equivalent to the $(n - 1)$ input gate obtained by removing the lead with the 1 signal. Similarly if an AND input s-a-0 is undetectable the AND gate can be removed and replaced by a 0 signal which can then also be removed from any gate to which it is an input. These simplification rules are summarized in Figure 2.30.

Undetectable fault	Simplification Rule
AND(NAND) input s-a-1	Remove input
AND(NAND) input s-a-0	Remove gate, replace by 0(1)
OR(NOR) input s-a-0	Remove input
OR(NOR) input s-a-1	Remove gate, replace by 1(0)

Figure 2.30   Simplification of Redundant Circuits

The determination of redundancy is a difficult problem. If no test exists for a given fault then the circuit is redundant. However a great amount of computation is required to show that no test exists for some fault. It would be desirable to develop other characterizing properties of redundant circuits. Hayes [16] has proven the following simple characterizing properties: If C is an irredundant combinational circuit with n primary input variables, the maximum gate fanin of C is $2^n - 1$ (See Problem 2.16(a)). Furthermore no fanout-free subnetwork of C may have more than $2^{2^n} - 2$ primary inputs. However these results are primarily of theoretical interest.

Although the presence of a redundant fault will not affect the circuit behavior, it is important that the existence of redundancy be determined and eliminated for the following reason. It is implicit in the single fault assumption that any fault will be detected before a second fault occurs. For a redundant circuit this may be impossible since the first fault may be undetectable. For such circuits, generation of tests for all detectable single faults is inadequate. Specifically, for a redundant circuit C and a set of tests $\{T\}$ which detects all detectable single faults in C, there may exist a sequence of faults α, β such that α is undetectable and the multiple fault (α, β) is detectable but is not detected by $\{T\}$.

Consider the circuit of Figure 2.31. The fault β (b s-a-0) is detectable

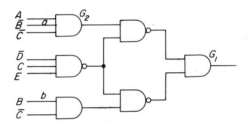

Figure 2.31

by $AB\overline{C}$. However, in the presence of the undetectable fault α (a s-a-1), the fault b s-a-0 is not detectable by $AB\overline{C}$. The reason for this is as follows. In order to detect the fault b s-a-0 the test must generate a 1 on the top input to gate G_1. This is done for the test $AB\overline{C}$ by setting line a to 0 and thus producing a zero output from gate G_2. However, since the fault a s-a-1 is not detectable, this path will be deactivated for the test $AB\overline{C}$ if this undetectable fault occurs, and the test $AB\overline{C}$ will not detect the fault b s-a-0. This fault can be detected only by $\overline{A}B\overline{C}$ in the presence of a s-a-1. The set of tests $\{A\overline{B}CD, \overline{A}\overline{B}\overline{C}, A\overline{B}\overline{C}\overline{D}E, AB\overline{C}\overline{D}E, BCD\}$ detects any detectable single fault in the original circuit but does not detect b s-a-0 in the presence of the undetectable fault a s-a-1.

Thus in deriving a complete test set for a redundant circuit we must generate tests for any multiple fault which can arise due to a sequence of undetectable faults. This greatly increases the difficulty of test generation for redundant circuits. Many other problems can arise in redundant circuits including the following: (1) if α is a detectable fault and γ is an undetectable fault, fault α may be undetectable in the presence of fault γ (see Problem 2.13). The latter fault is called a *second-generation* redundant fault. (2) An undetectable fault α may become detectable in the presence of another undetectable fault β (See Problem 2.14). Therefore, a complete test set must contain a test which detects the multiple fault (α,β) although it does not detect any of the corresponding single faults in the original redundant circuit. (3) If α and β are two distinguishable faults and γ is an undetectable fault, faults α and β may become indistinguishable in the presence of fault γ (See Problem 2.15).

Because of the difficulties inherent in test generation for redundant circuits, it is desirable to eliminate such redundancy via circuit simplification as specified in the table of Figure 2.30. However, in general there is no simple manner to determine redundancy in combinational circuits other than proving that no test exists for some fault or faults. Furthermore, it is also noteworthy that in a combinational circuit in which all single stuck faults are detectable a multiple stuck fault may be undetectable (See Problem 2.8).

Redundancy with respect to shorted diode and bridge faults introduces similar problems. A shorted diode fault may be undetectable in circuits for which all single stuck-type faults are detectable as demonstrated by fault α, the diode short on input a of G_1 in the circuit of Figure 2.32(a). Furthermore, the occurrence of this undetectable shorted diode causes the previously detectable fault b s-a-0 to become undetectable. The presence of undetected shorted diode faults can also affect the detection of stuck-type faults.

Undetectable shorted diode faults can be eliminated from a circuit in a rather straightforward manner. Referring to Figure 2.33 it is easy to show that if such a fault on input a of gate G_1 is undetectable the fanout from the input of gate G_1 can be replaced by fanout from the output of G_1 as shown in Figure 2.33(b). In Figure 2.33(a), $z_2 = A_n B_1 \ldots B_p$. If a is shorted, z_2 becomes $z_2' = A_1 \ldots A_n B_1 \ldots B_p$. If a shorted is undetect-

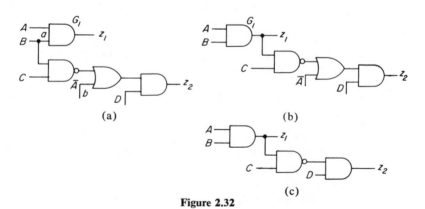

Figure 2.32

able then the response z_1, z_2 is identical to the response z_1, z_2'. In Figure 2.33(b) $z_1^* = z_1$ and $z_2^* = z_2'$. Thus the output of the circuit of Figure 2.33(b) is identical to that of Figure 2.33(a) if a shorted is undetectable.

In this way, undetectable shorted diode faults can be eliminated by replacing fanout points at the input of a gate G with fanout points from the output of G (repeatedly) if such a change does not alter the function realized by the circuit. Applying this transformation to the circuit of Figure 2.32(a) results in the circuit of Figure 2.32(b). This circuit is redundant and can be further simplified as shown in Figure 2.32(c).

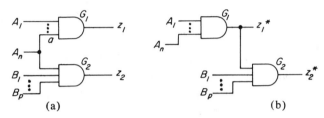

Figure 2.33

As shown in Chapter 1 (Figure 1.18), it is also possible to have shorted diode faults which cannot be detected because all tests for that fault cause oscillations. This type of fault induced oscillation can only occur if there is reconvergent fanout from a signal A with one of the paths a direct connection from A (Figure 2.34(a)). Furthermore in order that the shorted

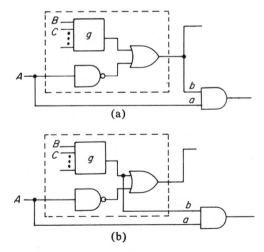

Figure 2.34

diode fault on a lead to an oscillation, b must be 1 if $a = 0$. Therefore $b = \bar{A} + g(B,C, \ldots)$. In general this difficulty can be eliminated by transforming the realization of Figure 2.34(a) into that of Figure 2.34(b). Again we observe that undetectability of shorted faults corresponds in some sense to the ability to move fanout points without changing (or with resultant simplification of) the circuit realization. In this case the fanout point is moved from the output of a gate G to an input of G, without changing the function realized by the circuit. For the circuit of Figure 1.18(a) this transformation enables gate G_1 to be eliminated and replaced by G_1 and G_2 which results in the equivalent circuit of Figure 2.35.

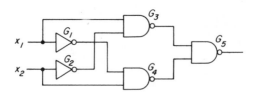

Figure 2.35

For stuck-type faults, redundant circuits can be simplified. However this is not necessarily true for short-type faults. Thus in a general theory of redundancy the two basic concepts of undetectable faults and circuit simplification without functional change are only equivalent for certain fault models.

Undetectable BRIDGE faults can also occur. In the circuit of Figure 2.32(a) an AND bridge on the inputs of gate G_1 is undetectable whereas all stuck-type faults are detectable. In this case the undetectable BRIDGE fault corresponds to the ability to move the point of fanout from the input to the output of an AND gate without changing the functions realized.

Hayes [16] has defined a more general class of redundancy which includes both undetectable stuck and short-circuit type faults. A circuit C is redundant if it is possible to cut a set of r lines in C and connect $q \leq r$ of the cut lines to some other signals in the circuit. Under this more general definition it can be shown that if a combinational circuit C having n primary input variables has more than $2^{2^n} - 2$ gates, then C is redundant (See Problem 2.16(b)).

2.8 TEST GENERATION FOR OTHER FAULT MODELS

Up to now we have only considered test generation for the single stuck fault model. Of course other faults may occur in practice. The first question to be resolved with respect to such faults is whether they will also be detected by a test set which detects all single faults.

2.8.1 Multiple Stuck Faults

One imporant class of faults is the multiple stuck type fault. As observed previously there are many more multiple faults than single faults. Although a single fault test set detects most multiple faults it may not detect all of them. Consider the circuit of Figure 2.36. For the multiple fault $\{B \text{ } s\text{-}a\text{-}1,$

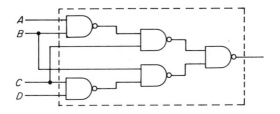

Figure 2.36

$C \text{ } s\text{-}a\text{-}1\}$ the faulty output is defined by the function $f' = \overline{AD} = \overline{A} + \overline{D}$ while the normal output function is $f = (\overline{A} + \overline{B})C + (\overline{C} + \overline{D})B$. Hence the set of tests which detect the multiple fault is defined by the Boolean expression

$$T' = f \oplus f' = \overline{A}\overline{B}\overline{C} + \overline{B}\overline{C}\overline{D} + AD(B\overline{C} + \overline{B}C).$$

The set of tests $\{ABCD, \overline{A}BCD, ABC\overline{D}, A\overline{B}CD, A\overline{B}C\overline{D}, \overline{A}B\overline{C}D\}$ detects all single faults and for all of these tests $T' = 0$. Therefore for this circuit there exists a set of tests which detects all single faults but not all multiple faults.

Much research has been done on multiple faults. However the results obtained are primarily of theoretical interest. For this reason, we shall only state, without proof, the most important of these results.

(1) In irredundant two-level combinational circuits, *any* set of tests which detects all single stuck faults also detects all multiple stuck faults.

(2) In fanout-free circuits (i.e., circuits where each primary input and each gate output are inputs to at most one gate), there exists a single stuck fault test set of minimal cardinality which detects all multiple stuck faults.

(3) The *checkpoints* of a combinational circuit consist of all inputs and branches of fanout points. A set of tests which detects all multiple stuck faults on the checkpoints of a circuit will detect all multiple stuck faults in the circuit.

(4) In a combinational circuit C any set of tests which detects all single stuck faults will also detect all multiple stuck faults unless C contains a subcircuit corresponding to the circuit shown within dotted lines in Figure 2.36 [27].

We shall now consider the extension of the single fault test generation procedures to multiple fault detection. In addition to being of relevance for testing combinational circuits we shall see that the problem of testing sequential circuits for single faults is analogous to the detection of multiple faults in combinational circuits.

In a combinational circuit with a multiple fault, a faulty signal (D or $\overline{D}$) may be propagated onto a line which itself is faulty. (Each of the faults in a multiple fault is assumed to be present simultaneously). The net effect of these two faults is easily determined. For example if a D propagates onto a line the normal circuit will have a 1 signal on that line, and the faulty circuit will have a 0 signal. If the line is s-a-1 however this 0 will become a 1 and both the normal and faulty circuits will have a 1 on that line. In this case the effect of the multiple faults cancel each other. If the line is s-a-0 the faulty circuit has a 0 and hence the signal values on the normal and faulty circuit are represented by D. The table of Figure 2.37 specifies the resultant signal when a D or $\overline{D}$ propagates onto a faulty line. The following example illustrates the use of the path sensitization procedure to generate tests which detect multiple faults.

Value of Fault Signal Propagated onto line ℓ	Fault on line ℓ	Resultant Signal on line ℓ
D	s-a-0	D
D	s-a-1	1
$\overline{D}$	s-a-0	0
$\overline{D}$	s-a-1	$\overline{D}$

Figure 2.37

Example 2.12:   Consider the circuit of Figure 2.38(a) and the multiple fault $\{A\ s\text{-}a\text{-}1,\ h\ s\text{-}a\text{-}1\}$.

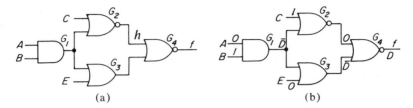

Figure 2.38

To generate a $\overline{D}$ at the output of G_1 we specify $A = 0$, $B = 1$. To propagate along the path G_2G_4 we specify $C = 0$, thus generating a D on the faulty line h. From the table of Figure 2.37 the propagation of a D onto a $s\text{-}a\text{-}1$ line results in a 1 signal. Thus the fault cannot be propagated along this path. Alternatively to propagate the $\overline{D}$ along G_3G_4 we specify $E = 0$. In justifying the input to G_4 we determine that the signal on h cannot be set to 0 but can be made $\overline{D}$ by specifying $C = 1$. Thus the test $\overline{A}BC\overline{E}$ detects the multiple fault. Figure 2.38(b) shows the resultant signal propagation. □

   The D-algorithm can be modified to handle multiple faults by modifying the implication and line justification subroutines to handle faulty elements, and considering primitive D-cubes of the fault for each of the faulty elements.

   The Boolean difference of a function f with respect to an input x_i, df/dx_i, represents all input conditions for which the value of f is determined by the value of x_i. Second degree Boolean differences may be defined as follows:

$$\frac{d^2f}{d(x_ix_j)} = f(x_1,\ \ldots,x_{i-1},0,x_{i+1},\ \ldots,x_{j-1},0,x_{j+1},\ \ldots,x_n)$$
$$\oplus f(x_1,\ \ldots,x_{i-1},1,x_{i+1},\ \ldots,x_{j-1},1,x_{j+1},\ \ldots,x_n)$$

and

$$\frac{d^2f}{d(x_i\overline{x}_j)} = f(x_1,\ \ldots,x_{i-1},0,x_{i+1},\ \ldots,x_{j-1},1,x_{j+1},\ \ldots,x_n)$$
$$\oplus f(x_1,\ \ldots,x_{i-1},1,x_{i+1},\ \ldots,x_{j-1},0,x_{j+1},\ \ldots,x_n).$$

Using this notation the set of all tests which detect the multiple fault $(x_i\ s\text{-}a\text{-}0,\ x_j\ s\text{-}a\text{-}0)$ is defined by the Boolean expression

$$x_i x_j \frac{d^2 f}{d(x_i x_j)} \quad + \quad x_i \bar{x}_j \frac{df}{dx_i} \quad + \quad \bar{x}_i x_j \frac{df}{dx_j}.$$

sensitize path	sensitize path	sensitize path
from x_i and x_j	from x_i only	from x_j only

The set of tests which detect the multiple fault (x_i s-a-0, x_j s-a-1) is defined by the Boolean expression

$$x_i \bar{x}_j \frac{d^2 f}{d(x_i \bar{x}_j)} + x_i x_j \frac{df}{dx_i} + \bar{x}_i \bar{x}_j \frac{df}{dx_j}.$$

In a similar manner we can define Boolean differences of degree k, for $k > 2$, which can be used to derive tests for multiple faults of degree k.

Example 2.13: For the circuit of Figure 2.38 and the multiple fault $\{A$ s-a-1, h s-a-1$\}$, the complete set of tests which detect this fault is defined by the expression

$$\bar{A}\bar{h} \frac{d^2 f}{d(Ah)} + \bar{A}h \frac{df}{dA} + A\bar{h} \frac{df}{dh}$$

where $f = \overline{h + AB + E} = \overline{\overline{AB + C} + AB + E}$ and $h = \overline{C + AB}$. Hence $\frac{df}{dA} = BC\bar{E}, \frac{df}{dh} = \bar{E}(\bar{A} + \bar{B})$, and $\frac{d^2 f}{d(Ah)} = \bar{E}$. The complete set of tests is defined by the expression

$$\bar{A}(C + AB)\bar{E} + \bar{A}(\overline{C + AB}) (BC\bar{E})$$
$$+ A(C + AB) (\bar{E}(\bar{A} + \bar{B}))$$
$$= \bar{A}C\bar{E} + A\bar{B}C\bar{E}$$
$$= C\bar{E}(\bar{A} + \bar{B}). \qquad \square$$

2.8.2   Shorted Diode and Bridge Faults

In this section we consider the problem of generating tests which detect shorted diode and bridge faults as well as stuck type faults.* In general a complete set of tests for stuck-type faults may not detect all shorted diode

---

*The probability of a given short circuit fault occurring will in general depend on the circuit layout. A "good" set of tests should detect those faults which have significant probability of occurrence.

and bridge faults. However it is relatively easy to incorporate constraints in the process of deriving tests for stuck-type faults so as to also detect all detectable shorted diode and bridge faults.

We will first consider shorted diode faults. Frequently for a given stuck-type fault in a circuit, there exist tests in which one or more inputs x_i are left unspecified. We shall now show how this degree of freedom can be used to generate a set of tests which detects all stuck-type faults as well as all shorted diode faults by a simple modification to the path sensitizing test generation procedure. The procedure will also determine if some shorted diode fault is undetectable.

Consider the situation depicted in Figure 2.39(a) where the line A fans out to 2 (or more) gates. In generating a test for A s-a-0 the circuit inputs would be specified so as to apply 1 to A and to propagate the fault signal

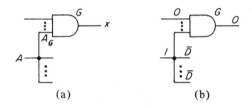

(a)   (b)

Figure 2.39

along any path (or set of paths) from A to an output. If one of the gates to which A fans out is an AND gate G, then (assuming positive logic) a shorted diode fault on the lead A_G is detected by applying the input combination 1 to A,0 to some other input to G, and propagating the faulty signal along any fanout path from A except through G. The resultant signal values are shown in Figure 2.39(b). Now suppose when generating a test for A s-a-0 we add a constraint that the output of G be 0. This forces us to set some input to G to 0 and to propagate the fault A s-a-0 along some path (paths) excluding G. This results in exactly the same set of signal values (Figure 2.39(b)) as the shorted diode fault on A_G. Hence, with this added constraint, in the process of generating a test for A s-a-0, we generate a test which also detects a shorted diode on A_G if this fault is detectable. (Similarly for negative logic with G an OR gate, if when generating a test for A s-a-1 we add the constraint that the output of G be 1, the shorted diode fault A_G will be detected.) If A fans out to several AND (or NAND) gates it may be necessary to generate several tests for line A to ensure detection of shorted diode faults on all such gates. The following example illustrates the application of these constraints to the test generation procedure.

Example 2.14:   Consider the circuit of Figure 2.40 and let us attempt to generate tests for stuck-type faults which also detect shorted diode faults on the fanout points of a and b. The presence of inverters on the $\overline{A}$ connection to G_2 and the $\overline{B}$ connection to G_5 prevents shorted diode faults on these leads from affecting the fanout points on G_3, G_4 or G_1.

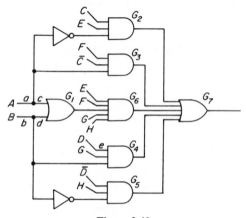

Figure 2.40

To detect the shorted diode fault on G_3 when deriving a test for a s-a-0 we add the constraint that the output of G_3 be 0. The complete set of tests satisfying these constraints is defined by the expression

$$A(C + \overline{F})\,(CE \oplus \overline{B}EFGH)\,(\overline{B} + \overline{D} + \overline{G})\,(B + D + \overline{H}).$$

$\underbrace{}$ $\underbrace{}$ $\underbrace{}$
added   propagate through   justify G_4 and G_5
constraint G_2 or G_6 but
        not both

The shorted diode fault on the B connection to G_4 can be simultaneously detected by the tests defined by the expression

$$AB(C + \overline{F})\,(\overline{D} + \overline{G})\,(C\overline{D}EH)\,(\overline{E} + \overline{F} + \overline{G} + \overline{H}) = ABC\overline{D}EH(\overline{F} + \overline{G}).$$

$\underbrace{}$ $\underbrace{}$ $\underbrace{}$
added   propagate   justify G_6
constraints   through
          G_2 and G_5

□

Tests derived for stuck type faults can also be modified to detect bridge faults. We first consider the problem of test generation for bridge faults between signals which are input to the same gate. Let us first consider the case when lines a and b are shorted and there is no fanout from either lead, and determine whether this bridge fault can be detected by a test for some stuck-type fault. For the case of Figure 2.41(a), a test for the fault a s-a-1 (a_1) requires the input condition $\overline{A}BC$ to generate an incorrect output from gate G, while the fault b s-a-1 (b_1) requires the input condition $A\overline{B}C$ to generate that incorrect output. The OR bridge fault* is detected by either of these conditions and therefore, in a combinational circuit, a set of tests which detect a_1 or b_1 will also detect the bridge fault (assuming no fanout from a or b) and it is unnecessary to consider that fault explicitly in the test generation process. In the circuit of Figure 2.41(a) the bridge fault dominates a_1 and b_1 and for fault detection purposes it is unnecessary to explicitly generate tests in a combinational circuit for a fault which dominates some other fault in the circuit.

Now suppose there is fanout from one of the two shorted leads as shown in Figure 2.41(b). Boolean expressions for the fault detection tests for some of the stuck-type faults and the OR bridge fault (BR) are shown below with the outputs to which the fault is propagated indicated as a parenthesized subscript:

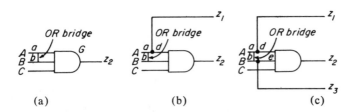

Figure 2.41

$$T_{a_1} = \overline{A}(\overline{B} + \overline{C})_{(z_1)} + \overline{A}BC_{(z_1, z_2)}$$

$$T_{b_1'} = A\overline{B}C_{(z_2)}$$

$$T_{d_1} = \overline{A}BC_{(z_2)}$$

$$T_{BR} = \overline{A}B\overline{C}_{(z_1)} + \overline{A}BC_{(z_1, z_2)} + A\overline{B}C_{(z_2)}.$$

---

*The AND bridge fault in this case is trivially undetectable.

From these tests we see that the bridge fault dominates b_1. Therefore any set of tests which detects b_1 will also detect the bridge fault and it is unnecessary to consider it separately in the test generation process.

In the most general case there is fan-out from both of the shorted leads as shown in Figure 2.41(c). In this case:

$$T_{a_1} = \overline{A}(\overline{B} + \overline{C})_{(z_1)} + \overline{A}BC_{(z_1, z_2)}$$

$$T_{b_1} = \overline{B}(\overline{A} + \overline{C})_{(z_3)} + A\overline{B}C_{(z_2, z_3)}$$

$$T_{d_1} = \overline{A}BC_{(z_2)}$$

$$T_{e_1} = A\overline{B}C_{(z_2)}$$

$$T_{BR} = \overline{A}B\overline{C}_{(z_1)} + A\overline{B}C_{(z_2, z_3)} + A\overline{B}\,\overline{C}_{(z_3)} + \overline{A}BC_{(z_1, z_3)}.$$

The OR bridge fault does not dominate any of the stuck faults a_1, b_1, d_1, e_1. In this case it is possible to have a complete set of tests for stuck-type faults in a circuit which does not detect a bridge fault if *fanout is present from both of the shorted inputs*. An example of such a circuit is that of Figure 2.40. One set of tests for the stuck faults a_0, b_0, c_0, d_0 is

$$T_{a_0} = ABCDE\overline{F}\,\overline{G}\overline{H}$$

$$T_{b_0} = ABCD\overline{E}\overline{F}G\overline{H}$$

$$T_{c_0} = A\overline{B}CDEFGH$$

$$T_{d_0} = \overline{A}B\overline{C}DEFGH.$$

All other stuck faults in the circuit have tests with $A = B = 1$ or $A = B = 0$. In order to detect the AND bridge fault between a and b it is necessary to have $A = 1$, $B = 0$, or $A = 0$, $B = 1$. The only faults whose tests must have this property are c_0 and d_0 and neither of the tests T_{c_0}, T_{d_0} detect the AND bridge fault since for that fault T_{c_0} (T_{d_0}) sensitizes the two paths $G_1G_6G_7$ and G_2G_7 (G_5G_7) with opposite polarity. This circuit can therefore have a complete set of tests for stuck-type faults which fails to detect the bridge fault shown.

Undetected bridge faults can create problems similar in nature to undetected stuck-type faults. Consider the fault e_1 (on the D lead of gate G_4) of Figure 2.40. The test $\overline{A}B\overline{C}D\overline{E}FG\overline{H}$ will detect this fault. However, in the presence of the AND bridge fault on the inputs of G_1 this test will fail to detect e_1 (and of course this test will fail to detect the bridge fault above). Hence undetected bridge faults can create problems in tests for stuck faults.

As for the shorted diode fault, it is relatively simple to generate tests for stuck-type faults which will also detect bridge faults (if they are detectable) by adding constraints to the test generation process. Consider a circuit with an AND gate G and an OR bridge fault between two inputs A and B with fanout from both inputs (Figure 2.42(a)). A test for A s-a-1 would be derived by specifying inputs so as to apply 0 to A and 1 to B and propagate along all fanout paths from A, or apply 0 to A and 0 to B and propagate along all fanout paths from A except that path containing G. The signal values in these two cases are shown in Figure 2.42(b) and (c).

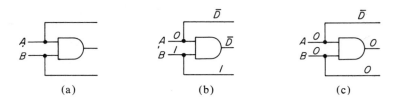

Figure 2.42

A test for the OR bridge fault between A and B would apply value 0 to A and 1 to B (or vice versa) and propagate along all fanout paths of $A(B)$. Consequently if when generating a test for A s-a-1, we add the constraint that $B = 1$, the test for A s-a-1 will automatically detect the OR bridge fault also. This can also be achieved by generating a test for B s-a-1 with the added constraint that $A = 1$. (Similarly for an AND bridge on an OR gate with fanout from two inputs A and B when testing one input (A) for s-a-0, if we add the constraint that the other input (B) be 0, the AND bridge fault will be detected by the generated test.) Applying this added constraint to the circuit of Figure 2.40 we would derive the following expression as the test condition for a_0.

$$\underbrace{A\bar{B}}_{\substack{\text{added} \\ \text{constraint}}} \quad \underbrace{(CE(\bar{F} + \bar{G} + \bar{H})(D + \bar{H})}_{\substack{\text{propagate through} \\ G_3 \text{ and justify} \\ G_6 \text{ and } G_5}} + \underbrace{\bar{C}F(\bar{E} + \bar{G} + \bar{H})(D + \bar{H}))}_{\substack{\text{propagate through} \\ G_2 \text{ and justify} \\ G_6 \text{ and } G_5}}.$$

This test will also detect the AND bridge fault on the inputs of gate G_1.

For an AND bridge fault on an AND gate the output of the faulty gate G is unchanged but all fanout points from the shorted inputs A and B are affected. Hence, the fault is undetectable if there is no fanout from A or B. If there is fanout from one of these inputs (say A) then the faulty signal can be propagated along the fanout paths of A (excluding paths containing G) by the excitation $A\bar{B}$. If there is fanout from both A and B the excitation $A\bar{B}$ will propagate the fault along the fanout of A (excluding G) and the excitation $\bar{A}B$ will propagate the fault along the fanout of B (excluding G). If in deriving a test for A s-a-0 we add the constraint that $B = 0$, this leads to the same signal pattern as the bridge fault (Figure 2.43(a)) and the bridge fault will be detected (assuming fanout from A and/or B). A similar analysis for the case of an OR bridge on an OR gate leads to a test for A s-a-1 with the added constraint $B = 1$ (Figure 2.43(b)). For these cases, to assure detection of bridge faults the added constraints must be applied when generating tests even for gates which have fanout from only one input lead.

(a)

(b)

Figure 2.43

The preceding results are only applicable to bridge faults affecting input leads to the same gate. The results on test generation for shorted diode and bridge faults are summarized in the table of Figure 2.44.

In combinational circuits bridge faults between leads to a gate are automatically detected by tests for stuck faults unless there is fanout from one or both signals. However this is not true for sequential circuits. Also, in combinational circuits more general bridge faults (i.e., where the bridge signals are not inputs to the *same gate*) may cause the circuit to become sequential. We shall consider these aspects of test generation in Chapter 3.

Fault Type	Fanout Condition	Gate Type	Relevant Stuck Fault	Extra Constraints for Test Generation	Figure
Shorted diode fault on input a of gate G	a is a fanout branch of A	AND, NOR	A s-a-0	$G = 0$	
		OR, NAND	A s-a-1	$G = 1$	
Bridge fault between inputs A, B on gate G	No fanout from A or B	AND, NAND (OR Bridge)	A s-a-1 B s-a-1	None	
		OR, NOR (AND Bridge)	A s-a-0 B s-a-0		
Bridge fault between inputs A, B on gate G	Fanout from A but not B	AND, NAND (OR Bridge)	B s-a-1	None	
		OR, NOR (AND Bridge)	B s-a-0		
Bridge fault between inputs A, B on gate G	Fanout from both A and B	AND, NAND (OR Bridge)	A s-a-1	$B = 1$	
			B s-a-1	$A = 1$	
		OR, NOR (AND Bridge)	A s-a-0	$B = 0$	
			B s-a-0	$A = 0$	

Figure 2.44 Summary of extra test generation constraints required for short-circuit faults

2.9 GENERATION OF TESTS WHICH DISTINGUISH FAULTS

In this section we consider the problem of generating a test to distinguish between two faults α and β. Such a test must detect α and not β on some output or vice-versa. The D-algorithm can be generalized to handle this problem. Let us use the symbols $D, \overline{D}$ to represent the faulty signals resulting from the propagation of the effects of α, and the symbols $E, \overline{E}$ to represent the faulty signals resulting from the propagation of the effects of β. Both of these pairs of signals are propagated in identical manner when they interact with 0 and 1 signals and the objective is to propagate a D (or $\overline{D}$) or an E (or $\overline{E}$) but not both to some output. However when these two signals appear on different inputs to the same gate, some differences arise in defining how they propagate through the gate. Specifically it must be remembered that even though we are propagating two single faults, at most one fault is present. Thus if the inputs to an OR gate are D and $\overline{E}$, this represents the situation where the normal inputs are 1 and 0 respectively, the inputs with α present are 0 and 0 and the inputs with β present are 1 and 1. The normal gate output is 1, the output with α present is 0, and the output with β is 1. Hence only the D propagates to the output $(D + \overline{E} = D)$. Similarly an AND gate with inputs D and E would have normal output 1 and output 0 with either α or β present and hence both D and E propagate to the gate output denoted by D,E $(D \cdot E = D,E)$. The tables of Figure 2.45 represent the signal propagations for AND and OR gates. Note that a pair of values may be assigned to some lines. The following

AND

	E	$\overline{E}$
D	D, E	$\overline{E}$
$\overline{D}$	$\overline{D}$	0

(a)

OR

	E	$\overline{E}$
D	1	D
$\overline{D}$	E	$\overline{D}, \overline{E}$

(b)

Figure 2.45

example demonstrates the generation of tests to distinguish between faults.

Example 2.15: For the circuit of Figure 2.46, we wish to derive a test to distinguish the "D" fault A s-a-1 and the "E" fault C s-a-0. We begin by trying to propagate a faulty signal from A s-a-1. Setting $A = 0$, $B = 1$,

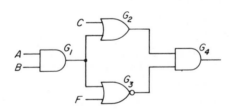

Figure 2.46

results in $G_1 = \overline{D}$. If we attempt to propagate this $\overline{D}$ through G_2 we observe that if $C = 0$ the output of G_2 is $\overline{D} + 0 = \overline{D}$. However if $C = 1$ the output of G_2 is $\overline{D} + E = E$. Similarly the output of G_3 is D if $F = 0$ and is 0 if $F = 1$. Thus the input $\overline{A}BC\overline{F}$ results in an output of G_4 equal to $E \cdot D = D,E$ which does not distinguish the faults. The input $\overline{A}B\overline{C}F$ results in G_4 equal to $\overline{D} \cdot D = 0$ which does not distinguish the faults, and the inputs $\overline{A}BF$ result in the output 0. Hence the faults cannot be distinguished if the error signal D is propagated from A s-a-1. We must thus propagate a faulty signal E from C s-a-0. Setting $C = 1$, $B = 0$ results in the output of G_2 of $E + 0 = E$. Setting $F = 0$ results in the output of G_4 of $E \cdot 1$ $= E$. Thus $\overline{B}C\overline{F}$ distinguishes the faults. If $B = 1$ the output of G_1 is 1 if $A = 1$ and is $\overline{D}$ if $A = 0$. In either case no distinguishing test can be generated. Hence the only tests which distinguish these faults are defined by the Boolean expression $\overline{B}C\overline{F}$. □

The application of a test input to a combinational circuit with k outputs may result in any of 2^k possible output responses, only one of which is the response of the fault-free circuit. For fault detection purposes all faulty responses can be jointly considered as a non-normal response. Given a sequence of tests $t_1, t_2, \ldots, t_r$, the response of the circuit can be represented by a tree as shown in Figure 2.47, where A_i is the set of faults detected by t_i *but not detected by* $t_1, t_2, \ldots t_{i-1}$. In this case once a faulty output occurs the fault has been detected and the remaining part of the

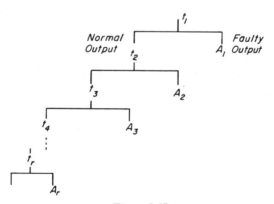

Figure 2.47

test sequence need not be applied. However if we wish to *diagnose* the fault all 2^k possible outputs must be individually considered. Let A_{ji}, $0 \leq i \leq 2^k - 1$ to be the set of faults which produce each of the 2^k possible responses to the test t_j. The remaining part of the test sequence may be designed to distinguish amongst the faults in A_{ji} if the corresponding output is produced to t_j. Thus the jth test applied may depend on the responses of the first $j - 1$ tests. The *diagnosis tree* of Figure 2.48, represents the use of such *adaptive testing* for fault diagnosis where $k = 2$. The first test applied is t_1. Depending on the response, test t_{20}, t_{21}, t_{22} or t_{23} is applied next, where these tests are intended to distinguish between the sets of faults A_{10}, A_{11}, A_{12} and A_{13} respectively. Similarly the next test applied will in general depend on the responses to the previous tests. Although it is possible to diagnose a fault in a combinational circuit by a *preset* test sequence where the next test applied is independent of the previous responses, the

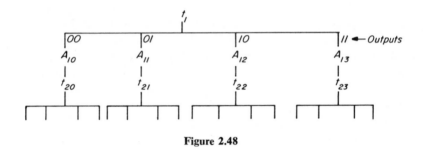

Figure 2.48

use of adaptive testing may substantially decrease the average number of tests required for fault diagnosis.

2.10   SPECIAL CLASSES OF CIRCUITS

Much research has been done on testing problems associated with special classes of circuits. While of limited practical significance in their own right, the study of such circuits is intended to lend insight to more general testing problems. These results are primarily of research interest. We will therefore only summarize the major results and references associated with this topic.

2.10.1   Fanout-Free Circuits

A fanout-free circuit is one in which the output of each gate and each circuit input is an input to at most one gate. Many results have been proven for this class of circuits which are not valid for more general circuits. These include the following:

(1) There exists a set of tests which detect all single and multiple stuck faults and is of minimal cardinality among all test sets for single faults [14].

(2) The number of tests required to detect all stuck type faults is bounded above by $n + 1$ and is bounded below by $2\sqrt{n}$ where n is the number of circuit inputs [14].

(3) A set of tests which detect all stuck faults on circuit inputs will detect all single stuck faults.

2.10.2 Circuits Realizing Unate Functions

Another special class of circuits which has been considered are those irredundant circuits which realize unate functions. A function $f(x_1,x_2, \ldots,x_n)$ is *positive* (*negative*) in a variable x_i if and only if there exists a minimal sum of products expression for f in which $\bar{x}_i(x_i)$ does not appear. A function is *unate* if it is positive or negative in each variable. Thus $f_1 = x_1x_2 + \bar{x}_3\bar{x}_4$ is unate, but $f_2 = x_1x_2 + \bar{x}_2x_3$ is not unate since it is neither positive or negative in x_2. For a unate function a *minimal 1-point* is a 1-point $\mathbf{x}_i = (a_1,a_2, \ldots,a_n)$ such that changing any positive variable from 1 to 0 or any negative variable from 0 to 1 changes $\mathbf{x}_i$ to a 0-point. The set of all minimal 1-points is denoted by S_1. Similarly a *maximal 0-point* is a 0-point $\mathbf{x}'_i = (a'_1,a'_2, \ldots,a'_n)$ such that changing any positive variable from 0 to 1 or any negative variable from 1 to 0 changes $\mathbf{x}'_i$ to a 1-point. The set of all maximal 0-points is denoted by S_0. Betancourt [3] has shown that for a unate function f, any realization of f containing only AND and OR gates can be tested for all stuck-type faults by the test set $\{S_0,S_1\}$.

Akers [1] and Reddy [23] have shown that a similar result holds for circuits which are positive or negative in some subset of the variables. An interesting theoretical question is as follows: Given a function $f(x_1, \ldots,x_n)$ which is not positive or negative in any variable, for any input combination $\mathbf{x}_i = (a_1,a_2, \ldots,a_n)$, $a_i = 0$ or 1, does there exist an irredundant circuit realization of f which requires the input $\mathbf{x}_i$ as a test in order to detect all stuck-type faults. To date this conjecture has yet to be proven but no counterexample has been discovered (See Problem 2.9).

2.10.3 Linear Combinational Circuits

A combinational function whose value is 1 if and only if an odd number of inputs are 1 (or if and only if an even number of inputs are 1) is said to be *linear*. A realization of a linear function is a linear circuit. A two level realization of an n-variable linear function requires all 2^n possible input combinations as tests to detect all single stuck type faults. A multiple level realization of a linear function consisting of k interconnected linear sub-circuits with $(n_1, n_2, \ldots, n_k)$ inputs respectively requires 2^p tests to detect all single stuck faults where $p = \max (n_1, n_2, \ldots, n_k)$. Thus for any value of n there exists a linear n variable circuit realization which requires only four tests to detect all single stuck faults. For an irredundant linear circuit with inputs $x_1, \ldots, x_k$, an error on any signal input x_i is propagated to the output for any value of x_j, $j \neq i$, i.e., $\dfrac{dF}{dx_i} = 1$ (See Problem 2.10).

2.10.4   Iterative Arrays

A one-dimensional unilateral iterative array consists of a linear cascade of identical combinational modules (cells) as illustrated in Figure 2.49. The controllable inputs, $x_1, x_2, \ldots, x_p$, and y_0 are assumed independent. The number of cells of the array, p, is assumed arbitrarily large but finite. The observable outputs are $z_1, \ldots, z_p$ and y_p. Such structures occur in many common circuits, such as parallel adders, and are also used to model sequential circuits. Consequently it is of interest to identify special properties for testing these circuit structures.

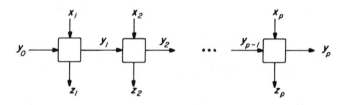

Figure 2.49   A One-Dimensional Iterative Array

Kautz [18] first studied the fault detection testing problems of such arrays under the assumptions that at most one cell is faulty and *that* cell can correspond to any other combinational circuit with the same number of inputs and outputs. He was able to characterize necessary and sufficient properties of the basic module for an arbitrarily long array of such modules to be testable under these assumptions. Menon and Friedman [21] also considered and solved the fault detection problem under the assumption of single stuck type faults, and derived necessary and sufficient conditions for fault location in such arrays. They also showed that the basic module could be augmented by adding one x input to each cell so that any fault could be located to within 2 cells [4].

For some iterative arrays the number of tests required for fault detection is independent of p, the size of the array. Friedman [12] has derived sufficient conditions on the basic module for an array to be easily testable in this sense (C-testable) and has shown that any combinational module may be augmented to be C-testable.

Kautz [18] also studied the problems associated with the testing of two-dimensional arrays of $p \times q$ identical combinational cells arranged in a rectilinear pattern as shown in Figure 2.50.

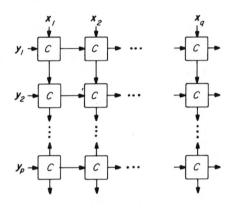

Figure 2.50

The problem of determining whether all faults in an array of this type of arbitrary size are detectable is probably *undecidable*.* Kautz [18] and Menon and Friedman [21] developed some sufficient conditions for complete fault detection in such arrays and Boelens [4] considered the problem of fault location.

REFERENCES

[1] Akers, S. B., "Universal Test Sets for Logic Networks," Proceedings Switching and Automata Theory Symposium, pp. 177–184, October 1972.

[2] Armstrong, D. B., "On Finding a Nearly Minimal Set of Fault Detection Tests for Combinational Logic Nets," *IEEE Transactions on Electronic Computers,* vol. EC-15, pp. 66–73, February 1966.

---

*A problem is undecidable if there exists no effective general procedure for its solution, i.e., a procedure which either terminates having found a solution or terminates indicating that no solution exists.

[3] Betancourt, R., "Derivation of Minimum Test Sets for Unate Logical Circuits," *IEEE Transactions on Computers,* vol. C-20, pp. 1264–1269, 1971.

[4] Boelens, O. C., Friedman, A. D. and P. R. Menon, "Fault Location in Iterative Logic Arrays," Symposium on Fault-Tolerant Computing, pp. 1.2–1.7, June 1974.

[5] Bossen, D. C. and S. J. Hong, "Cause-Effect Analysis for Multiple Fault Detection in Combinational Networks," *IEEE Transactions on Computers,* vol. C-20, pp. 1252–1257, November 1971.

[6] Chang, A. C. L., Reed, I. S., and A. V. Banes, "Path Sensitization, Partial Boolean Difference and Automated Fault Diagnosis," *IEEE Transactions on Computers,* vol. C-21, pp. 189–194, February 1971.

[7] Chang, H. Y., "A Method for Digitally Simulating Shorting Input Diode Failures," *Bell System Technical Journal,* vol. 48, pp. 1957–1966, 1968.

[8] Clegg, F. W., "Use of SPOOF's in the Analysis of Faulty Logic Networks," *IEEE Transactions on Computers,* vol. C-22, pp. 229–234, March 1973.

[9] Dandapani, R., "Derivation of Minimal Test Sets for Monotonic Logic Circuits," *IEEE Transactions on Computers,* vol. C-22, pp. 657–661, July 1973.

[10] Dandapani, R. and S. M. Reddy, "On the Design of Logic Networks with Redundancy and Testability Considerations," *IEEE Transactions on Computers,* vol. C-23, pp. 1139–1149, November 1974.

[11] Friedman, A. D., "Fault Detection in Redundant Circuits," *IEEE Transactions on Electronic Computers,* vol. EC-16, pp. 99–100, February 1967.

[12] Friedman, A. D., "Easily Testable Iterative Systems," *IEEE Transactions on Computers,* vol. C-22, pp. 1061–1064, December 1973.

[13] Friedman, A. D., "Diagnosis of Short-Circuit Faults in Combinational Circuits," *IEEE Transactions on Computers,* vol. C-23, pp. 746–752, July 1974.

[14] Hayes, J. P., "A NAND Model for Fault Diagnosis in Combinational Logic Networks," *IEEE Transactions on Computers,* vol. C-20, pp. 1496–1506, December 1971.

[15] Hayes, J. P., "On Realizations of Boolean Functions Requiring a Minimal or Near-Minimal Number of Tests," *IEEE Transactions on Computers,* vol. C-20, pp. 1506–1513, December 1971.

[16] Hayes, J. P., "On the Properties of Irredundant Logic Networks," *IEEE Transactions on Computers,* (to appear), 1976.

[17] Ibarra, O. H. and S. K. Sahni, "Polynomially Complete Fault Detection Problems," *IEEE Transactions on Computers,* vol. C-24, pp. 242–249, March 1975.

[18] Kautz, W. H., "Testing for Faults in Cellular Logic Arrays," *Proceedings Switching and Automata Theory Symposium,* pp. 161–174, 1967.

[19] McCluskey, E. J. and F. W. Clegg, "Fault Equivalence in Combinational Logic Networks," *IEEE Transactions on Computers,* vol. C-20, pp. 1286–1293, November 1971.

[20] Mei, K. C. Y., "Bridging and Stuck-at-Faults," *IEEE Transactions on Computers,* vol. C-23, pp. 720-727, July 1974.

[21] Menon, P. R. and A. D. Friedman, "Fault Detection in Iterative Logic Arrays," *IEEE Transactions on Computers,* vol. C-20, pp. 524-535, May 1971.

[22] Poage, J. F., "Derivation of Optimum Tests to Detect Faults in Combinational Circuits," *Proc. Symposium on Mathematical Theory of Automata,* Polytechnic Institute of Brooklyn, pp. 483–528, 1963.

[23] Reddy, S. M., "Complete Test Sets for Logic Functions," *IEEE Transactions on Computers,* vol. C-22, pp. 1016-1020, November 1973.

[24] Roth, J. P., "Diagnosis of Automata Failures: A Calculus and a Method," *IBM Journal of Research and Development,* vol. 10, pp. 278–291, July 1966.

[25] Roth, J. P., "An Algorithm to Compute a Test to Distinguish between two Failures in a Logic Circuit," *Proceedings IEEE International Computer Group Conference,* Washington, D.C., pp. 247–249, June 1970.

[26] Rutman, R. A., "Fault Detection Test Generation for Sequential Logic by Heuristic Tree Search," *IEEE Computer Group Repository,* R 72–187, 1972.

[27] Schertz, D. R. and G. Metze, "On the Design of Multiple Fault Diagnosable Networks," *IEEE Transactions on Computers,* vol. C-20, pp. 1361-1364, November 1971.

[28] Schertz, D. R. and G. Metze, "A New Representation for Faults in Combinational Digital Circuits," *IEEE Transactions on Computers,* vol. C-21, pp. 858–866, August 1972.

[29] Schneider, R. R., "On the Necessity to Examine D-Chains in Diagnositic Test Generation," *IBM Journal of Research and Development,* vol. 11, p. 114, January 1967.

[30] Sellers, F. F., Hsiao, M. Y., and C. L. Bearnson, "Analyzing Errors with the Boolean Difference," *IEEE Transactions on Computers,* vol. C-17, pp. 676–683, July 1968.

[31] Thomas, J. J., "Automated Diagnostic Test Programs for Digital Networks," *Computer Design,* pp. 63–67, August 1971.

[32] Yau, S. S. and Y. S. Tang, "An Efficient Algorithm for Generating Complete Test Sets for Combinational Logic Circuits," *IEEE Transactions on Computers,* vol. C-20, pp. 1245–1251, November 1971.

PROBLEMS

2.1 a) Consider the circuit shown in Figure 2.51(a), where f_1 and f_2 are combinational circuits defined by the Karnaugh maps of Figure 2.51(b). Find all tests which detect the fault α in f_1 which transforms f_1 to f_1' (shown in Figure 2.51(c)).

b) Find all tests which detect the fault β in f_2 which transforms f_2 to f_2' (shown in Figure 2.51(d)) assuming f_1 is fault free.

c) Find all tests which detect the multiple fault α and β (i.e., f_1 becomes f_1' and f_2 becomes f_2').

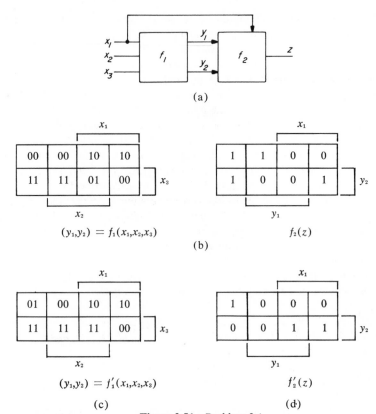

(a)

$(y_1,y_2) = f_1(x_1,x_2,x_3)$

$f_2(z)$

(b)

$(y_1,y_2) = f'_1(x_1,x_2,x_3)$

$f'_2(z)$

(c)   (d)

Figure 2.51   Problem 2.1

2.2 For the circuit of Figure 2.52 consider a fault which causes gate G_7 to generate a 1 output if and only if both of its inputs are 0 or both are 1. Find tests which detect this fault by finding the primitive D-cube of the fault and using path sensitization. (Hint: It is easier to find inputs which are *not* tests.)

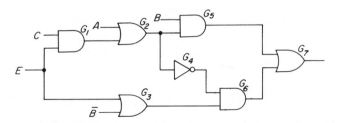

Figure 2.52   Problems 2.2 and 2.3

2.3   For the circuit of Figure 2.52, find all tests which detect the multiple fault A s-a-1, G_6 s-a-0. Use path sensitization.

2.4   For the circuit of Figure 2.53 find all tests which detect the faults

a) A s-a-0

b) b s-a-1

c) G_2 s-a-1

d) the multiple fault b s-a-1, G_2 s-a-1.

e) Repeat (a) and (b) using the D-algorithm. (Hint: once a test is found, backtrack to the last choice.)

2.5   a) For the circuit of Figure 2.53 find all tests which distinguish A s-a-0 from G_2 s-a-1.

b) Is there an input which sensitizes both A s-a-0 and G_2 s-a-1 at the same time? If so, will this input be a test for the multiple fault A s-a-0, G_2 s-a-1?

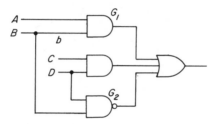

Figure 2.53   Problems 2.4, 2.5 and 2.12

2.6   For the circuit of Figure 2.54

a) Find all tests which detect the fault A s-a-1.

b) Find all tests which detect the fault b s-a-0.

c) Find all tests which detect the multiple fault A s-a-1, b s-a-0.

d) Find all tests which distinguish the faults A s-a-1 and b s-a-0.

2.7   For the functional logic block f of Figure 2.54

a) Determine the primitive cubes.

b) Determine all propagation D-cubes for errors on single input lines.

c) Determine all primitive D-cubes for the single faults A s-a-0 and b s-a-1.

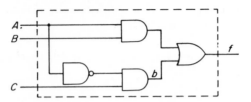

Figure 2.54   Problems 2.6 and 2.7

2.8   For the circuit [10] of Figure 2.55

a) Show that all single faults are detectable.

b) Show that the multiple fault (a_0, b_1, c_0, d_1) is undetectable.

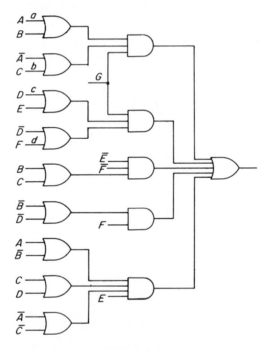

Figure 2.55

2.9   Consider the function $f(x_1,x_2,x_3) = x_1x_2x_3 + \bar{x}_1\bar{x}_2\bar{x}_3$. Show that for any input combination x_i there exists a circuit which requires x_i as a test to detect all stuck type faults. (Hint: Consider the sum of products and product of sums realizations.)

2.10 The circuit of Figure 2.56(a) is a realization of an n bit parity check function, where the basic module is as shown in Figure 2.56(b). Show that there exists a set of 4 tests which detect all single stuck type faults independent of n.

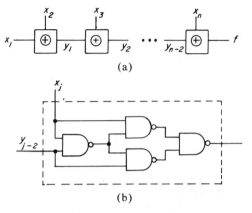

(a)

(b)

Figure 2.56   Problem 2.10

2.11 Consider a type of fault which causes a NAND gate to produce a 1-output if and only if an odd number of its inputs are 0. For the circuit of Figure 2.13 find a set of tests to detect all such detectable faults of this type.

2.12 For the circuit of Figure 2.53

   a) Find the set of all tests which detect the shorted diode fault on input b of gate G_1.

   b) Find the set of all tests which detect the OR bridge fault on the inputs of G_1.

2.13 For the circuit of Figure 2.57

   a) Find the set of all tests which detect the fault c s-a-1.

   b) Find the set of all tests which detect the fault a s-a-0.

   c) Find the set of all tests which detect the multiple fault (c s-a-1, a s-a-0).

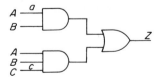

Figure 2.57

2.14 For the circuit of Figure 2.58

a) Find the set of all tests which detect the fault a s-a-0.

b) Find the set of all tests which detect the fault b s-a-0.

c) Find the set of all tests which detect the multiple fault (a s-a-0, b s-a-0).

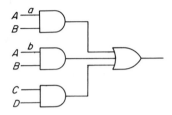

Figure 2.58

2.15 For the circuit of Figure 2.59

a) Find the set of all tests which detect the fault b s-a-1.

b) Find the set of all tests which distinguish the faults a s-a-0 and c s-a-0.

c) Find the set of all tests which distinguish the multiple faults (a s-a-0, b s-a-1) and (c s-a-0, b s-a-1).

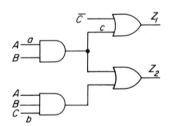

Figure 2.59

2.16 a) Prove the following theorem:

For a combinational circuit C having n primary input variables, if C has a gate with $q \geq 2^n$ inputs then C is redundant.

b) Prove the following theorem:

For a combinational circuit C having n primary input variables, if C has more than $2^{2^n} - 2$ gates then C is redundant (using the generalized concept of redundancy).

2.17 Specify a procedure for determining implication of D and $\overline{D}$ signal values for general complex elements.

2.18 A decoder is a combinational circuit containing n inputs and 2^n outputs, labeled respectively $(x_0, x_1, \ldots, x_{n-1})$, and $z_0, z_1, \ldots z_{2^n-1}$. The circuit functions as follows: If $(a_0, a_1, \ldots a_{n-1})$ is a binary input vector, representing the integer k, then $z_k = 1$ and $z_j = 0$ for all $j \neq k$. Based upon the functional operation of this device, determine a minimal set of tests which will detect any single fault on an input or output line of this device.

2.19 A multiplexer is a combinational circuit C having the structure shown in Figure 2.60.

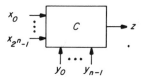

Figure 2.60

If $(a_0, a_1, \ldots a_{n-1})$ is an input vector, representing the integer k, applied to $(y_0, y_1, \ldots, y_{n-1})$, then $z = x_k$, where $0 \leq k \leq 2^n - 1$. That is, input line x_k is connected to the output z. Based upon the functional operation of this device, determine a minimal set of tests which will detect any single stuck fault on an input or output line of this device.

2.20 Prove that in an irredundant realization of a combinational function $f(x_1, \ldots, x_n)$, no single stuck-at-fault can change the output to correspond to the function $\overline{f}(x_1, \ldots, x_n)$.

Chapter 3

TEST GENERATION FOR
SEQUENTIAL CIRCUITS

Generating tests for sequential circuits is usually considerably more difficult than for combinational circuits. Usually a test sequence is required, rather than a single input vector, and the response of a sequential circuit is a function of its initial state.

We will first illustrate a very general form of test for a sequential circuit. Let $\mathbf{T}$ be a test sequence, and $\mathbf{R}_\alpha$ be the set of responses to $\mathbf{T}$ from a circuit having a fault α, starting in all allowable initial states. We denote the fault free situation by $\alpha = 0$. We say that $\mathbf{T}$ *strongly detects* fault α if and only if $\mathbf{R}_\alpha$ and $\mathbf{R}_0$ are disjoint, and $\mathbf{T}$ *strongly distinguishes* faults α and β if and only if $\mathbf{R}_\alpha$ and $\mathbf{R}_\beta$ are disjoint.

Example 3.1: For the synchronous circuit of Figure 3.1(a) whose behavior is described by the state table shown, and the input sequence $\mathbf{T} = 10111^*$ the fault free circuit generates the output sequences shown in Figure 3.1(b), and the circuit with single faults α (line a s-a-1) and β (line b s-a-0) generate the output sequences shown in Figure 3.1(c) and 3.1(d) respectively.

Since all sequences of Figure 3.1(d) are different from those of Figure 3.1(b), $\mathbf{T}$ strongly detects β. Since the sequences of the fault free circuit in initial state $B(y_1 = 0, y_2 = 1)$ and the circuit with fault α in initial state B are identical, $\mathbf{T}$ does not strongly detect α. Also $\mathbf{T}$ does not strongly distinguish the faults α and β because 01010 is an allowable output sequence for both cases. $\square$

---

*Read from left to right.

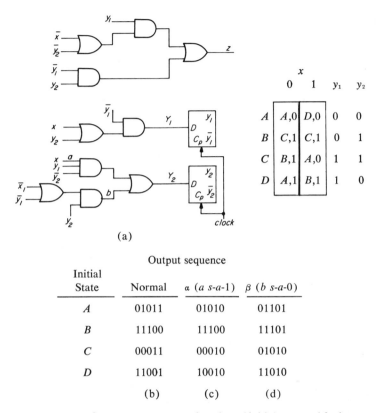

Figure 3.1 Output sequences as a function of initial state and fault.

In this example, despite the fact that **T** strongly detects β, the error symptom cannot be simply specified. That is, we cannot say that at some point in the output sequence the normal circuit will have a 1 output and the faulty circuit a 0 output, or vice-versa. Instead, we must list all possible responses of the normal and faulty machines. The usefulness of such tests for circuits with a large number of memory elements (and hence a large number of possible initial states and possible responses) is limited and the derivation of such a test is computationally difficult. Therefore, in the remainder of this book we will consider the derivation of a less general type of fault detection test which results in an output sequence which at some instant of time has a 1 output if the circuit has the fault α, and a 0 output if the circuit is fault free (or vice-versa). We say that such a test **T** *detects* the fault α.

In this chapter we will be primarily concerned with static testing, which is defined by the following steps.

1. Apply an input (vector) when circuit is in stable state.
2. Observe output when circuit is in stable state.
3. Repeat steps 1 and 2 for each input in the test sequence.

We will first consider synchronous circuits, and then asynchronous circuits. Aspects of fault dominance peculiar to sequential circuits will be illustrated. Also the topics of checking sequences, random test generation, transition count testing, and testing of semiconductor memories will be dealt with.

3.1 TEST GENERATION FOR SYNCHRONOUS SEQUENTIAL CIRCUITS

In this section we will show that a synchronous circuit can be modeled by a pseudo combinational circuit having a special structure. By carrying out this transformation, most techniques for generating a test for a combinational circuit can be extended to apply to sequential circuits. This transformation is more accurate for synchronous circuits than for asynchronous circuits because, for the latter case, timing is a critical factor.

A general model of a synchronous sequential circuit S is shown in Figure 3.2(a). For the purpose of test generation it is convenient to deal with the iterative array of Figure 3.2(b), which is logically equivalent to the sequential circuit in the following sense. If an input sequence $x(0)\ x(1)\ldots x(k)$ is applied to S in initial state y_I generating the output sequence $z(0)\ z(1)\ldots z(k)$, and state sequence of $y(1)\ y(2)\ldots y(k+1)$, then the iterative array will generate the output $z(i)$ from cell i, $1 \leq i \leq k$, in response to the input $x(i)$ to cell i, $1 \leq i \leq k$ if $y(0) = y_I$. In this transformation the clocked flip-flops are modeled as combinational elements, referred to as pseudo flip-flops. For a JK flip-flop the inputs of the combinational model are the present state q of the flip-flop, and the excitation inputs J and K, and the outputs are the next state q^+ and the device outputs y and $\bar{y}$. The y outputs of cell i of the iterative array, corresponding to time frame i, are denoted as $y(i)$. The present state q of the flip-flops in cell i must be equal to the q^+ output of the flip-flops in cell $i - 1$. The combinational element model corresponding to a JK flip-flop is defined by the truth table in Figure 3.3(a). Note that in this case $q^+ = y = (\overline{\bar{y}})$. The general flip-flop model will be represented as shown in Figure 3.3(b). For simple fault free elements, such as flip-flops, the q's can be replaced by y's. However, for more complex sequential devices the outputs and internal states may not be the same. Also, due to faults internal to a device, it may be necessary to distinguish

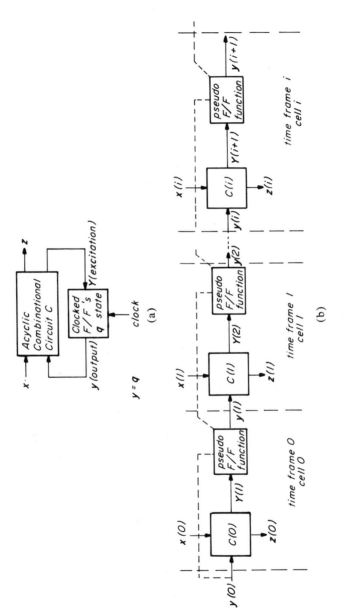

Figure 3.2   (a) General form of a synchronous sequential circuit S (b) Equivalent combinational iterative array

its state from its outputs. The pseudo flip-flop model can also be extended to include the clock as an additional input.

Since the flip-flop has been modeled as a combinational element, the circuit of Figure 3.2(b) is combinational and consequently most of the techniques discussed in Chapter 2 can be applied to this model. In effect the time domain response of the sequential circuit is mapped into a space domain response of the combinational iterative array model. A single fault in the sequential circuit corresponds to the multiple fault consisting of the same fault in every cell of the iterative array.

q	J	K	q^+	y	$\bar{y}$
0	0	0	0	0	1
0	0	1	0	0	1
0	1	0	1	1	0
0	1	1	1	1	0
1	0	0	1	1	0
1	0	1	0	0	1
1	1	0	1	1	0
1	1	1	0	0	1

(a)

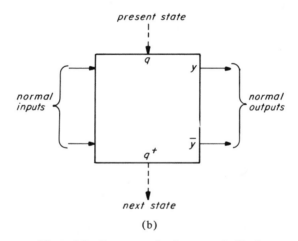

(b)

Figure 3.3   Representation for a pseudo flip-flop

In the next sections we will illustrate how the D-algorithm and the Critical Path procedure can be used to derive a test for a fault using the model just derived. The Boolean Difference procedure can also be applied to this model.

3.1.1   Extension of D-algorithm to Sequential Circuits

To derive a test for a fault in the circuit model of Figure 3.2(b), we desire to propagate a D or $\overline{D}$ to some output line. For simplicity, assume the output of C consists of a single line. We shall first consider this test generation problem when the initial state y_I is completely specified for both the fault free and faulty circuits. For example, if the initial state of the fault free circuits is $y^0 = (0, 0, 1)$, and that of the faulty circuit is $y^\alpha = (1, 0, 0)$, then the composite initial state is $y_I = y^0/y^\alpha = (\overline{D}, 0, D)$. If $y^0 = y^\alpha$ then no components of y_I will have D's or $\overline{D}$'s. For a fault α, if we can specify an input of $x(0) = a$ which, with $y(0) = y_I$, propagates a D $(\overline{D})$ to $z(0)$, then $x(0) = a$ is a test which detects the fault α from initial state y_I. A circuit can then be tested for α, independent of the initial state, by a test sequence Ia, where I is a sequence which causes the fault free and faulty circuits to enter state y_I independent of their initial states (if such and I exists). I is said to initialize the circuit to state y_I.

In order to propagate a D $(\overline{D})$ to some output, it may be necessary to first propagate a D $(\overline{D})$ through some flip-flops. Since a flip-flop can be modeled as a combinational element, we can develop primitive cubes, propagation D-cubes and primitive D-cubes of failures for it, just as we do for other combinational elements. For example, in Figure 3.4(c) we indicate propagation D-cubes for a T flip-flop.*

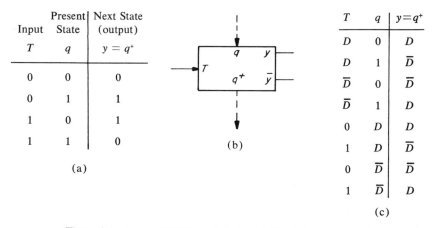

Figure 3.4   Pseudo T flip-flop (a) truth table (b) representation
(c) propagation D-cubes

---

*Note that the propagation of D's through a T, D, or JK flip-flop can be determined from the characteristic equations of the flip-flops.

Note that each component of the state vector $y(i)$ will have one of five values, namely $(0, 1, \times, D, \bar{D})$. If a test exists, the $\times$'s can be replaced by 0's and 1's, hence only four values need be considered. It is clear that in testing a circuit it is never necessary to enter the same state twice, hence each $y(i)$ can be restricted to be unique, and there are only 4^n such unique states, where n is the number of state variables.

We will now present the extension of the D algorithm for generating a test to detect a fault α in a synchronous circuit, assuming a composite initial state vector y_I.

Procedure 3.10 *(Test generation algorithm for synchronous circuits):*
1. Construct the iterative array model of Figure 3.2(b). Set $y(0) \leftarrow y_I$, and set $k \leftarrow 0$.
2. Ignoring all output lines except for those in $z(k)$, apply the combinational circuit D algorithm (Procedure 2.2)*. Restrict each state vector $y(j)$, $j = 1, 2, \ldots, k$ to be unique. If no test is found, increment k by one and repeat (2). Terminate when $k > 4^n$, where n is the number of state variables (flip-flops). If no test is found the circuit is redundant. □

In general, when choices exist in this procedure, it has been found advantageous to first select those alternatives which drive D's ($\bar{D}$'s) into the memory elements, i.e., it is easier to generate an incorrect output ($z = D$ or $\bar{D}$) from an incorrect state than from the correct state.

In propagating a fault in a sequential circuit, a signal which has the value D (or $\bar{D}$) may propagate onto a wire which is itself faulty. This is the same situation which occurred in generating tests for multiple faults in combinational circuits. As we have previously observed a single fault in a sequential circuit is logically equivalent to a multiple fault in the corresponding iterative array. This situation is discussed in Section 2.8.1.

Example 3.2: Consider the sequential circuit of Figure 3.5(a) and the gate input fault α (a s-a-1) on G_4. We will derive a test to detect this fault, assuming the initial state is $y_1 = y_2 = 0$.

Time frame 0: Since $y_2 = 0$ and a is s-a-1 we have a $\bar{D}$ at the location of the fault. Setting $x(0) = 1$ allows this $\bar{D}$ to propagate through G_4 and since $G_3 = 0$, we produce the next state vector $(0, \bar{D})$.

---

*This procedure requires minor modifications to deal with multiple faults and for the fact that y_I may contain D's.

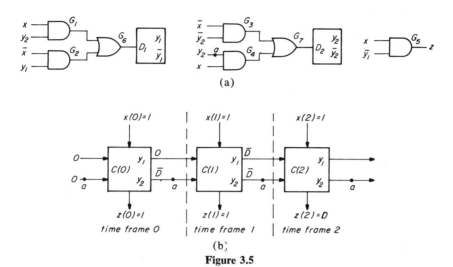

(a)

(b)

Figure 3.5

Time Frame 1: We cannot set $z = D$ or $\bar{D}$, hence we set $x(1) = 1$ and enter the state $(\bar{D}, \bar{D})$.

Time Frame 2: Since $\bar{y}_1 = D$, we set $x(2) = 1$ and obtain $z = D$ and hence a test sequence exists which detects this fault, namely $\mathbf{X} = 111$. □

It may be desired to observe the output both before and directly after clocking the flip-flops. For this case the computational model is modified to that shown in Figure 3.6. Here we use two copies of the circuit C in the

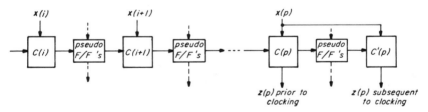

Figure 3.6 Array model when output is observed both prior to and subsequent to clocking

rightmost end of the iterative array. The first copy $C(p)$ computes the output based upon the current input and old state, while the second copy $(C'(p))$ computes the output based upon this same input and the new state.

When the number of state variables n is large one may have to cease seeking a test for a fault before the bound of 4^n is reached due to the fact that the computational time is becoming exorbitant. This typically occurs due to the problem of buried flip-flops. Consider the simple shift register shown in Figure 3.7. Here in response to each clock pulse the data in the flip-flop register shifts right one position, with the leftmost flip-flop accepting the value of the signal on input line w_1.

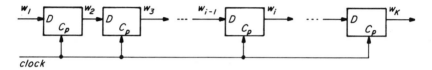

Figure 3.7   Shift register

Now consider the fault α (line w_{i-1} s-a-0), and the initial state where each flip-flop is reset to 0. The test sequence consists of a single 1 followed by $(K - 2)$ $\times$'s.* That is $w_1 = 1$ followed by the first clock pulse will set the first flip-flop to a 1. After $(i - 3)$ more clock pulses we have a D at line w_{i-1}. The remaining $(K - i + 1)$ clock pulses propagate the D through the register until it is finally observable at the output w_K. The total number of clock pulses is thus $K - 1$.

The difficulty in generating this test sequence is that it requires one input sequence to create the error, i.e., produce the first D or $\bar{D}$, and another sequence to propagate the error to an observable output. For this shift register it is relatively simple to construct a test. However, for complex sequential circuits which are not highly structured this test generation process can be quite complex. The major problem here is that the flip-flops are *buried*, i.e., (1) most of their inputs are controlled by the outputs of other flip-flops and not by primary input lines, and (2) most of their outputs feed other flip-flops and are not observable by primary output lines. In attempting to simplify test generation the degree to which flip-flops are buried should be minimized. This is often accomplished by the use of scan-in and scan-out circuitry (see Section 5.4).

Transfer Sequences

Assume we desire to construct an input sequence of length K which will drive a circuit from an initial state y_I to a final state y_f. We can solve this problem using the D-algorithm by setting up the condition y_f in the test

---

*The $\times$'s can be 0's or 1's.

cube for time frame K, and justifying the cube for time frame K under the restrictions imposed by y_I. Using this scheme a minimal length transfer sequence can be found by first using this model for $K = 0$, then $K = 1$, etc. until either a solution is found or an upper bound on K is met. This procedure is considerably more complex if faults are present since the existence of the D's and $\bar{D}$'s introduce another order of variability in selecting line values. For example, to justify a 1 on the output of a two input NAND gate it may be necessary to assign a D and a $\bar{D}$ to its inputs.

Implementation

In implementing the extension of the D-algorithm for sequential circuits, the iterative circuits shown in Figure 3.2 are not actually constructed. Only one copy of the circuit topology is constructed. The data base structure used to represent the circuit is similar to those which will be discussed in Section 4.4.3. A sequence of vector arrays is stored. There is an array $T(i)$ corresponding to time frame i. The j-th entry in this array indicates the logic value of line j for time frame i.

In addition to the implementation techniques described in Section 2.3, a number of additional techniques designed specifically for sequential circuits can be used to improve the efficiency of a test generation system. For example, certain state configurations within a circuit may be impossible to achieve. Thus, a 5-state counter implemented with 3 flip-flops may have 3 states which cannot be entered. During test generation, however, a subproblem may be established to justify one of these invalid states. A significant amount of time may be consumed before the test generation system recognizes that this state cannot be achieved. To help alleviate this situation, a table I/UNJ of invalid and unjustifiable states can be constructed. Initially, the designer or test engineer may make entries into this table. Subsequently, the system itself may make entries in one of two ways.

(a) If a state is found to be invalid, i.e., cannot be justified, it is added to the table I/UNJ.

(b) If a state is found to be unjustifiable within a time limit T specified to the system as an input parameter, then this state is added to the table I/UNJ.

Let v_1 and v_2 be two vectors whose elements are 0, 1 or $\times$. If some or all of the $\times$'s in v_1 can be replaced by 0's and/or 1's such that the resulting vector is identical to v_2, then we say that v_1 *covers* v_2. For example, $(\times,1,0,\times)$ covers $(1,1,0,0)$. Note that if v_1 cannot be justified, then neither can v_2 be justified, since v_2 is a more stringent restriction on the state space.

The table I/UNJ is used as follows. After processing a time frame and before going on to the next time frame, either forward or backward in time, the system first checks the values of the state variables in the circuit, e.g., the value of the feedback lines. This state vector is then matched with the entries in I/UNJ. If some entry in I/UNJ *covers* this state vector, then the state vector is either invalid or unjustifiable within the computational time period T, and the state vector is rejected, i.e., the program backtracks to some other choice.

This concept can be extended to cover solvable problems. For example, assume a state v_2 has been justified and it is now desired to justify the state v_1. If v_1 covers v_2, then the same input sequence which justified v_2 will also justify v_1, with some of the $\times$ components in v_1 replaced by 0's and/or 1's. Hence a table SOL of solved state justification problems can be created. Whenever a new state justification problem is encountered this table is searched to see if it has been previously solved. If so, the stored justification sequence is used. If this state is not in SOL and also not in I/UNJ then an attempt is made to justify it. If successful, the result is stored in SOL, otherwise a new entry is made in I/UNJ.

3.1.2   Initialization

In general, when power is first applied to a circuit, each flip-flop may stabilize in either the 0 or 1 state. Not only may the fault free circuit initialize to an arbitrary state S_0, but the faulty circuit can also initialize into some arbitrary state, say S_α. Hence the most general form of a test generation procedure must deal with this aspect of unknown initial state. Unfortunately, this aspect of testing introduces complexities which, as yet, have not been adequately solved.

In general, the problem of circuit initialization or synchronization deals with finding an input sequence which will drive a circuit, starting in an unknown state, to a fixed state. In test generation it is usually desirable to initialize not only the fault free circuit, but also the faulty ones. Of course, these circuits need not be driven to the same state.

We will first describe a common heuristic procedure used for solving this problem, which employs a new logic value denoted by u to represent the unknown state of a line. Our notation for the fault free, faulty, and composite circuits is summarized in Figure 3.8. The truth table for the logic system consisting of 0, 1 and u is identical to that for 0, 1 and $\times$. The only difference between an $\times$ and a u is the following. An $\times$ can be specified by the computational process to be a 0 or a 1; a u is already either a 0 or a 1 but its value is not known to the computational process. Hence we can think of a u as a special case of an $\times$ which cannot be set to either a 0 or a 1, i.e., a u must be left a u. For simplicity, we will temporarily restrict our attention to the composite logic values 0, 1, D, $\overline{D}$, $\times$, and u.

	fault free line value			
	0	1	u	$\times$
0	$0/0 = 0$	$1/0 = D$	$u/0$	$\times/0$
1	$0/1 = \bar{D}$	$1/1 = 1$	$u/1$	$\times/1$
u	$0/u$	$1/u$	$u/u = u$	$\times/u$
$\times$	$0/\times$	$1/\times$	$u/\times$	$\times/\times = \times$

faulty line value

line value for composite circuit

Figure 3.8

In order to construct a test for a fault when S_0 and S_α are unknown, we can set the initial state vector $\mathbf{y}_I$ equal to $(u,u, \ldots,u)$ and apply a modified version of Procedure 3.1.

The general form for the computational model required to generate a self initializing test sequence is shown in Figure 3.9. Assume p and q are arbitrary predefined nonnegative integers. The computation for a test proceeds as follows. Starting in an arbitrary cell, say cell $C(q)$, corresponding to time frame q, and letting $\mathbf{y}(q)$ be the vector $(\times,\times, \ldots,\times)$, it is attempted to drive a D to the output vector $\mathbf{z}(q + p)$ corresponding to time frame $q + p$. If successful, all line settings must be justified including those now existing at $\mathbf{y}(q)$. This is done by carrying out line justification on cells $C(q - 1)$ through $C(0)$, and insuring that $\mathbf{y}(0) = \mathbf{y}_I = (u,u, \ldots,u)$. If the attempt to drive a D to $\mathbf{y}(p + q)$ fails, then p should be incremented by one and the procedure repeated. If the attempt to justify the resulting $\mathbf{y}(q)$ fails, then another test for the fault which requires a different $\mathbf{y}(q)$ to be justified should be found. If no such $\mathbf{y}(q)$ can be justified, q is increased by one and the attempt to justify the $\mathbf{y}(q)$'s previously encountered is repeated.

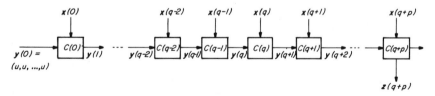

Figure 3.9 General form of computational model for test generation for synchronous circuits requiring self initialization sequences

Hence, test generation consists of a process of selecting various values for p and q. Initially one can select $p = q = 0$.

On following page, we summarize the process just discussed.

Procedure 3.2 *(Construction of a self initializing test sequence):*

    (1) Determine the maximum values P and Q for p and q. Usually P and Q are user specified, where $P + Q \leq n^s$ and n is the number of state variables.

    (2) Select initial values for p and q (usually $p = q = 0$).

    (3) Construct the corresponding iterative array model corresponding to p and q, and attempt to generate a test for the fault α insuring that $y(0)$ retains the value $y_I = (u,u, \ldots,u)$. If a test is found exit, otherwise continue.

    (4) Select the next set of values for p and q, if they exist, and return to step 3, otherwise exit with no test.   □

Step 4 of procedure 3.2 can actually be quite complex and is a function of how the D-algorithm is implemented. The main objective here is to modify the values of p and q in such a way as to reuse as much of the previous computation as possible. Note also that it is not necessary that the initial state be $(u,u, \ldots,u)$, i.e., this procedure can be easily modified such that each component in the initial state vector can be an element from the set $\{0,1,D,\bar{D},\times,u\}$.

Example 3.3:   Consider the circuit shown in Figure 3.10(a) and the fault α (a s-a-0). We first attempt a solution with $p = 0$ (the fault is on an output line) and $q = 1$.

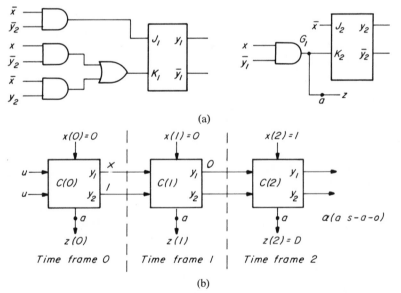

(a)

(b)

Figure 3.10

Time frame 1: To detect α we require $G_1 = 1$, hence $x(1) = 1$ and $\bar{y}_1(1) = 1$. This produces $z = D$ and a D has been propagated to the output using $p = 0$. (Note that if $q = 0$, since $y_1(0) = y_2(0) = u$ the condition $\bar{y}_1(0) = 1$ cannot be satisfied.)

Time frame 0: For this time frame we have that the present (initial) state of y_1 is u, and its next state must be 0. To achieve this condition we can attempt to justify the line settings $J_1(0) = 0$ and $K_1(0) = 1$. This can be done by setting either
   (a) $x(0) = 1$ and $\bar{y}_2(0) = 1$ or
   (b) $x(0) = 0$ and $y_2(0) = 1$.
However, since $y_2(0) = \bar{y}_2(0) = u$, no test exists.

We must therefore attempt a solution using $q = 2$. The iterative array for this case is shown in Figure 3.10(b).

Time frame 1: We can now justify the condition $y_1(2) = 0$ by either $J_1(1) = 0$, $K_1(1) = 1$ or by assuming $y_1(1) = 0$. We first try the former condition. To satisfy this condition we will first try condition (a) stated previously, i.e., we attempt to justify $\bar{y}_2(1) = 1$.

Time frame 0: To justify $\bar{y}_2(1) = 1$ we require $J_2(0) = 0$ (hence $x(0) = 1$) and $K_2(0) = 1$. But the output of G_1 cannot be set to 1 since $\bar{y}_1(0) = u$. We therefore must backtrack to an earlier choice.

Time frame 1: We next try to justify the setting $J_1(1) = 0$ and $K_1(1) = 1$ by setting $y_2(1) = 1$, as shown in Figure 3.10(b).

Time frame 0: Now by setting $x(0) = 0$ we obtain $J_2(0) = 1$ and $K_2(0) = 0$ and hence $y_2(1) = 1$ independent of the initial state of $y_2(0)$.

The generated self initializing test sequence is $\mathbf{X} = 001$, and requires $q = 2$ and $p = 0$.   □

Unfortunately, the procedure just illustrated does not guarantee generating a test for a fault when one exists. Consider the circuit shown in Figure 3.11. If line x has the value u and $y = z = 1$, then G_1 has output $1 \cdot u = u$ and G_2 has output $1 \cdot u = u$ and hence f has the value $u \cdot u = u$. However, $f(x,y,z) = xy + \bar{x}z$ and $f(x,1,1) = x + \bar{x} = 1$. Thus f has the value 1 independent of the value of x if $y = z = 1$. The difficulty arises because signals a and b have opposite values even though both are unknown and only u is used to denote an unknown value. One might think that this problem could be solved by using the additional logic value $\bar{u}$, and the logical identities $u \cdot \bar{u} = 0$ and $u + \bar{u} = 1$. However, this extension does not lead to a general solution since, if there are two lines initially at unknown values, it is not known whether to assign them the value u or $\bar{u}$.

Due to this problem many common circuits cannot be initialized by the simple extension of the *D*-algorithm presented. One such circuit is the classical nine NAND gate model of the *JK* flip-flop (see Figure 1.14(b)). Other models for this device can be developed, however, which are initializable by using a single unknown value. Other examples of noninitializable circuits using a single unknown value are discussed in Chapter 4.

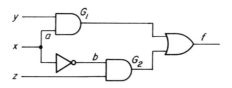

Figure 3.11

Finally, it should be noted that some circuits have no initialization sequence. They must be tested by employing a homing sequence, i.e., a sequence such that the state of the circuit is deduced by observing the output to the input sequence. A simple example of such a circuit is a *T* (trigger) flip-flop. A more general form of this circuit is a ring counter, i.e., a counter which goes through the periodic state sequence 0,1,2, ...,*N*,0,1,2, ...

It was stated earlier that the values $\times$ and *u* have similar properties. Therefore, in many systems, rather than use the logic values 0, 1, *D*, $\bar{D}$, $\times$ and *u*, only the values 0, 1, *D*, $\bar{D}$ and $\times$ are used. The computer implementation of the algorithm automatically compensates for the lack of a *u* by not allowing any of the $\times$ components in the initial state vector $y(0) = y_I = (\times, \times, ..., \times)$ to ever be changed to a 0 or 1.

Figure 3.8 specifies 16 logic values, of which only 6 have been used so far. Procedure 3.2 can be readily extended to handle these 16 logic values. This extension offers some additional versatility, though this advantage does not seem to outweigh the disadvantages of handling a much more complex set of cubes. The main advantage of using the 16 valued logic system is that some faults can now be detected which could not be detected using only the 6 valued system (see Problem 3.9).

A procedure which guarantees producing an initialization sequence, when one exists, requires the use of multiple unknown values. This leads to the processing of large Boolean switching expressions, and appears to be computationally feasible for only small circuits. We will briefly expand on this concept in sections 3.2.4 and 4.3.5.

Due to the complex problem of initialization it is often necessary to either design circuits which can be easily initialized, or it is necessary to have the test engineer supply the initialization sequence to the test generation system, and then apply Procedure 3.1 starting in a known initial state. The simplest technique used to aid initialization is to design the circuit with either a preset or reset line going to each flip-flop. Then a single input vector can initialize the fault free circuit, and in most cases will initialize the faulty circuits. The only problem with this approach is that the initial state of each faulty circuit may not be readily known. For this situation the logic values $1/u$ and $0/u$ are·useful.

3.1.3 Extension of Critical Path Test Algorithm to Synchronous Sequential Circuits

The Critical Path test generation algorithm discussed in Section 2.4 can also be extended to apply to sequential circuits. In general there are several ways in which a critical signal at a flip-flop output can be driven back through the circuit. The tables of Figure 3.12 specify these alternatives for JK and T flip-flops.

Flip-flop Critical Value on y output — time $t+1$	Previous State —time t	Input Excitation	
		J	K
0^c	0^c	0^c	0
	0	0^c	1
	1^c	1	1^c
	1	0	1^c
1^c	0^c	1^c	1
	0	1^c	0
	1^c	0	0^c
	1	1	0^c

(a)

Flip-flop Critical Value on y output	Previous State	Input Excitation
		T
0^c	1^c	1^c
	0^c	0^c
1^c	0^c	1^c
	1^c	0^c

(b)

Figure 3.12 Critical Cubes for JK and T flip-flops

The first four lines of the table of Figure 3.12(a) indicate four state/ excitation combinations which result in a critical 0-output from a JK flip-flop. In each case an input signal is critical if a change in that signal alone will change the flip-flop output to a 1.

To generate a test from a known initial state y_I, we backward drive through the corresponding iterative array (equivalent to time frames) until all state variables in the last time frame can be set to the values as specified in y_I. To generate a test from an unknown initial state, it is necessary to backward drive until all state variables can be left unspecified. We start with an arbitrary time frame, say n, and keep working back through preceding time frames until the initial state condition is satisfied.

Example 3.4:   Consider the circuit shown in Figure 3.13 for which we wish to derive a test, assuming the initial state is $y_1 = y_2 = 0$.

Time frame n: We arbitrarily initially define $z(n) = 1^c$. We then backward drive (denoted by $\leftarrow$) through gate G_1 by specifying $x(n) = 1^c$ and $y_1(n) = 1^c$.

Time frame n − 1: To justify $y_1(n) = 1^c$, we can specify $y_1(n − 1) = 0$, $J_1 = 1^c$ and $K_1 = 0$. These assignments imply (denoted by $\rightarrow$) that $x(n − 1) = 0^c$ and $\bar{y}_2(n − 1) = 1^c(y_2(n − 1) = 0^c)$.

Time frame n − 2: The condition $y_2(n − 1) = 0^c$ can be justified by specifying $y_2(n − 2) = 1^c$ and $K_2 = 1^c$. This latter condition can be justified by the setting $x(n − 2) = 1$ and $y_1(n − 2) = 0^c$. These line values imply $J_1 = 0$ and $K_1 = 0^c$ which, along with $y_1(n − 2) = 0^c$, is sufficient for justifying the requirement that $y_1(n − 2) = 0$.

Time frame n − 3: The critical signals $y_1(n − 2) = 0^c$ and $y_2(n − 2) = 1^c$ can be simultaneously justified by specifying $y_1(n − 3) = y_2(n − 3) = 0$, and $J_1 = 0^c$, which implies $x(n − 3) = 1^c$.

We have thus created the test sequence $X = 1101$ with respect to the initial state $y_1 = y_2 = 0$. After noting all lines which have critical values, we can next backtrack to wherever previous choices existed. We select those choices which set lines to critical values which have not yet been made critical, and in this way we can construct a whole set of test sequences which constitute the test set for this circuit.   □

Given a collection of test sequences for a circuit it is important to determine all faults not detected by these tests. This can be determined with the use of a fault simulator which will be considered in Chapter 4.

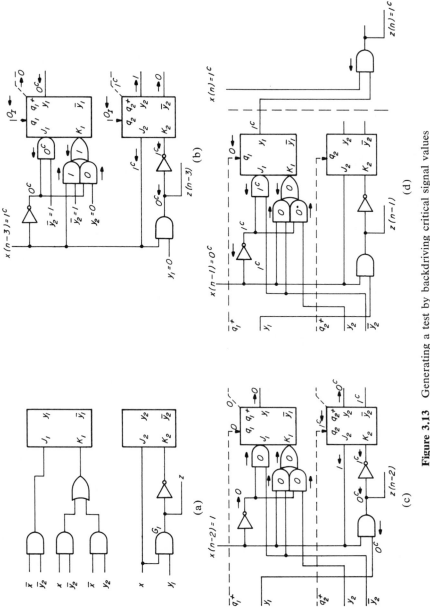

Figure 3.13 Generating a test by backdriving critical signal values

3.1.4   Test Set Reduction

Typically at the completion of test generation for a sequential circuit the final test consists of a set of self initializing test sequences $\{X_1, X_2, \ldots, X_n\}$. The final test sequence X can be constructed by concatenating these tests, e.g., $X = X_1 X_2 \ldots X_n$. Often, however, the length of this final test sequence can be substantially reduced by using one of several test consolidation procedures. These procedures typically take advantage of the fact that most test vectors contain many $\times$ components. These $\times$'s can be changed to 0's or 1's without invalidating the test, and in fact, additional faults are usually detected when the $\times$'s are replaced by 0's and 1's. Of course, the $\times$'s must be replaced by 0's and 1's before the test can be applied by the test equipment.

In one common procedure used to reduce the length of X, pairs of test sequences X_i and X_j are compared, vector by vector, to see if they can be merged into one test sequence. Often, the $\times$'s must be changed to 0's or 1's to accomplish this task.

Example 3.5:   Consider the two test sequences shown below. We will try to merge X_j with X_i. Note that the intersect of x_1^j with x_1^i and x_2^i does not exist. However, $x_1^j \cap x_3^i = 1\ 1\ 0\ 1\ 1\ \times$ and $x_2^j \cap x_4^i = 1\ 0\ 1\ 1\ 0\ 1$. Hence we can consolidate X_i and X_j into a new test X_k shown below.

$X_i = x_1^i x_2^i x_3^i x_4^i$	$X_j = x_1^j x_2^j x_3^j$
$x_1^i = 0 \times 1\ 0\ 1 \times$	$x_1^j = \times \times 0\ 1\ 1 \times$
$x_2^i = 0 \times \times 1\ 1 \times$	$x_2^j = \times 0 \times 1\ 0\ 1$
$x_3^i = 1\ 1 \times \times 1 \times$	$x_3^j = \times 1\ 1\ 1\ 0 \times$
$x_4^i = 1\ 0\ 1 \times 0 \times$	

$$X_k$$

$$x_1^k = 0 \times 1\ 0\ 1 \times \ (= x_1^i)$$
$$x_2^k = 0 \times \times 1\ 1 \times \ (= x_2^i)$$
$$x_3^k = 1\ 1\ 0\ 1\ 1 \times \ (= x_1^j \cap x_3^i)$$
$$x_4^k = 1\ 0\ 1\ 1\ 0\ 1\ (= x_2^j \cap x_4^i)$$
$$x_5^k = \times 1\ 1\ 1\ 0 \times \ (= x_3^j) \qquad \square$$

Once two tests are consolidated, they are replaced by the resulting test and the procedure repeated. The length of the final test sequence may be a small fraction of the length of the original sequence. It should be noted, however, that test consolidation has an adverse effect on fault location if fault dictionaries are used. The reason for this is that by consolidating tests, more faults are detected per test vector, hence fewer unique fault signatures exist and therefore fault resolution is degraded.

3.2 TEST GENERATION FOR ASYNCHRONOUS CIRCUITS

For several reasons, generating tests for asynchronous circuits is considerably more difficult than for synchronous circuits. First, asynchronous circuits often contain races and are susceptible to improper operation due to hazards. Secondly, to obtain an iterative model of the circuit requires the identification of all feedback lines, which is not always a simple task. Finally, correct circuit operation is often a function' of delays intentionally placed in the circuit, but which are ignored by most test generation algorithms. In this section we will consider these problems. We will develop procedures for the generation of hazard-free tests. We will also investigate how races effect the validity of a predicted test. We will introduce a more accurate iterative array model to be used for asynchronous circuits. Finally, two ways in which delays can be dealt with more effectively in the test generation process will be described. The first procedure discussed will again employ the iterative array model, while the second procedure will employ an equation generation technique which does not require feedback lines to be identified. Finally, once we see how to deal with delays in test generation, we will show how tests for delay faults can be constructed. We will assume a static mode of testing in which once an input is applied, the output is not sampled, and the next input is not applied until the circuit stabilizes.

In the following example we illustrate the importance of delay on circuit operation. The circuit in this example is intended to generate a pulse.

Example 3.6:   Consider the circuit shown in Figure 3.14. Analysis of this circuit shows that CLOCK $= x \oplus \bar{x} = 1$. Hence it appears that the *JK* flip-flop is never clocked, and consequently it will never change state. If we employed the *D*-algorithm to generate tests for this circuit we would find that CLOCK $= 1$. If we applied the backward drive testing procedure to justify a critical 0 on CLOCK, we would find that there is no solution.

However, with the use of hazard analysis it is apparent that the CLOCK line has a hazard whenever the input x changes value and consequently it may be possible to clock the flip-flop. If there is appreciably more delay in the path through the three inverters than through the direct connection from x to the exclusive-OR element, then there will be a pulse on CLOCK every time x changes value. This pulse will trigger the flip-flop. If the oper-

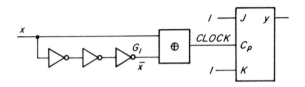

Figure 3.14   Simple Clock Generating Circuit

ation of the rest of the circuit, driven by y, is dependent on y changing state, then it is imperative that the pulses on CLOCK be accurately predicted. Hence a test generation algorithm must be capable of dealing with the concept of time, and delays.   □

3.2.1   Iterative Array Model for Asynchronous Circuits

Analogous to the approach taken for treating synchronous circuits, one common technique for dealing with asynchronous circuits is to develop an iterative array combinational circuit model and then use test generation procedures such as those discussed in Chapter 2. However, there are a few differences between the models used for synchronous and asynchronous circuits. In Figure 3.15(a) we show the classical model of an asynchronous circuit, and in Figure 3.15(b) the corresponding iterative array model. In Figure 3.15(c) we indicate the structure of one cell, $C(i)$, of the model of Figure 3.15(b).

Note that an asynchronous circuit may, in response to an input change, go through a sequence of internal state changes $\mathbf{y}(i) \rightarrow \mathbf{y}^1(i) \rightarrow \mathbf{y}^2(i) \rightarrow \ldots \rightarrow \mathbf{y}^{I_i}(i)$ in going from an initial stable state $\mathbf{y}(i)$ to a final stable state $\mathbf{y}^{I_i}(i) = \mathbf{y}(i + 1)$. In the model of Figure 3.15(b, c) we account for the unique aspects of asynchronous circuits in the following way:

(1) Fundamental mode input

   (a) The input is not allowed to change until the circuit has stabilized. This condition is satisfied by requiring $\mathbf{y}^{I_i-1}(i) = \mathbf{y}^{I_i}(i)$.

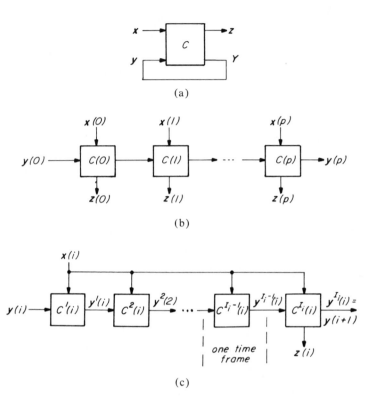

Figure 3.15   a) Classical (cyclic) Model for an Asynchronous Circuit
b) Iterative Array Model
c) One cell ($C(i)$) in Iterative Array Model

(b) We require $x(i) \neq x(i + 1)$. (To minimize race conditions it is sometimes useful to restrict $x(i)$ and $x(i + 1)$ to differ in only one component position.)

(2) Static output response.

To insure a static mode of testing and also to avoid erroneous indications of tests which are delay dependent, the output z is only observed once the circuit has stabilized. In this model input $x(i)$ is associated with I_i time frames.

Problem 3.10 illustrates difficulties encountered if the synchronous model of Figure 3.2(b) is used in place of that of Figure 3.15(b,c).

Example 3.7:   Consider the machine defined by the flow table of Figure 3.16(a)*. Assume that the initial total stable state is $(x,y) = (0,A)$, and that the fault changes the output in total state $(0,E)$ from a 1 to a 0.

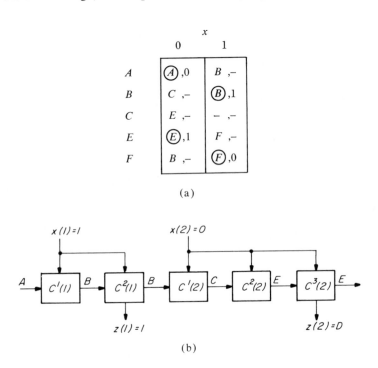

(a)

(b)

Figure 3.16   Test generation in an asynchronous circuit

To generate a test for this fault we will employ a D-algorithm procedure in the iterative array shown in Figure 3.16(b). We first set $x(1) = 1$ and attempt to drive a D to an output. This fails, so we try to drive a D to a feedback line. This also fails and we find that the circuit must be sent into a new stable state B. We then set $x(2) = 0$ and find that the circuit stabilizes in state E and $z(2) = D$.   □

In this example we have processed the circuit model in a forward direction. It is also possible to process the circuit model in the reverse direction.

_____

*In this example, for simplicity, we use a flow table model rather than the circuit realization for the machine.

For example, starting with an arbitrary cell $C^{I_i}(i)$ we attempt to find an input $x(i)$ such that $z(i)$ contains a D component and $y^{I_i-1}(i) = y^{I_i}$. If the fault is not redundant, such a condition always exists. We then attempt to work back to our total initial state condition $(x(0), y_I)$. We first try to establish that $(x(i), y^{I_i-1}(i))$ is a valid initial total state for the array $C(i)$. This is the case if there exists an input $x(i - 1)$ such that $(x(i - 1), y(i - 1))$ is a stable total state, where $y(i - 1) = y(i)$. If this is not the case, then it is necessary to work back one cell and calculate $y^{I_i-2}(i)$ for $x = x(i)$. We proceed working backward until a valid initial total state is encountered, at which time the input can be changed.

In both of these procedures, the computation is complicated by the fact that the value of I_i which ensures circuit stability is not known *a priori*.

Identification of Feedback Lines

Another difficulty associated with this model is that of identifying what lines should constitute the state variables (feedback lines). At least one line in each cyclic path in the circuit must be a feedback line. In addition, any line or element associated with a delay required for correct functional circuit operation can be made a feedback line. Hence even a combinational circuit can be modeled with feedback lines. In the circuit of Figure 3.14, if the output of G_1 is considered to be a feedback line (state variable), then in the corresponding iterative array model it is possible to generate a 0 on the CLOCK line, and hence the flip-flop can be triggered.

Normally the feedback lines of a circuit are not explicitly identified. The circuit is usually described as an interconnection of elements, such as gates and flip-flops, or by the interconnection of "macro" elements, such as SSI, MSI and LSI circuits. To construct an iterative array model for such a circuit requires the identification of feedback lines. This problem can be transformed into a graph-theoretic form in the following way. We can associate with the circuit S, assumed to be sequential, a graph G, where each element e_i in S corresponds to a node n_i in G. G will contain a directed edge from node n_i to node n_j if and only if an output signal from element e_i is an input signal to e_j. If there is a closed path or loop in this graph, the graph is said to be *cyclic*. Our original problem now reduces to that of removing edges, called *cuts*, from graph G so that the resulting graph is *acyclic*. The identification of the minimal number of *cuts* is a difficult problem whose complexity grows exponentially with the number of nodes in G. One algorithm for solving this problem is reported by Smith and Walford [31]. Many approaches to this problem require the identification and/or enumeration of the loops in G [20], [32]. Due to the complexity of this problem, several heuristic procedures have been developed for identifying near minimal edge cuts [26], [35]. Since this problem pertains to model construction rather than test generation, we will not consider it further. In many test generation systems this aspect of model construction is done manually. Before leaving this subject, however, it should be pointed out that the following two aspects of this problem have direct bearing on the resulting iterative array, namely:

(1) The number of feedback lines identified; and
(2) Which lines are selected as feedback lines.

If races exist in the circuit, these two factors can influence the results obtained from the test generation process.

Example 3.8:   Consider a modulo 8 ripple counter (Figure 3.17) in which each flip-flop triggers when a 0 to 1 transition occurs at its clock input. Since this is an asynchronous circuit having three flip-flop (state variables), it can be modeled by a circuit with three feedback loops corresponding to these three flip-flops. In the corresponding iterative array structure, for the worst case condition, four cells (time frames) are necessary to process one input vector period, say $x(i)$. That is, when $\bar{y}_1 = \bar{y}_2 = \bar{y}_3 = 0$, and $x(i)$ becomes a 1, $\bar{y}_1$ will change to a 1 causing $\bar{y}_2$ to change to a 1 which in turn causes $\bar{y}_3$ to change to a 1. We see that this model deals with time at a very detailed level. Since each flip-flop in the original circuit can be modeled by a pseudo combinational flip-flop element, this circuit can also be modeled without feedback. In this model only one time frame per input vector period is required, hence time is quantized at a much coarser level.   □

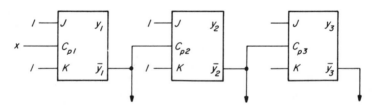

Figure 3.17   Ripple counter

The Effects of Races in Test Generation

Races occur in circuits due to signal delays. Many asynchronous circuits contain noncritical races which most test generation procedures cannot adequately handle.

Referring back to our original model for an asynchronous circuit, if we assume that we can lump all circuit delays into the feedback lines of the circuit, and that the delay in feedback line y_i has Δ_i units (integer), then we can develop a new iterative model which will incorporate these delays and in which we assume that each cell (time frame) corresponds to one unit of delay. In this model, if line y_i has Δ_i units of delays, then the output Y_i of $C(j)$ is the y_i input to $C(j + \Delta_i)$. We illustrate this concept in Figure 3.18, where $\Delta_1 = 1$ and $\Delta_2 = 2$.

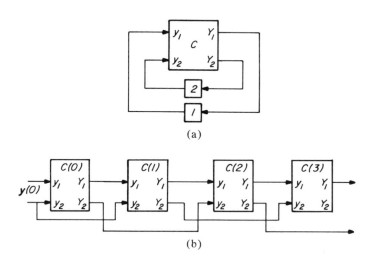

(a)

(b)

Figure 3.18 Model for Unequal Delays

We can now summarize some of the properties of this model.

Case 1: If all delays are known and included in the model, then this computational model is a valid representation of the circuit behavior.

Case 2: If the test activates only race free transitions* in both the fault free and faulty circuit, then this model is still valid even when the relative values of the delays are not known, i.e., modeled by setting $\Delta_i = 1$ for all i.

Case 3: If a race occurs for some transition, and the relative values of the delays are not known, then the test may not necessarily be valid. This situation occurs since the actual circuit may enter a state not predicted by the model.

Unfortunately, some circuits have noncritical races whose relative delay values are not known. If it is desired to handle these cases more accurately

---

*Only one feedback line changing at a time.

during test generation, then a more general delay model must be used. Breuer [8] has shown how ambiguous delay and inertial delay models can be incorporated in the test generation model. These techniques extend the class of circuits which can be correctly processed by automatic test generation systems.

3.2.2   Generation of Critical Hazard Free Tests

Most test generation models for sequential circuits make little use of circuit delay information. Consequently, tests which contain hazards may be generated. These hazards may invalidate the tests, i.e., the faults the tests were intended to detect may in fact remain undetected. Consider, for example, the circuit shown in Figure 3.19. Consider the input sequence

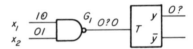

Figure 3.19   Hazard produces a steady state error

$x(0)x(1)$, where $x(0) = (x_1,x_2) = (1,0)$, and $x(1) = 0,1)$. Due to delays in the circuit it is possible that line x_2 changes prior to x_1, hence producing $(x_1,x_2) = (1,1)$ and a momentary pulse on line G_1, i.e., line G_1 has a static 0 hazard. This pulse, if it occurs, may possibly trigger the flip-flop. Hence the final value of y is not known, i.e., it is a 0 if no hazard occurs, but may be a 1 if the flip-flop is triggered. Since this hazard may cause a steady state error, we refer to it as a *critical hazard*. Not all hazards cause steady state errors. Since we are considering only static testing, hazards which do not cause steady state errors can be ignored.

In this section we will present methods by which existing test generation procedures can be modified so that generated tests will not contain critical hazards. For illustrative purposes, we will consider techniques for critical hazard elimination within the framework of the *D*-algorithm. The basic concepts, however, are also applicable to other test generation procedures.

The techniques to be presented are applicable to circuits which satisfy the following properties:

*P*1: All circuit elements are either gates, such as AND, OR, NAND, etc., or flip-flops.

*P*2: All cyclic paths in the circuit must be pseudo-loops [34], i.e., in response to an input change no signal change can propagate through the circuit and back onto itself.

$P3$: Data inputs of clocked flip-flops (such as J and K) are not allowed to change value when the clock line is changing.

The main reason for properties $P1$ and $P2$ are that the techniques to be presented have not yet been extended to handle the most general form of asynchronous circuits. Hence, for example, latches and flip-flops must be modeled functionally, $(P1)$, and global feedback lines must, in some sense, be logically cut $(P2)$. Property 3 is used to simplify functional analysis for a clocked flip-flop. Hazard analysis is carried out during test generation by carrying along with the computation, not only the logic value of a line but also a flag which indicates whether or not a hazard is present on the line.

Hazards occur between two steady state conditions. Hence we will use a 27 valued logic system of the form $(a\ b\ f)$ where a and b are two successive steady state values of a line, and f is a flag which indicates the status of a hazard on the line. We let $a,b \in \{0,1,\times\}$ and $f \in \{*,d,\text{"blank"}\}$, where $f = *$ indicates the existence of a hazard for the transition from a to b; $f = \text{"blank"}$ denotes the fact that the transition from a to b is hazard free; and $f = d$ indicates that the hazard status condition is not known. This latter condition occurs when either a or b or both are $\times$, or when the hazard status flags on the input to a gate do not convey enough information to remove a d flag on the output of a gate. In Figure 3.20 we indicate the logic values corresponding to the case $a,b \in \{0,1\}$ and $f \in \{*,\text{"blank"}\}$.

	Logic Symbol		
a	b	* or "blank"	Interpretation
0	0		steady state 0
1	1		steady state 1
0	1		hazard free transition from 0 to 1
1	0		hazard free transition from 1 to 0
0	0	*	static 0 hazard
1	1	*	static 1 hazard
0	1	*	dynamic hazard
1	0	*	dynamic hazard

Figure 3.20   Eight valued logic used for hazard analysis

If the logic values at the input to an element at times $t(i)$ and $t(i + 1)$ are known, then the output logic values can be calculated. In addition, if the hazard status of the inputs are known, the hazard status on the outputs can be determined. In effect, we can propagate the hazard status flag through an element similarly to propagating D's through an element. The table of Figure 3.21 indicates the truth table for a NAND gate for the 8 valued logic system of Figure 3.20.

NAND	11	00	01	10	11*	00*	01*	10*
11	00	11	10	01	00*	11*	10*	01*
00	11	11	11	11	11[c]	11[c]	11[c]	11[c]
01	10	11	10	11*[a]	10*[b]	11*	10*	11*
10	01	11	11*[a]	01	01*[b]	11*	11*	01*
11*	00*	11[c]	10*[b]	01*[b]	00*	11*	10*	01*
00*	11*	11[c]	11*	11*	11*	11*	11*	11*
01*	10*	11[c]	10*	11*	10*	11*	10*	11*
10*	01*	11[c]	11*	01*	01*	11*	11*	01*

Figure 3.21 Truth Table for NAND gate

In Figure 3.21, the entries labeled "a" indicate the *creation* of static hazards while entries labeled "b" indicate the *creation* of dynamic hazards. When one of the inputs is 00, no hazard can propagate through the gate (see for example entries labeled "c"). For this case we say that the hazard is masked. For the remaining entries, hazards on the inputs are propagated to the outputs.

For a NAND latch, a similar truth table can be produced for this 8 valued logic [9]. Due to its complexity, however, we shall only indicate a small portion of this table. In the table of Figure 3.22 we have shown just two entries for the truth table for an *SR* flip-flop (NAND latch). Here we assume the input and output sequences $S = 11$, $R = 00$, $y = 00$, and $\bar{y} = 11$.

S	R	y	$\bar{y}$
11*	00	00*	11
11*	00*	00*	11*
11	00*	00	11
11	00	00	11

Figure 3.22 Portion of truth table for NAND latch

For this latch, as for gates, the following three cases occur:
(1) Propagation and creation of hazard status flags f.
(2) Propagation of hazards
(3) Justification of hazard-free status requirements.
In addition, a hazard can cause a steady state error in a latch, e.g., if $S = R = 11*$.

The procedure used to generate a critical hazard free test uses the following concepts:
(1) Propagation and creation of hazard status flags f.
(2) Specification of hazard free (hf) status requirements.
(3) Justification of hazard-free status requirements.
For simplicity we will illustrate these concepts only on the following elements: NAND gates, SR flip-flops, JK clocked master-slave flip-flops.

Creation and Propagation of Hazard Status Flags

Example 3.9: Consider the circuit shown in Figure 3.23, and the input sequence x(0)x(1), where x(0) = (0,1,0,1,0) and x(1) = (1,0,1,1,0). The

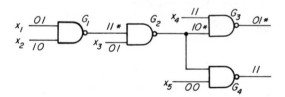

Figure 3.23 Creation and propagation of hazards

resulting logic values and hazard status flags are as shown. We assume that the primary inputs are hazard-free. At the output of G_1 there is a static 1 hazard; at G_2 a dynamic hazard; and at G_4 a hazard has been masked. □

Hazard Free Status Requirements

Since hazards can cause steady state errors in latches and flip-flops, these conditions must be avoided. Consider the situation shown in Figure 3.24.

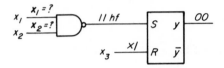

Figure 3.24   The need for a hazard-free status requirement

Assume we require the *SR* (NAND) latch to hold its state of 0, given the logic values shown. To insure this condition we require line *S* to be hazard-free, denoted by *hf*, since a momentary value of 0 may set the latch. Hence we flag the *S* input 11 *hf*. Below we summarize those conditions which require hazard-free conditions on the input to a latch which must hold its state.

Case	S	R	y	
1	11 *hf*	×1	00	(hold a 0)
2	×1	11 *hf*	11	(hold a 1)

If a latch is to change state, then no hazard-free requirements exists on its input lines.

For a *JK* master-slave clocked flip-flop, where the master is enabled when $C_p = 1$, we have the following cases.

Case (a): $C_p = 0$: The clock must be hazard-free under the following conditions:

Case	J	K	y
1	× 1	× ×	00
2	× ×	× 1	11

Case (b): $C_p = 1$: The *J* and *K* lines must be hazard free under the following conditions.

Case	J	K	y
1	0 0 *hf*	×0	00
2	×0	0 0 *hf*	11

A hazard free (*hf*) requirement on a line can only be justified if this line also carries the hazard status flag "blank."

Extended *D*-algorithm for Hazard Free Test Generation

For test generation we must consider signal values in the normal and faulty circuit simultaneously. Thus if a line is labeled 01* in the fault free circuit, and 11 in the faulty circuit, then by composition this line is labeled $\bar{D}1*/$. The label *hf/hf* implies that we require a line in both the fault free and faulty circuit to be fault free. The following abbreviations are used: $d/d = d$, $*/* = *$, and $hf/hf = hf$.

We have thus far presented the additional tools useful for carrying out hazard analysis during test generation. As stated earlier, these tools are intended to be used in conjunction with a conventional test generation algorithm. We will now briefly discuss how these concepts can be imbedded within the framework of the *D*-algorithm. Initially all lines which are known to be hazard free (such as primary inputs and outputs of memory elements) are assigned the hazard status "blank"; all other lines are assigned the flag d. During execution of the *D*-algorithm lines are set to values via *D*-drive, implication or line justification. When a line is set to a value (i.e., an × changed to a 0, 1, D or $\bar{D}$) at time frame i, the value of this line at time frame $i - 1$ can be queried. Based upon this information it may be possible to assign to a new hazard status flag (* or blank) for time frame i. In addition a check can be made to see if a *hf* requirement flag should also be assigned to this line. If the line is assigned both the flags * and *hf*, then a conflict exists and the test generation procedure must backtrack in the normal fashion. If no conflict in flags exists, then the procedure should continue in the usual manner.

Example 3.10: Consider the circuit shown in Figure 3.25(a). The value of every line (initial state) at time frame t and $t + 1$ is shown, along with the initial value of the hazard status flags. We desire to derive a critical hazard free test for the fault a s-a-0. The computation proceeds as follows for time frame $t + 1$ (see Figure 3.25(b)). Here, step (*i*) in the computation to be described next is denoted by (*i*).

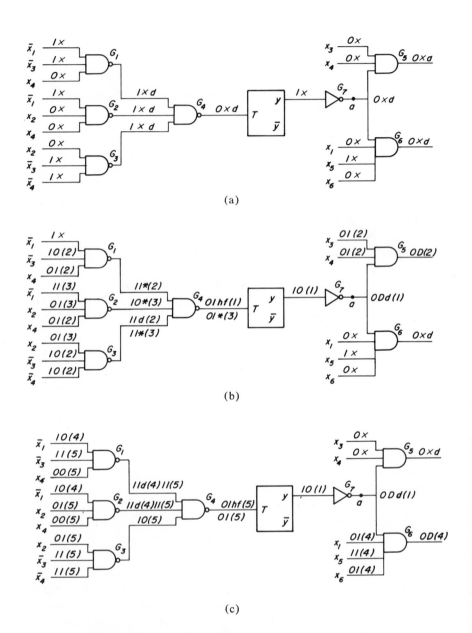

(a)

(b)

(c)

Figure 3.25   Example of critical hazard free test construction

Step 1. Set $G_7 = D$. This implies $y = 0$, which implies $G_4 = 1$, i.e., the 0 to 1 transition at T will trigger the flip-flop. We now add the requirement that $G_4 = 0\ 1$ be hazard free since multiple transitions at T may leave $y = 1$. There are no further implications.

Step 2. We arbitrarily decide to D-drive through G_5, producing $G_5 = D$, and $x_3 = x_4 = 1$. By implication we have that $G_1 = 1\ 1\ *$ and $G_3 = 1\ 1\ d$. The hazard status flag of G_3 is not known since x_2 still has the value $\times$.

Step 3. We now justify the value $G_4 = 1$. We require $G_2 = 0$, which implies that $\bar{x}_1 = 1$ and $x_2 = 1$. This results in $G_2 = 1\ 0\ *$, and $G_3 = 1\ 1\ *$, which implies $G_4 = 0\ 1\ *$. But $G_4 = 0\ 1\ *$ does not justify $G_4 = 0\ 1\ hf$. Hence we must backtrack to the last point a choice existed, i.e., we should D-drive through G_6 rather than G_5.

The remainder of the computation is shown in Figure 3.25(c).

Step 4. We D-drive through G_6 producing $G_6 = 0\ D$ and $x_1 = x_5 = x_6 = 1$. By implication we get $G_1 = G_2 = 1\ 1\ d$.

Step 5. To justify $y = 1\ 0$ we require $G_4 = 0\ 1\ hf$. By implication (or line justification), we require $G_3 = 0$ which implies $x_2 = \bar{x}_3 = \bar{x}_4 = 1$. This implies $G_3 = 1\ 0$ as well as $G_1 = G_2 = 1\ 1$. Hence all line values are justified and the hf condition on line G_4 is also justified.   □

3.2.3   Test Generation for Delay Faults

Delays are added to many circuits to ensure reliable operation. Some examples are for filtering out unwanted spikes, fixing races, compensating for essential hazards, and synchronization between circuits. For these situations (and others), the values for the delay elements may be critical in order to obtain the desired operation.

Let the delay of an element be Δ. Due to factors such as aging, leakage, temperature, humidity, etc., the value of this delay may become $\Delta' \neq \Delta$. We refer to such a change as a *delay fault*.

Unger [34] has shown that there is a class $\mathcal{A}$ of asynchronous circuits whose steady state operation is correct for any finite value of stray delays. This class consists of those circuits which contain no critical races, essential hazards, or d-trios (nonessential hazards). From this result we obtain the following theorem.

Theorem 3.1:   For a class $\mathcal{A}$ circuit, a delay fault causes no detectable static error; it may cause a detectable transient error.   □

Hence some delay faults, like some stuck-at-faults, are undetectable. We will now show how delay faults can be modeled as stuck-at-faults. As a consequence, tests for these faults can be generated using the procedures for stuck-at-faults.

Consider the circuit shown in Figure 3.26, where each gate is assumed to be fault free. If line a is fault free, then $z(t) = x(t - \Delta)$ while for the fault a s-a-0, $z(t) = x(t - \Delta')$.

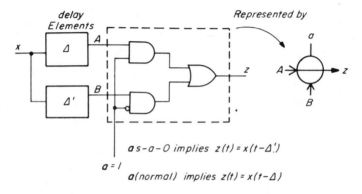

Figure 3.26   Model used to "Switch In" a delay fault

Hence this stuck-at-fault can be used to switch from one delay value to another, and thus model a delay fault. In Figure 3.27 we show how this model is included in our general model of an asynchronous circuit. When line a is normal, we have an asynchronous circuit with Δ units of delay in the feedback path, while if a is s-a-0 we have Δ' units of delay. We have previously illustrated how different delay values are dealt with in an iterative array model.

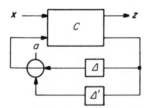

Figure 3.27   Asynchronous circuit having a delay fault

3.2.4   Circuit-Time Equations

In the preceding sections we have shown how the parameter of delay could be incorporated into the computational test generation model of a circuit in order to generate a valid (race and hazard free) test. Classical test generation techniques, such as the D-algorithm and Boolean difference, can be applied to these models.

We will now present another approach for generating tests for asynchronous circuits. In this method Boolean equations are developed for the outputs of the circuit in terms of the inputs. From these equations, all test sequences for detecting a specific fault, up to a specified sequence length, can be computed. The equations are developed under the assumption that each gate has one unit of delay. Hence, some race conditions can be dealt with. Feedback lines need not be identified (the iterative array concept is used implicitly rather than explicitly). This procedure utilizes the three valued $(0,1,u)$ logic system previously described.

In manipulating ternary valued logic expressions the laws of commutativity, associativity, absorption $(A + AB = A)$, and De Morgan's Law of ordinary Boolean algebra are valid. However, because the variables are three valued, we have the following results which are different from those in Boolean algebra (see Problem 3.17).

  i) $AB + A\bar{B} \neq A$
 ii) $A + \bar{A}B \neq A + B$
iii) $AB + \bar{A}C + BC \neq AB + \bar{A}C$

Hence, some care must be taken in manipulating 3 valued logical expressions.

The logic equation to be derived, called *circuit-time equations,* are denoted by G_t, where G_t is the value of line G at time t. In general, G_t is represented by a ternary valued expression in terms of the input sequence $\mathbf{X} = x(0)\ x(1)\ x(2)\ \ldots\ x(p)$. The subscript t denotes the unit of time (gate delay) under consideration rather than which input vector is applied.

We will illustrate the generation of these equations using the circuit shown in Figure 3.28. Let $x(0) = (A,B,C,1)$ and initially set $E_0 = F_0 = G_0 = u$.

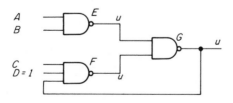

Figure 3.28

Since each gate is assumed to have one unit of delay, we have that $E_1 = \bar{A} + \bar{B}$ and $F_1 = \bar{C} + 0 + \bar{u} = \bar{C} + u$. For time $t = 2$ we have $G_2 = AB + Cu$. Now G has a new value (expression) associated with it, since its initial value was u. Since G fans-out to gate F, we recompute the equation for F, i.e., $F_3 = \overline{C} + \overline{AB + Cu} = \overline{C} + u(\overline{A} + \overline{B})$. Now F has a new value, so we recompute the value of G, namely $G_4 = \overline{\overline{A} + \overline{B}} + \overline{\overline{C} + u(\overline{A} + \overline{B})} = AB + Cu = G_2$. Hence at time $t = 4$ the circuit has stabilized and we have thus computed the complete transient as well as steady state description for the line values in this circuit under the condition $D = 1$. To set $G = 1$ we require $A = B = 1$; to set $G = 0$ we require $C = 0$ and either A or B equal to 0.

In Figure 3.29 we illustrate a flow chart for computing the circuit-time

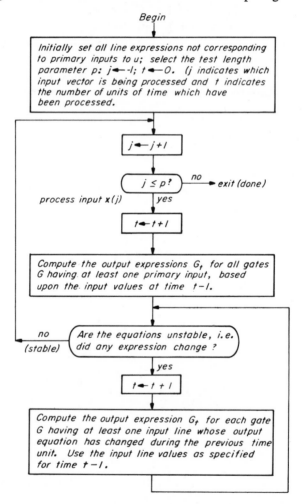

Figure 3.29   Generation of circuit-time equations

equations for an arbitrary circuit. Note that each component $x_i(j)$ of input vector $\mathbf{x}(j)$ is either a variable represented symbolically as $x_i(j)$, or a constant $(0,1$ or $u)$.

Note that in developing the equations, it is possible that some of the primary inputs or internal signal lines have fixed values, namely $0,1$, or u. In this case the equations use these values rather than the signal name, and hence can be greatly simplified. It is also possible that the equations, while processing input $\mathbf{x}(j)$, may oscillate (not stabilize). If this situation is detected, then one can set the value of those lines which are oscillating to the value u.

We will now consider how these equations can be developed in the presence of faults. Let f_i be a fault in the circuit, and assume it is associated with line a. Let f_i^p and f_i^n be binary variables associated with fault f_i such that $f_i^p (f_i^n)$ equals 1 if and only if f_i is present (not present) in the circuit. Then $f_i^p, f_i^n \epsilon \{0,1\}$ and $f_i^p = 1 - f_i^n$. Since $\bar{f_i^p} = f_i^n$, only one of these variables is necessary.

The normal logic equations for a NAND gate having inputs A, B and output C are now modified as shown in Figure 3.30, in order to reflect the presence or absence of faults.

Fault	Circuit-Time Equation
$f_1(A \text{ s-a-1})$	$C = \overline{AB} + Bf_1^p$
	$= \bar{B} + \bar{A}f_1^n$
$f_2(C \text{ s-a-0})$	$C = (\bar{A} + \bar{B})f_2^n$
$f_3(C \text{ s-a-1})$	$C = \bar{A} + \bar{B} + f_3^p$

Figure 3.30   Logic equations for NAND gate under fault conditions

When developing the circuit-time equation for a circuit having fault f_i, the appropriate modified logic equation for the element associated with the fault should be used. Note that the modified logic equations for an element are valid even when the fault identifiers f_i^n and f_i^p are present in the input expression to the faulty element (see Problem 3.18).

The general form of a circuit-time equation is

$$G_t = \alpha + \beta f^p + \gamma f^n \qquad (1)$$

where α, β and γ are expressions over the input variables $x_i(j), j = 0, 1, \ldots, p$ and u. In order to generate a test to detect a stuck-at-fault f at line

a, we require that $G_{t+\tau}|_{f^p=1, f^n=0} \neq G_{t+\tau}|_{f^p=0, f^n=1}$ which implies the conditions

i) $\alpha = 0$
ii) $\beta \oplus \gamma = 1$.

For this case $G = 0(1)$ if the fault is present, and $1(0)$ if it is not. This condition corresponds to taking the Boolean difference of G with respect to the fault f.

Example 3.11:   We now consider the case of the latch shown in Figure 3.31 (ignore input and output line values). We will develop a test for the

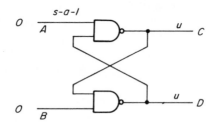

Figure 3.31   An SR latch with fault A s-a-1

fault $f = A$ s-a-1. The initial value (state) of lines C and D is denoted by $C(0)$ and $D(0)$. If the initial state of the latch is unknown, then $C(0) = D(0) = u$. The computation is shown in Figure 3.32.

j	time t	A	B	$C_t = \overline{A} + \overline{D}$	$D_t = \overline{B} + \overline{C}$
0	0	$A(0) + f^p$	$B(0)$	u	u
0	1	,,	,,	$\overline{A(0)}f^n + u$	$\overline{B(0)} + u$
0	2	,,	,,	$\overline{A(0)}f^n + B(0)u$	$\overline{B(0)} + u(A(0) + f^p)$
0	3 (stable)	,,	,,	$\overline{A(0)}f^n + B(0)$ $(u + \overline{A(0)}f^n)$ $= \overline{A(0)}f^n + B(0)u$	$\overline{B(0)} + (A(0) + f^p)$ $(\overline{B(0)} + u)$ $= \overline{B(0)} + u(A(0) + f^p)$
1	4	$A(1) + f^p$	$B(1)$	$\overline{A(1)}f^n + B(0)$ $(u + \overline{A(0)})f^n$	$\overline{B(1)} + (A(0) + f^p)$ $(\overline{B(0)} + u)$
. . .	. . .	. . .	. . .	. . .	. . .
1	7 (stable)	,,	,,	$\overline{A(1)}f^n + B(1)\overline{D}_3^*$	$\overline{B(1)} + \overline{C}_3(A(1) + f^p)*$

*In practice $\overline{D}_3$ and $\overline{C}_3$ would be replaced by their values (expressions) as defined at time 3.

Figure 3.32   Development of Circuit-Time Equations

At time $t = 0$, the first input vector ($A(0)$ and $B(0)$) is applied. Note that at time $t = 3$ the equations have stabilized, i.e., $C_3 = C_2$, and $D_3 = D_2$.

Consider line C to be an output. To detect the fault f at this point we require

i) $(\alpha = 0)$: $(B(0) \cdot (\overline{D(0)})) = 0$

and

ii) $(\beta \oplus \gamma = 1)$: $\overline{A(0)} \oplus 0 = 1$

  or $A(0) = 0$.

For case i) we have the following two subcases:

1) $B(0) = 0$

or

2) $\overline{D(0)} = 0 \; (D(0) = 1)$.

If the initial state of the latch is u, then condition i) implies that $B(0) = 0$, which is the same as case 1. We illustrate these results in Figure 3.31.

If a test cannot be generated after applying the first test vector, i.e., if conditions i) and ii) cannot be satisfied, then another test vector can be applied and the equations developed further.

We illustrate the beginning of this process in Figure 3.32. Here, at time $t = 4$ we apply the second input vector $A(1)$, $B(1)$ and determine the equations for C and D in terms of $A(1)$ and $B(1)$ and the previous steady states values for C and D, namely C_3 and D_3.   □

A self-initializing test can be generated if the conditions $\alpha = 0$ and $\beta \oplus \gamma = 1$ required for a test can be satisfied independently of the initial values of the internal signal lines. Unfortunately, this procedure suffers from the same difficulties as those previously described. That is, due to the use of only a single unknown value u, a test for a fault may sometimes not be found even though it exists. If we assign a unique u_i value to each line i, then this difficulty can be circumvented. However this extension greatly increases the complexity of this procedure.

We have seen that the general procedure for obtaining a test for a specific fault f is to construct the equation

$$G_t = \alpha + \beta f^p + \gamma f^n$$

and then solve the equations

$$\alpha = 0 \text{ and } \beta \oplus \gamma = 1.$$

Several heuristic versions of this procedure exist for obtaining a set of tests which generally detect a large percentage of the faults in the circuit which are detectable by a test sequence of length $p + 1$. Two variants of a procedure which simplifies the equation generation processing by not using the f^p and f^n variables will now be described. Procedure 3.3 is used to detect stuck-at-faults at the input lines of the circuit under test.

Procedure 3.3 (*Circuit-Time Equation Heuristic*):
(1) Select an arbitrary input line x_i and output line z_j, and calculate the circuit-time equation for $(z_j)_t$ for an input sequence of length $p + 1$. (p is a user specified input parameter.)

(2) Set $x_i(0) = x_i(1) = \ldots = x_i(p) = x_i$. Factor $(z_j)_t$ into the form

$$(z_j)_t = \alpha + \beta x_i + \gamma \bar{x}_i.$$

Determine, if possible, one or more test sequences of length $p + 1$ or less for each of the two stuck-at input faults on line x_i by solving the equations $\alpha = 0$ and $(\beta \oplus \gamma) = 1$.

(3) Repeat step 2 for each input-output line pair (x_i, z_j).

(4) The set of tests so constructed represents the desired test sequence set.   □

A slight variation of this procedure, suggested by Chappell [12], has been found to be quite effective. In this procedure no permanent stuck-at-fault is considered, but rather the test appears to be constructed around the concept of line x_i being stuck-at-0 or 1 only for the last input vector. The procedure is essentially identical to procedure 3.3, except step 2 is modified to read as follows:

2(Modified). Factor $(z_j)_t$ into the form

$$(z_j)_t = \alpha + \beta x_i(p) + \gamma \bar{x}_i(p).$$

Determine, if possible, one or more test sequences of length $p + 1$ or less satisfying the following equations:

i) $\alpha = 0$

ii) $(\beta \oplus \gamma) = 1$

iii) $x_i(p) = 0$ and then 1.

The property of the test sequences generated by this latter procedure is that they tend to highly stimulate the circuit, i.e., they propagate signals from inputs to outputs via most of the circuit paths. Such test sequences typically detect a high percentage of the circuit faults.

Once tests from either of these procedures have been found, they can be processed through a fault simulator. Any faults not detected by these tests can then be processed explicitly using the more general procedure (Equation 1).

There are a number of difficulties related to the use of circuit-time equations, a few of which will be listed below:

(1) Equation Oscillation — it is possible that a stable equation will never be reached, though this seldom happens.

(2) Memory Span — like other techniques, it is never known, a priori, how many input vectors are required before the conditions of a test can be satisfied. As the number of inputs increases, the complexity of the circuit-time equations grows significantly.

(3) Initialization — unless multiple u_i values are used, this procedure may fail to initialize an initializable circuit.

(4) Races at latches and flip-flops — race conditions at the inputs of memory devices cannot be easily avoided.

However these procedures have been found to be effective for moderate size circuits consisting of hundreds of elements. The depth of buried flip-flops is a critical factor in equation complexity. In many respects, one can consider this procedure to be the extension of the concept of Boolean difference to asynchronous circuits.

The circuit-time equation technique presented here is due to Chappell [12]. However, rather than using ternary expressions for the signal lines, Chappell associates two Boolean expressions with each line (similar to the expressions P_a and $\bar{P}_a$ of Poage [25]). By using this technique all expressions are positive, i.e., no complemented variables appear, which leads to an efficient implementation scheme.

3.3 REALIZATION INDEPENDENT TEST GENERATION PROCEDURES

The test generation procedures we have considered so far make use of specific fault models and consider the specific circuit realization being tested. Sometimes these techniques may not be applicable. For example, often the function of a circuit is known, but its circuit realization is not. This situation is common with LSI circuits. Also, the fault modes associated with some elements are not always known. Frequently a device, such as a RAM, is too large to handle by conventional gate level modeling. These types of problems can sometimes be dealt with by *functional testing*. The related concept of *checking sequences* is of theoretical interest.

3.3.1   Functional Testing
Functional testing refers to the selection (usually manual), of tests which will validate the functional operation of a device. For example, a functional test for a flip-flop may consist of the following:
(1) Validate that the flip-flop can be set (0 to 1 transition), and reset (1 to 0 transition).
(2) Validate that the flip-flop'can hold its state.
Problems 2.18 and 2.19 are related to functional tests for decoders and multiplexers. Functional testing of large semiconductor memories, such as random access memories (RAM's), has become an important problem on which much work has been carried out. This work is discussed in Section 3.5. The main concept of functional testing is to attempt to verify the fault free functional behavior of the device test. If specific fault modes are known, then tests which detect these faults, i.e., produce an erroneous output, are selected.

3.3.2   Checking Sequences
A more formal approach to functional testing which has application to sequential circuit testing and the related problem of circuit verification is the derivation of an input/output sequence which distinguishes a given n-state sequential machine M from all other machines with the same inputs, outputs and *at most n* states. The existence of such sequences is based on the following theorem [22].

Theorem 3.2:   For any reduced strongly connected n-state sequential machine M, there exists an input-output sequence pair $\mathbf{T} = (\mathbf{I}, \mathbf{O})$ which can be generated by M but cannot be generated by any other sequential machine M' with n or fewer states.   □

Such an input-output sequence is called a *checking sequence*. Note that the checking sequence only depends on the state table of M and is independent of the particular circuit realization and fault model assumed, with the restriction that no fault increases the number of states. Such a sequence can be used for testing for classical and non-classical faults, as well as for circuit verification, and constitutes a *functional test* in the strictest sense of the term. However, since it requires the complete state table to be generated, its usefulness is limited to very small circuits. Since checking sequences are primarily of theoretical interest we will only consider them briefly. The interested reader can find a more comprehensive treatment of this topic elsewhere [14].

We will discuss the application of checking sequences to synchronous circuits. However, the basic approach is also applicable to asynchronous circuits [4].

Example 3.12: Consider the following input-output sequence generated by a 3-state machine having one input x and one output z. Denote the states of this machine as q_1, q_2, q_3.

	1	2	3	4	5	6	7	8	9	10	11	12	13	14	15
Input Sequence:	0	0	0	0	0	1	0	0	1	0	0	0	1	0	0
Output Sequence:	0	1	0	0	1	1	1	0	0	1	0	0	0	0	1

Let us denote the state when the ith input was applied as $S(i)$. We arbitrarily label the initial state $S(1)$ as q_1. Since $S(2)$ responds to a 0 input with a 1 output while $S(1)$ responds to the same input with a different output, $S(2) \neq S(1)$ and we arbitrarily label $S(2)$ as q_2. Therefore, $N(q_1, 0) = q_2$, $Z(q_1, 0) = 0$, and $Z(q_2, 0) = 1$. Similarly, $S(3) \neq S(2)$ and since $S(3)$ responds to the input sequence 00 with an output sequence 00 while $S(1)$ responds to the same input sequence with the output sequence 01, $S(3) \neq S(1)$, and hence $S(3)$ must be q_3 (since the circuit has at most 3 states). Therefore, $N(q_2, 0) = q_3$ and $Z(q_3, 0) = 0$. In a similar manner $S(4) \neq S(2)$ and $S(4) \neq S(3)$. Since the machine has only three states, $S(4) = S(1) = q_1$ and hence $N(q_3, 0) = q_1$. At this stage the partial state table of Figure 3.33(a) has been derived. From this table we can determine that $S(5) = q_2$, $S(6) = q_3$ and $S(7) = q_2$ (since the 0 input applied to $S(7)$ produces a 1 output). Therefore, $N(q_3, 1) = q_2$ and $Z(q_3, 1) = 1$. Similarly, $S(8) = q_3$, $S(9) = q_1$, and $S(10) = q_2$. Therefore $N(q_1, 1) = q_2$ and $Z(q_1, 1) = 0$. Similarly $S(11) = q_3$, $S(12) = q_1$, $S(13) = q_2$, and $S(14) = q_1$. Therefore, $N(q_2, 1) = q_1$ and $Z(q_2, 1) = 0$ and the sequential machine of Figure 3.33(b) has been derived as the only three-state machine which can generate this input-output sequence. □

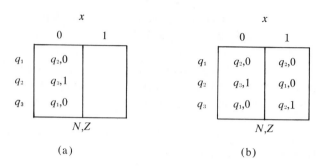

Figure 3.33   State table corresponding to given input-output sequence

We now consider the inverse of the problem just studied, namely, the construction of a checking sequence for a machine M. There exists algorithmic procedures for constructing such sequences. The complexity of both the algorithms and the checking sequences derived depend primarily on whether or not M has a *distinguishing sequence*. Since if M does not have a distinguishing sequence it is usually a simple task to modify M so that it possesses such a sequence, we will only consider this case.

Let X_D be an input sequence to M, and let Z_i be the response to X_D of M starting in state q_i. If Z_i is unique for each $i = 1,2, \ldots, n$, then X_D is said to be a *distinguishing sequence*. The important aspect of X_D is that by observing the response of M to X_D one can determine the state M was in when X_D was applied.

There are three aspects to constructing a checking sequence T for M, namely:

(1) Initialization, i.e., driving M to a given starting state
(2) Verifying that M has n states, and
(3) Verifying the next state and output entries for each state-input pair in the state table for M.

A checking sequence $T = (I,O)$ consists of an input sequence I and the corresponding output sequence O. If I is applied to a circuit realization M^* of M, then if M^* is not logically equivalent to M, due either to an arbitrary hardware fault or error in design, then the response will not be O. Because of this property T can be used to verify the design of circuits.

Conceptually a checking sequence T has the form $T_1 T_2 T_3$ where $T_1 = (I_1, -)$, $T_2 = (I_2, O_2)$, and $T_3 = (I_3, O_3)$.

1. The sequence I_1 is used to initialize M to some starting state, say q_a.
2. I_2 is an input sequence which, when applied to state q_a of M, causes M to generate an output sequence which contains as subsequences all

responses to X_D, i.e., T_2 contains the n input-output sequences (X_D, Z_i) for $i = 1, 2, \ldots, n$. Thus T_2 verifies that M^* has n distinct states and that X_D is a distinguishing sequence for this circuit.

3. T_3 makes use of this knowledge to verify each individual transition of M^*. A transition $N(q_i, I_m) = q_j$, $Z(q_i, I_m) = z_k$ is verified by having two subsequences in T_3 of the following form

$$X_D X X_D \text{ and } X_D X I_m X_D$$

$$Z_p Z Z_i \qquad Z_p Z z_k Z_j$$

where the input sequence X is such that $X_D X$ applied to state q_p takes M to state q_i with output $Z_p Z$. The first subsequence verifies that the machine under test behaves in the same manner for this input sequence. From this we can conclude that for the second subsequence the state of the machine under test when I_m is applied is q_i. After I_m is applied we apply X_D, thus verifying the state table entries $N(q_i, I_m) = q_j$ and $Z(q_i, I_m) = z_k$.

The length of the checking sequence can frequently be reduced by overlapping the subsequences T_2 and T_3.

A *synchronizing sequence* is an input sequence which when applied to M results in a unique final state q_i, independent of the initial state. For the machine of Example 3.12, the sequence 100100 initializes M to state q_1. Every checking sequence should begin with a synchronizing sequence to ensure the correct initial state. For machines which have no synchronizing sequence, a homing sequence (an input sequence the output response to which uniquely determines the final state) may be used for initialization purposes. Hence I_1 consists of either a synchronizing or homing sequence. Effective procedures exist for determining the existence and constructing (when they exist), distinguishing, synchronizing and homing sequences. Every reduced machine has a homing sequence [14].

3.4 FAULT DOMINANCE AND NON-CLASSICAL FAULTS

The dominance relation used in fault collapsing for combinational circuits (Section 2.5) is not valid for sequential circuits. Because of this, Theorems 2.2 and 2.3 are not applicable, and fault collapsing becomes a much more difficult task. Similarly bridge faults are much harder to test (since dominance relations were used to simplify the testing problem for such faults).

In this section we shall demonstrate these problems. Unfortunately no computationally effective procedures currently exist to handle these problems. Thus this section primarily contains negative results, pointing out problems but no solutions.

Consider the portion of the circuit shown in Figure 3.34. Assume that initially $y = 1$ and consider the test sequence shown in the figure. For the normal circuit the output sequence generated is $Z = 0000$. For the fault $\alpha(x_2\ s\text{-}a\text{-}1)$ the first input erroneously resets y and the fourth input propagates this error to z. Thus the generated output sequence is 0001 and x_2 $s\text{-}a\text{-}1$ is detected. Now consider the same test sequence and the fault $\beta(G_1,\ s\text{-}a\text{-}0)$, which dominates α in a combinational circuit sense. The first input again erroneously resets y. However, the fourth input generates an erroneous 0 at G_2 and the two effects of this single fault cancel each other $(z = D \cdot \overline{D} = 0)$ and the fault is not detected. Thus fault collapsing techniques based on fault dominance on gates (such as Theorems 2.2 and 2.3) are not applicable to sequential circuits. Of course collapsing techniques based on fault equivalence on gates can still· be used.

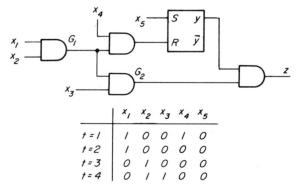

	x_1	x_2	x_3	x_4	x_5
$t=1$	1	0	0	1	0
$t=2$	1	0	0	0	0
$t=3$	0	1	0	0	0
$t=4$	0	1	1	0	0

Figure 3.34

The same example can also be used to demonstrate that bridge faults between leads to a gate, both of which do not have fanout, can also cause problems in sequential circuits. Consider the bridge fault between inputs x_1 and x_2 on gate G_1. In a combinational circuit, this fault would dominate the fault $x_2\ s\text{-}a\text{-}1$ and hence would not have to be explicitly considered. Unfortunately the bridge fault is not detected by the test sequence defined in Figure 3.34.

As shown by the circuit of Figure 1.19, it is possible for a bridge fault to convert a combinational circuit to a sequential circuit. Such a fault is called a *feedback bridging fault*. It is possible that such faults will not be detected by a set of tests for stuck-type faults.

Consider the circuits of Figure 3.35 and the stuck-type fault test set $T = \{1011,1101,1010,0101\}$.

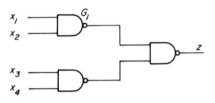

Figure 3.35

If these tests are applied in the order listed, the output sequence generated by the normal circuit is 1100. For the AND bridge fault between x_1 and z, the same output sequence is generated and hence the fault is not detected. Note that if the first and third tests are interchanged the fault-free circuit generates the output sequence 0110 and the circuit with the aforementioned bridge fault generates the output sequence 0010 and the fault is detected.

Mei [21] has considered the problems associated with testing for feedback bridging faults in fanout-free circuits. For such circuits a single feedback bridging fault creates a single feedback loop. If this loop has an odd number of inversions, any single fault test set will also detect the fault. If the loop has an even number of inversions, as in the fault considered for the circuit of Figure 3.35, this is not true. However, it is possible to define a stuck fault test set which will detect all feedback bridging faults (for fanout-free circuits). This is done by restricting justification of a 0(1) output from an AND(NAND) gate to application of all 0 inputs, similarly 1(0) outputs from an OR(NOR) gate must be justified by the application of all 1 inputs. A test set with this property is said to *optimally desensitize* the circuit. For the circuit of Figure 3.35, and the test set $T = \{1011, 1101, 1010, 0101\}$, the first test detects x_3 s-a-0 and x_4 s-a-0, but does not optimally desensitize the circuit since it applies $x_1 = 1, x_2 = 0$ to produce a 1 output from G_1. This test should be replaced by 0011. Similarly, the second test (which has the same problem) should be replaced by 1100, the third test by the two tests 1000 and 0010, and the fourth test by 0100 and 0001 resulting in the test set $T' = \{0011, 1100, 1000, 0010, 0100, 0001\}$. In response to T' the fault-free circuit generates the output sequence 110000. However, the circuit with the AND feedback bridging fault between x_1 and z generates the output sequence 000000 and hence this fault is detected.

We shall now prove these results.

Theorem 3.3:   In a fanout-free circuit,
   (a) A feedback bridging fault with odd inversion will be detected by any stuck fault test set.
   (b) A feedback bridging fault with even inversion will be detected by an optimally desensitized stuck fault test set.

Proof: (a) Consider the general case shown in Figure 3.36, with the AND feedback bridging fault between a and b,* and any test t which detects

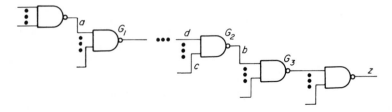

Figure 3.36

the fault a s-a-1. Such a test results in $a = 0$ in the normal circuit and $b = 1$ (due to the odd number of inversions between a and b). In the circuit with a s-a-1, $b = 0$. Similarly, in the circuit with the bridging fault $b = 0$. Furthermore, this faulty signal must be propagated to z by t and hence the bridging fault is detected by t.

(b) Consider the general case shown in Figure 3.36 with the AND feedback bridging fault between a and b. Let t' be any optimally desensitized test which detects the stuck fault c s-a-1. Such a test results in $c = 0$, $d = 1$ and $b = 1$ in the normal circuit. Since there is odd inversion between a and d, and t' optimally desensitizes the circuit, $G_1 = 1$ and $a = 0$. Hence the output of G_3 for both the bridging fault and c s-a-0 is the opposite value than that in the normal circuit, and therefore t' detects the bridging fault.   □

---

*Since NAND is a universal element, this result can be extended to circuits composed of arbitrary elements. A similar proof holds for OR bridge faults.

For more general circuits, the generation of tests for feedback bridge faults is much more difficult. No computationally effective algorithms currently exist. From empirical results [17], it seems that tests for stuck-type faults seem to be fairly good for detection of bridge faults (non-classical faults in general) but are inadequate for the location of such faults.

3.5 TESTING OF SEMICONDUCTOR RANDOM ACCESS MEMORIES

A component which is becoming widely used in digital circuits is the semiconductor random access memory (RAM). Single chips containing up to 4096 bits (4K) are being produced and in the near future this density will reach 64K. These memories typically are manufactured using one of two technologies, bipolar and metal oxide semiconductor (MOS). The MOS memories have a higher circuit density and hence have a larger memory capacity. Unfortunately, these memories store·their data via the charge across a capacitor. Due to circuit leakage, this charge must be re-established at fixed intervals, or else the value of the bit stored will be lost. The maximum period of time the data can be stored without re-establishing its value is called the *hold time*, t_d. While t_d is a function of temperature, at normal operating temperatures $t_d \cong 2$ ms. The process of re-establishing the data in the memory is called *refreshing*. Memories which require refreshing are called *dynamic*. Currently, all 4K RAM's are dynamic MOS memories. Such a chip has over 13000 MOS devices.

Figure 3.37 shows the typical functional circuit configuration for a RAM. Assume the RAM has an n bit capacity, i.e., we can read and/or write a bit of information into n different locations, called cells, each randomly addressable. This requires s address bits where $s = \lceil log_2 n \rceil$. Typically the s-bit address is partitioned into an r-bit field and a q-bit field, where $r + q = s$. The memory array is then constructed using 2^r columns of 2^q cells each, (or vice-versa). The r-bit-field is used to address a column in the memory, and the q-bit-field addresses a row. The cell addressed is that in the column and row addressed. Typical array configurations for a 4K memory are 64×64, 32×128 and dual 16×128.

Refreshing, usually carried out on an entire column or row of an array in one cycle, requires 64 cycles in a 64×64 array chip, but only 16 cycles in a dual 16×128 array configuration. To write a 1 in every cell of a 4K chip having a read cycle time of 500 ns per bit requires about 2 ms. If the hold time is 2 ms, then by the time we have finished writing into the last bit, the data written into the first bit may have been lost.

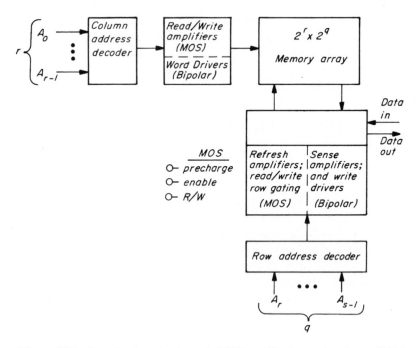

Figure 3.37   Organization of a dynamic MOS and bipolar semiconductor RAM

Hence the following parameters have a significant effect on how the memory is to be tested.

1. Total capacity
2. Array configuration
3. Addressing layout
4. Refresh parameters

In this section we will consider the problem of testing RAM's in the manufacturing environment.

Categories of Memory Faults

Faults can occur in the memory matrix, decoders, input buffers, read/write circuitry, data input circuitry or sense amplifiers. These internal faults can lead to functional failures such as the inability to read or write, to erroneous data storage, to d.c. parametric failures such as unacceptable output levels, or to dynamic failures such as slow access times. More specifically, these semiconductor memories exhibit malfunctions such as the following:

(1) *Opens and shorts.*

(2) *Open decoders* — the total memory cannot be truly addressed.

(3) *Multiple writes* — in the act of writing in one cell the chip actually writes in more than one cell.

(4) *Pattern sensitivity* — the contents of a cell become complemented due to read and write operations in "electronically adjacent" cells. Such an error may be a function of (a) the information being read and written; (b) the cells being addressed, and (c) the sequence in which these cells are addressed.

(5) *Write recovery* — memory may not produce information at the specified access time when each read cycle is preceded by a write cycle.

(6) *Sense amplifier sensitivity* — memory may not respond with the proper information after reading a long series of similar data bits followed by a single transition of the opposite data value.

(7) *Sleeping Sickness* — memory loses information in less than the stated hold time.

The problem of pattern sensitivity arises primarily due to the high component density which exists in RAM's and the related effect of unwanted interacting signals. Because of this problem the following situation may occur: (1) store (write) a value in cell *i*; (2) read this value several times to verify that it is indeed stored in cell *i*; (3) read and write in cells other than cell *i*; (4) read cell *i* and find the value is now wrong. This effect can occur even though each cell is capable of being correctly addressed and individually can store a 0 and a 1.

To prove that a read/write RAM is completely functional, the following aspects must be verified.

1. Every cell of the memory must be capable of storing a 0 and a 1.
2. The cell addressing circuits, or decoders, must correctly address every cell.
3. The sense amplifiers must operate correctly.
4. There must be no interaction between cells.
5. For dynamic MOS memories, the cells must be capable of storing data for a specified time without being refreshed.

It is a complex task to design tests to cover these 5 factors given the possible fault modes previously defined. Tests must also take into consideration the chip configuration and electronic characteristics, since each design exhibits its own unique failure characteristics. It is often very difficult to determine exactly what fault modes exist in these chips. Presently, no formal test procedure exists for determining whether or not a memory is fault free. Instead, ad hoc test procedures are used, as will be discussed in the section on Testing Patterns.

Test Mode Categories

As with other digital chips, there are three classes of tests which are carried out on memories, namely functional, DC parametric, and AC parametric (or dynamic). DC parametric testing deals with the measurement of voltage and signal values, rise and fall times, etc. Functional testing refers to verifying the chips internal logic, i.e., the logical function of the chip. It is carried out by applying 0's and 1's to input pins and observing the output responses. In AC testing, measurements are made on access times, set-up and hold times, and cycle times. In essence, an AC test is run at the circuit's designed operational speed and hence is considered a dynamic test. Combining functional tests and dynamic tests leads to real time functional testing. This type of testing is most important for dynamic memories and will be considered almost exclusively in the remainder of this section.

Testing Patterns

Numerous classes of canonical test pattern sequences have been devised for testing RAM's. These tests can be classified under a number of categories, such as complexity and function. Function refers to what fault mode the test is primarily designed to detect. Complexity refers to the number of operations (READ or WRITE) required to carry out the test, as a function of the memory size n. Most current tests are either of order $\mathcal{O}(n)$, $\mathcal{O}(n^{3/2})$, or $\mathcal{O}(n^2)$.* Note that the number of possible patterns (states) in a memory is 2^n, hence, in practice, exhaustive testing is infeasible.

Another factor to be considered in designing a test is the difficulty in computing the sequence of addresses, of input data bits, and READ and WRITE control inputs. These factors influence the complexity of the test generation algorithm and the cost of the tester.

In the discussion of test procedure, the following notation will be used. The statement

$$\text{WRITE: } c_i \leftarrow \delta$$

implies that cell i (i is the address) should be set to the value δ, $\delta \in \{0,1\}$. The statement

$$\text{READ: } c_i(=\delta)$$

implies that cell i is read, and the value read should be δ.

---

*$\mathcal{O}(n^k)$ means "of the order n^k". For example a test of order n^2 contains Cn^2 steps for some constant C.

To illustrate some aspects of the complexity of testing a RAM, consider the following simple procedure, which we will call Memory Scan (MSCAN).

MSCAN Test Procedure

For $i = 0,1,2, \ldots, n - 1$ (addresses) in turn, do the following.

$$\text{WRITE: } c_i \leftarrow 0$$
$$\text{READ: } c_i(=0)$$
$$\text{WRITE: } c_i \leftarrow 1$$
$$\text{READ: } c_i(=1).$$

This test sets (WRITE) each cell to a 0 and 1, and verifies via a READ that the cell contains the desired piece of information. Analysis indicates that there is very little information gained from this test procedure. All that is known at the end of this procedure is that there is at least one cell in the RAM which can be set to a 0 and 1, and in which this data can be read. This is because a fault could have occurred in the address decoder modifying the logic of the RAM so that the same cell is always referenced. Since this test requires four operations per bit, its complexity is $4n$.

Many common functional test procedures used for RAM's are presented in the Appendix. The table of Figure 3.38 lists these procedures and summarizes their important attributes.* Total test time is important since it is not economical to tie up test equipment for a long period of time in testing a high volume inexpensive product. However, the cost to the customer of using a defective chip could be quite high. The growing use of LSI devices and the fact that densities are increasing at a significant rate increase the importance of testing for pattern sensitivity and low signal-to-noise (S/N) ratios. Pattern sensitive faults may become the predominant fault mode in such devices. These faults are not restricted to memory chips, but occur in the most general chips, such as microprocessors. In fact, tests such as GALPAT (see Appendix) are already being used to test the memory parts (general registers, scratchpads, etc.) in microprocessor chips.

Theoretical Aspects of Testing RAMs

A RAM can be modeled as a finite state sequential machine M_n with $N = 2^n$ states. Theoretically it is possible to construct a test to detect permanent faults in M_n using the checking sequence approach discussed

---

*Calculations used in this section assume a 4K memory with a 500 ns cycle time and 2 ms hold time.

Test	Complexity	Test Time (seconds) for a 500 ns cycle 4K RAM	Purpose
1 Column bars	$4n$	.008	Shorts between columns; refresh
2 Checkerboard	$4n$	.008	Refresh
3 Volatility	$4n$	.008	Refresh
4 Marching 1's/0's	$12n$	.024	Minimal functional test, simple multiple select
5 Shifted Diagonal	$4n^{3/2}$	.5	Test for slow recovery in sense amplifiers
6 Ping-pong*	n^2 (full) $n^{3/2}$ (row/column)	8 .128	Procedure to pair off a test bit with other bits in the array
7 Walking 1's/0's	$2n^2 + 6n$	16	Verify that each cell can be set to both 0 and 1 without causing interference
8 Galloping 1's & 0's (GALPAT I)	$2n^2 + 8n$	16	Test all possible read/write combinations (multiple selects)
9 Galloping 1's & 0's (GALPAT II)	$4n(2n - 1)$	64	Test all possible read/write combinations (multiple selects)

*Ping-pong is not a test but a procedure used in tests 7, 8, and 9.

Figure 3.38   Summary of RAM Test Characteristics

in Section 3.3.2. Such a test may not detect all dynamic problems, but it will detect all static pattern interference faults.

Let W_i^0 and W_i^1 be the normal operations of writing a 1 and 0, respectively, into cell c_i and let R_i be the operation of reading the contents of cell c_i.

In Figure 3.39 we show the state table for M_2. In general M_n has $3n$ inputs, namely W_i^1, W_i^0 and R_i for $i = 0,1,2, \ldots, n - 1$, and one output z, where if $Y_j = (y_{j0}, y_{j1}, \ldots, y_{j(n-1)})$ is the state of M_n, then

$$Z(R_i, Y_j) = y_{ji} \text{ and}$$
$$Z(W_i^a, Y_j) = -, a = 0,1.$$

Note that M_n is strongly connected, every sequence of n distinct READ operations identifies the internal state of M_n and therefore constitutes a distinguishing sequence for M_n, and the state of M_n can be changed to any other state by a sequence of at most n WRITE operations on distinct cells of M_n. Hence M_n possesses an initialization sequence.

	Input					
State $y_0 y_1$	W_0^1	W_1^1	W_0^0	W_1^0	R_0	R_1
00	10,—	01,—	00,—	00,—	00,0	00,0
01	11,—	01,—	01,—	00,—	01,0	01,1
10	10,—	11,—	00,—	10,—	10,1	10,0
11	11,—	11,—	01,—	10,—	11,1	11,1

$Y_0 Y_1, z$

Figure 3.39   State Table for M_2

Hayes [16] has shown how to construct a checking sequence for M_n of length $(3n^2 + 2n)2^n$. Though this checking sequence is not necessarily minimal in length, it is fairly efficient and uses the minimum number of WRITE's. Though some further reductions in its length may be possible, a checking sequence for M_n will always be of complexity $\mathcal{O}(2^n)$, and hence computationally infeasible except for very small memories.

In order to substantially reduce the length of the test for a memory, restrictions must be put on the type of faults that may occur. For example, rather than assume that a READ or WRITE operation on cell c_i can affect or be affected by an arbitrary cell c_j, we can restrict fault interference to occur only between *neighborhood* cells. The neighborhood of cell c_i might be defined to consist of the cell c_i itself and all other cells to its immediate left, right, top and bottom. Based upon the structure of these neighborhoods, a test sequence consisting of a checking sequence for each neighborhood may be sufficient or "almost" sufficient for testing M_n.

Tests like GALPAT use 2-cell neighborboods of the forms (c_i, c_j) where for each i, j is allowed to run over all cells. These tests do not apply all possible patterns and do not constitute a checking experiment.

Alternatively, the testing problem can be simplified by assuming only a single (local) pattern-sensitive fault in M_n, i.e., only one cell c_{i*} can be erroneously affected by one or more other cells. For this case, tests which are less complex and hence shorter than checking sequences can be employed.

3.6 RANDOM TEST GENERATION AND TESTING

3.6.1 Practice

Testers

There are two major categories of automatic test equipment (ATE), called *stored program* ATE and *random* or *comparison* type ATE. Stored programmed testers usually contain a minicomputer and back-up storage such as disc, and the test sequence is stored vector by vector, or as a high level program interpreted by the computer. Stored program ATE typically also store the expected response and (sometimes) a fault dictionary, which are usually generated by simulation. The actual test sequence can be obtained using an algorithmic procedure (e.g., the D-algorithm), manually (e.g., by a test engineer), or randomly (e.g., by a pseudo random pattern generator).

Since tests vectors must be processed through a minicomputer, the average rate of applying vectors to the unit under test (UUT) varies from about 200 K Hz to 20 K Hz. In burst modes, i.e., for short sequences, higher rates are possible. Because of a number of factors, such as the effectiveness of stored programs, the need for simulation processing, and the slow rate of test application, stored program test sequences are typically not of great length, varying from a few vectors to several thousand per UUT.

Random or comparison type ATE employ pseudo random patterns as test vectors. These patterns can be derived in many ways and are sometimes not totally random. These vectors are not stored in a minicomputer, but rather are generated via a hard-wired digital pattern generator. Hence vectors can be generated at very high rates, such as from 1-40 MHz. Testing a board at these high rates for a few seconds allows several million vectors to be applied. Errors on the output of the UUT can be detected using a comparison scheme as shown in Figure 3.40.

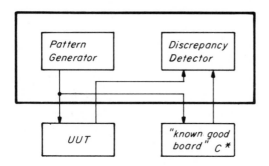

Figure 3.40   Comparison type ATE system

Here two circuit cards, the UUT and a known good copy of the circuit under test, denoted by C^*, are inserted into the ATE. The pattern generator then applies several million pseudo random patterns to both the UUT and C^*. The outputs of the boards are then compared by the discrepancy detector. A mismatch indicates a fault in the UUT.

Probing

By using a fault dictionary a fault may be identified to within its equivalence class. The set of physical faults associated with this equivalence class may be distributed over many components, such as IC's. In order to determine the exact site of a physical fault, probing techniques are required. By probing we mean the insertion of temporary outputs (test points).*

Most ATE have a probe used to sample non-primary output signals in a UUT. The test points employed are typically the pins of the individual IC chips. The probe may sample one signal at a time, or may consist of a test clip which samples all n pins of an n pin chip.

Probing is typically an interactive process between the test engineer and the ATE. The data base of the ATE contains a topological description (net interconnection) of the UUT, as well as the results from a fault free logic simulation. That is, a record is kept of the correct signal value at every chip pin for each input vector.

A simplified probing procedure called *guided probe*, in which the ATE determines the probing strategy, is as follows:

---

*Often a probe can be used to apply a signal to the circuit.

Procedure 3.4 *(Guided Probe):*

(1) ATE applies test sequence to UUT. If resulting output sequence is correct, then exit (no fault has been detected), otherwise continue. (This is called GO-NO GO testing.)

(2) ATE identifies a failing output pin, i.e., a pin with an erroneous signal value, and notes failing test step (vector i). Set $T \leftarrow i$.

(3) Based upon circuit topology the ATE identifies one or more chips* which may be producing the failing signal. These are called *source chips*. The test operator then probes the pins of one of these chips.

(4) The test is then reapplied from the beginning. Again, the first erroneous test step, j, is noted. If $j > T$ then either an error in testing has occurred (i.e., the wrong chip or pin has been probed), else an open conductor fault probably exists. If $j \leq T$, set $T \leftarrow j$.

    When probing a chip the following cases may arise:

    Case 1 — One of the input signals to a chip is in error.

    For this case, go to step 3.

    Case 2 — One of the output signals to a chip is in error, but all of its input signals are correct.

    For this case, the fault may be located in one of three places:

    (a) in the chip being probed;

    (b) along a signal line emanating from this source chip; or

    (c) at the input to a chip which is a *sink* to a signal in error.

    Some additional local probing and/or manual inspection can now be carried out to identify the exact cause of the fault. Note that a short to ground or power fault at a sink (source) usually effects the source (sink) while an open between a source and sink usually only affects the sink.

    Case 3 — No test fails.

    For this case, we return to other erroneous signal sources which have not yet been processed. If a chip, called the sink chip, has been identified which has an erroneous input signal, but each of its source chips passes the test, then the fault is localized to within one of the following cases:

    (a) the fault occurs along the interconnections between a source chip and the sink chip, but is not reflected back into a source chip, i.e., an open conductor.

    (b) the fault is at the input of the sink chip.   □

---

*"Dotted" or "wired AND's or OR's" can result in multiple signal sources.

Faults are particularly difficult to locate in asynchronous circuits because it is possible to find a connected closed chain of chips which all fail at the same test vector step. For this situation it may be necessary to replace each chip in the chain, one at a time, until the failing chip is identified.

Pseudo Random Vectors

Most circuits are functional, and hence their inputs can be categorized by function. For example, some lines are clocked lines and specific input sequences should be applied to these lines. Let the statement "CLOCK($n;p$)" represent a periodic binary sequence which consists of n 0's followed by p 1's. This statement can then be used to describe input sequences to lines driven by periodic square waves.

Some input lines are used as reset lines. These lines should be activated very infrequently. For example the statement "CLOCK(1;100,000)" represents an input sequence which activates (on 0) the reset line once every 100,001 vectors.

It may be desired to apply a random input sequence to some input lines which is *Gray coded.** We could represent this condition by the statement "GRAY." If no specific restriction between $x(i)$ and $x(i + 1)$ is required, then vectors can be generated completely randomly, and we denote this function by "RANDOM."

Example 3.13:   Consider a circuit having 10 input lines labeled 1,2, . . ., 10. Assume line 1 is a clock line, line 2 is a reset line, lines 3, 5, 9 form a group which are to be stimulated by Gray coded vectors, lines 4 and 6 form another group which are to be stimulated by Gray coded vectors, and the remaining lines can be stimulated by completely random vectors. We could specify a test for this circuit by the following set of statements:

> "PSEUDO RANDOM TEST SPEC"
> TEST LENGTH = 1,000,000
> 1 = CLOCK(1,1)
> 2 = CLOCK(1,1000)
> 3,5,9 = GRAY
> 4,6 = GRAY
> 7,8,10 = RANDOM
> END

We refer to such a list of line specifications as a *pseudo random test spec.*

---

*A sequence of vectors $X = x(0)x(1)$ . . . is said to be Gray coded if for each $i,x(i)$ and $x(i + 1)$ differ in only one coordinate position.

Stored Program Testers

As stated previously some stored program ATE use pseudo random test sequences. These sequences are normally generated in the following way (see Figure 3.41). A pseudo random test spec is developed for the UUT. This test spec is then processed by a computer and test vectors are generated. These vectors are processed through a fault simulator to determine the percent of faults detected. Typically, as each test vector $x(i)$ is generated, it is processed as follows: A value $V(x(i))$ is assigned to $x(i)$, usually based upon the number of faults detected by $x(i)$ which were not detected by the test sequence $x(0)x(1) \ldots x(i-1)$. Two cases typically occur.

Case 1: $V(x(i)) \geq T$ (a user specified threshold value)

For this case $x(i)$ is accepted as the ith input vector, i is incremented by one, and the next vector is processed.

Case 2: $V(x(i)) < T$.

For this case $x(i)$ is rejected as the ith input vector and another vector is generated and evaluated.

A vector can also be rejected if it leads to race and hazard conditions. Once the percent detection reaches a specific level, or the maximum allowable number of inputs vectors have been generated, the process terminates.

This type of test generation procedure exists as one alternative approach in many automatic test generation systems, and has been discussed in depth by Seshu and Freeman [29] and Breuer [6]. It is effective for moderate size circuits where initialization can be easily achieved.

Comparison Testers

In a comparison type ATE system, a pseudo random test spec is again developed, and then hard-wired into the ATE. The ATE then generates patterns according to this specification. The patterns are deterministic, i.e., whenever execution is restarted, the same patterns are generated.

There are several problems which must be confronted when employing this technique, the most serious being initialization, races and hazards. Since the UUT is being tested at a very high rate, and the input patterns are not necessarily functional, there is a chance that races or hazards may occur in either the UUT or C^*. In this case, it is possible that the UUT will be classified as faulty when in fact it is not. Careful programming of the input specifications will tend to minimize this problem.

Initialization is usually carried out in a comparison type tester using the concept of synchronization. That is, before processing any UUT's, two known good boards are inserted into the tester. A test sequence of length L

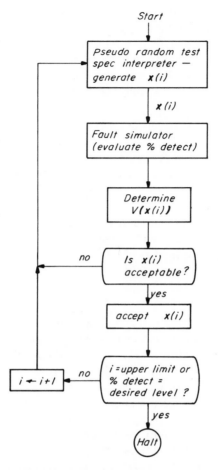

Figure 3.41   Generating a pseudo random test in an automatic test generation system

is then applied to the boards. This test consists of a prefix of length L', and a suffix of length $(L - L')$. The outputs are not compared by the discrepancy detector until the suffix test is applied. The concept here is that the prefix test sequence is intended to synchronize the two boards, i.e., drive them into the same identical state. The suffix test sequence is then used to detect faults. Typically the test sequence must be repeated several times before the value L' is determined which appears to synchronize the circuit. This process is only done once while the test parameters for a given circuit board type are being developed. Synchronization is achieved if the response to the suffix test sequence from the two boards agree. Of course, for boards which are difficult to initialize, one cannot be certain that the prefix test sequence actually synchronizes all fault free UUT's, independent of their initial state. Typically, L' may be several million.

The percent fault detection for a comparison type ATE can be estimated by physically injecting faults into one of the known good boards and determining whether or not the fault is detected. If the percent detection is too low, the value of L can be increased. Often it is difficult to inject all the faults of interest. Typically, only stuck-at faults can be injected at IC pin locations. Internal IC faults usually cannot be injected. Care must be taken in injecting faults so that the circuit is not permanently faulted.

Fault isolation can also be carried out by probing pins in the UUT and the corresponding pins in C^*. The ATE then carries out a comparison (discrepancy) test on these pins rather than the output pins of the circuits. The complexity of the ATE can be significantly reduced by comparing some function of the output sequences of the UUT and C^*, rather than the actual output sequences (see Section 3.7).

3.6.2   Theory

Several studies have been carried out in an attempt to predict analytically the effectiveness of applying random input patterns in testing a circuit [1-3], [5], [19], and [27]. Unfortunately, most of this analysis applies only to combinational circuits, and even for this case, restrictions on circuit topology are often required. For these cases, analytic expressions can be derived which will indicate the expected number of faults detected as a function of input vectors applied (see Problem 3.26). Also, for an arbitrary combinational circuit, one can determine the probability that a random input will drive the output to a 1 [23-24] (see Problem 3.27).

The extension of the theoretical aspects of probabilistic test analysis is just beginning to be carried out on sequential circuits [5, 27]. One goal in this area is the development of a measure to indicate whether random test patterns can effectively test a given circuit. These tools are also pertinent to the concepts of error latency [30], and signal reliability [26].

3.7   TESTING CIRCUITS BY TRANSITION COUNTING

Consider a digital circuit which, under fault-free conditions produces an output sequence Z_0 in response to an input sequence X. Upon applying X when testing a circuit, assume the output response observed is Z'. Now a fault is said to be detected if $Z' \neq Z$. There are two difficulties associated with this method of testing. First, the entire fault-free response Z_0 must be stored for comparison with Z'. Secondly, Z' must be compared with Z_0, bit by bit. This requires a fairly sizeable amount of hardware, especially if this comparison is to be made at the UUT's clock-rate.

In order to simplify this testing procedure, one can apply a function f to the output response of the UUT and only compare $f(Z_0)$ to $f(Z')$. Several different choices for the function f exist, such as "the number of 1's in the sequence" or "the number of 0 to 1 and 1 to 0 transitions in the sequence." The latter function is called the transition count (TC) and is employed in a number of very popular commercial testers. In this section, we will briefly review some of the properties of transition count testing.

Let $Z = z(1)z(2) \ldots z(m)$ be any m-bit binary sequence (for simplicity we assume that the circuit has only a single output). Then the *transition count* $c(Z)$ of Z is given by the equation

$$c(Z) = \sum_{i=1}^{m-1} z(i) \oplus z(i + 1)$$

where Σ denotes arithmetic summation, and $\oplus$ denotes exclusive-OR.

For example, consider the circuit shown in Figure 3.42. The input sequence and transition count for each signal are shown. The output sequence is $Z_0 = 1001$ and $c(Z_0) = 2$. If the output of G_2 is s-a-1, we obtain $Z' = 0001$, and $c(Z') = 1$. Thus this fault changes the transition count from 2 to 1 and hence the fault is detected.

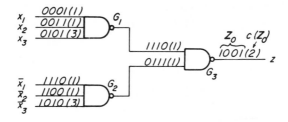

Figure 3.42 Circuit showing both binary sequences and associated transition counts

Note that this form of testing is quite simple since actual responses need not be stored, only transition counts. The transition count for the UUT can be determined by simply running the outputs of the UUT into counters.

Hence a very simple ATE can be used. For an m-bit output sequence an n-bit counter is required, where n is proportional to $\lceil \log_2 m \rceil$. Typically a circuit is tested using the transition count method by first applying a long test sequence to a fault-free copy of the circuit and recording the transition counts at each of the circuit outputs, some internal test points, and perhaps even at each IC terminal. This latter information is used in determining the location of a fault. The input sequence is generated via a hardware pseudo-random number generator. At 1 MHz, one million patterns (vectors) can be applied by the ATE in just one second. Typically several million patterns are used in testing a circuit.

Problems related to transition count testing are very similar to those dealing with comparison testers as discussed in Section 3.6.1.

There are several positive aspects to transition count testing. First, for a moderately complex synchronous circuit card of about 50 IC's (MSI's and SSI's) which has reset capabilities, one can quite easily construct and verify a complete test in about one man-day. No modeling and associated computer test generation and/or simulation is required. Secondly, the ATE equipment for transition counting is much simpler than that equipment which must process test programs and fault dictionaries. Finally, this ATE can operate at much higher test rates, hence (1) reducing station time, (2) producing operational conditions closer to functional operating conditions, and (3) processing more input patterns. For these reasons, test procedures based on transition count have been widely accepted.

Theoretical Aspects of Transition Counting Test Methods in Combinational Circuits

Very little theory exists concerning TC testing. In this section we will review some fundamental results dealing with TC testing in combinational circuits [15].

Let X be an input test sequence and $F = \{f_1, \ldots, f_n\}$ be a set of faults in a combinational circuit C. Let Z_0 be the response to X from C, and Z_i be the response to X from C when fault f_i is present. For simplicity we assume that C is a single output circuit. Then X is a *transition count* (TC) *test* for C with respect to F if $c(Z_0) \neq c(Z)$ for $1 \leq i \leq n$. Here, every fault is said to be *TC detectable*. Note that in general, not all logic faults are TC detectable. For example consider a fault which causes the output function realized by C to be changed from $f(x_1, \ldots, x_n)$ to $\bar{f}(x_1, \ldots, x_n)$. For this case the response to X will be $\bar{Z}_0$, that is, each bit in the output sequence will be complemented. But $c(\bar{Z}_0) = c(Z_0)$, hence this fault is TC undetectable even though every response bit is in error (see Problem 3.31).

Faults f_i and f_j are said to be *TC distinguishable* if there exists an input sequence **X** such that $c(\mathbf{Z}_i) \neq c(\mathbf{Z}_j)$. If $c(\mathbf{Z}_i) \neq c(\mathbf{Z}_j)$ for all $j \neq i$, and fault f_i is detectable, then fault f_i is said to be *TC locatable*. Transition count testing is weaker than the conventional testing procedure in the following senses:

(1) A fault in C is TC detectable only if it is detectable; the converse is not true.

(2) Two faults in C are TC distinguishable only if they are distinguishable; the converse is also false.

We will restrict our attention to TC testing of single and multiple stuck-type faults. Note that in an irredundant single-output combinational circuit C no single-fault can change the response $\mathbf{Z}_0$ to a complete test set to $\bar{\mathbf{Z}}_0$. Hence no single fault can change the output function $f(x_1 \ldots, x_n)$ to $\bar{f}(x_1, \ldots, x_n)$. It is conjectured that this result also holds true for multiple faults. However, for multiple faults in irredundant multiple output circuits, or for multiple faults in single output redundant circuits, it is possible for a fault to complement one of the output lines.

The following theorem specifies a constructive procedure for generating a complete TC test for a combinational network C.

Theorem 3.5:   Let T be a single-fault test set for an irredundant single-output combinational circuit C. Let $T^0(T^1)$ be all tests in T producing output $0(1)$. Construct a test sequence $\mathbf{X}^* \doteq t(1)t(2) \ldots t(p)$ as follows:

(1) $\mathbf{X}^*$ contains every element in T.

(2) $\mathbf{X}^*$ is an alternating sequence of tests from T^0 and T^1. If $|T^0| \geq |T^1|$, let $t(1) \in T^0$, otherwise $t(1) \in T^1$. If $t(i) \in T^d$, then select $t(i + 1) \in T^{\bar{d}}$ for $1 \leq i \leq p - 1$. The resulting sequence $\mathbf{X}^*$ is a single fault TC test for C.

Proof: The response $\mathbf{Z}^*$ to $\mathbf{X}^*$ is an alternating sequence of 0's and 1's. The only other sequence with this same transition count is $\bar{\mathbf{Z}}_0$. But $\mathbf{X}^*$ detects all stuck-at faults, and none of these faults can produce $\bar{\mathbf{Z}}_0$. Note that the length p of $\mathbf{X}^*$ is bounded by the inequalities $p \leq 2 \max\{|T^0|, |T^1|\} < 2(|T| - 1)$. In addition, if T is a minimal length test C, and if the difference D between $|T^0|$ and $|T^1|$ is at most 1, then $\mathbf{X}^*$ is a minimal length single fault TC test for C.   □

Thus, every single stuck type fault in a single output irredundant combinational circuit is TC detectable using less than twice the number of tests required by conventional testing. For $D > 1$, the problem of finding minimal length TC test is unsolved.

Fault Location

It is quite difficult to locate a fault in a single output combinational circuit using TC testing. Let $s(n)$ be the length of a minimal single fault TC location test for an n input NAND gate. Hayes [15] has shown that

$$s(n) \geq \frac{n^2}{8} + 1.$$

Systematic procedures exist for generating tests of length $(n(n + 1)/2) + 2$. From these results, one can construct a test to TC locate faults in an arbitrary irredundant circuit. The length of such a test is quite long. Due to this factor, in practice, fault location is accomplished by using additional test points and by detecting transition count errors at these points.

Thus TC tests for combinational circuits can be constructed from conventional test sets. The extension of conventional test generation procedures to produce TC tests for sequential circuits has not been carried out. In addition, there are no results dealing with the analysis of TC testing based upon random inputs, though in practice, this is the normal mode in which TC ATE is used.

APPENDIX: COMMONLY USED FUNCTIONAL RAM TEST PATTERNS

Test:

Column Bars (similar to checkerboard test)

Purpose: Tests for possible shorts between adjacent columns. For RAM's which are refreshed an entire row at a time, this pattern, or a checkerboard pattern*, may be used for worst case refresh tests.

Test Procedure:

   Step 1: WRITE 1's in all even columns and 0's in all odd columns
   Step 2: READ each column and row
   Step 3: Repeat steps 1 and 2 for complementary patterns (i.e., interchange 0's and 1's)

Complexity: $4n$

---

*A checkerboard pattern consists of alternate 0's and 1's in each row and column (analogous to the coloring of squares on a checkerboard).

Test:

Volatibility Test Pattern

Purpose: Checks for hold time in dynamic memories.

Test Procedure:

Step 1: Load memory with a test pattern (various different simple patterns are typically used)

Step 2: Pause T units of time* (inhibit all clocks)

Step 3: READ entire memory

Step 4: Repeat for complementary patterns

Complexity: $4n$

Test:

Marching 1's and 0's

Purpose: Minimal functional testing; detection of many decoder errors; minimal check on cell interactions.

Test Procedure:

Step 1: WRITE: $c_i \leftarrow 0$ for $i = 0,1, \ldots, n - 1$

Step 2: For $i = 0,1, \ldots, n - 1$ do
      READ: $c_i(=0)$
      WRITE: $c_i \leftarrow 1$
      READ: $c_i(=1)$

Step 3: For $i = n - 1, n - 2, \ldots, 0$ do
      READ: $c_i(=1)$
      WRITE: $c_i \leftarrow 0$
      READ: $c_i(=0)$

Step 4: Repeat steps 1-3 interchanging 0's and 1's. That is repeat for the complementary pattern.

Comment: As the memory is scanned in ascending order, any effect that writing in a cell has on a higher numbered cell is detected when the second cell is read. Similarly, when processing in descending order, effects on lowered numbered cells are detected. By leaving a trail of 1's behind each iteration in step 2 , it is known that we are addressing a new cell at each step. Therefore, this process guarantees that each cell exists and that every cell is capable of storing a 1 and a 0. Most of the decoder is tested.

Complexity: $12n$

---

*T is a function of the refresh and hold times which in turn are a function of temperature.

Test:

Shifted Diagonal Test

Purpose: This test is designed to identify slow recovery in sense amplifiers. That is, after reading a long sequence of the same bit value, switching to a new output value may be delayed.

Test Procedure: The test consists of placing a diagonal of 1's in the memory, all other cells storing 0's. This diagonal is then shifted one position at a time so that it sweeps through the memory.

   Step 1: Load memory with 0's in every cell except those on a diagonal (assuming a square array), where 1's are stored.

   Step 2: Repeat the following two steps $K = 2^r$ times (once for each column).

   2a: READ column k for $k = 1, 2, \ldots, K$

   2b: Shift the diagonal right one position. (The last shift can be deleted.)

   Step 3: Repeat steps 1 and 2 using a diagonal of 0's rather than 1's.

Comment: For a 64×64 array, the original pattern is set up by first applying a 1 after every 63 0's. We see that this test applies a long sequence of 0's (1's) followed by a single 1 (0) to the sense amplifiers during the READ operation.

Complexity: To load and read memory requires $2n$ operations. This procedure is done K times for the diagonals of 0's and 1's, hence $C = 4Kn$ test steps are required. For a square array (K maximum), $K = n^{1/2}$, hence $C = 4n^{3/2}$. The complexity for this test varies from $64n$ (for $K = 16$) to $4n^{3/2}$ (for $K = n^{1/2}$), and is often considered to be of order $n \log_2 n$.

   So far we have not considered testing for faults involving cell interaction, i.e., pattern sensitive faults. To do this, a sub-procedure, called ping-pong, has been devised. We will first discuss how this sub-procedure works, then present several tests which incorporate this ping-pong concept. Due to the complexity of the ping-pong process, all of these tests will be of complexity $\mathcal{O}(n^{3/2})$ or greater.

Sub-test:

Ping-Pong Procedure

   Ping-pong is a sub-test procedure used in several functional test patterns. Ping-ponging is used to test for the interaction between pairs of cells in the memory. In a full ping-pong (Figure 3.43(a)), one cell c_i is designated as the test bit. Now for all $j \neq i$ some sequence of READ and WRITE operations are done on cells c_i and c_j. If this procedure is repeated for each i, then a test of order n^2 results. Since tests using a full ping-pong procedure usually require a large amount of tester time, some simplifications are often employed. One common procedure is to assume that interference between cells occurs if they are either in the same "electrical" column or row. Note that these cells share common addressing and refresh circuitry. If we only ping-pong between cells in the same row and column in which the test bit resides, as shown in Figure 3.43(b), the test complexity is reduced to about $n^{3/2}$. The actual complexity of this procedure is a function of the array configuration.

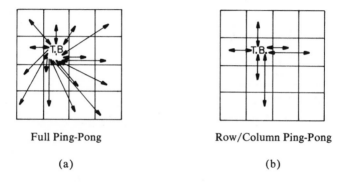

Full Ping-Pong   Row/Column Ping-Pong

(a)   (b)

Figure 3.43   Two versions of ping-pong

The following two test procedures employ ping-ponging.

Test:

Walking 1's and 0's
Purpose: Verifies that each cell can be set to both 0 and 1; that any cell can be set to either state without causing any other cell to change its state; and that decoder addressing is correct. Slow amplifier recovery is also detected by this test.

Test Procedure:
   Step 1: WRITE: $c_i \leftarrow 0$ for $i = 0,1, \ldots, n-1$
   Step 2: For $i = 0,1, \ldots, n-1$ carry out the following full ping-pong procedure on test bit c_i.
        2a: WRITE: $c_i \leftarrow 1$

2b: READ: $c_j(=0)$ for all $j \neq i$ (tests that no cell is disturbed).

2c: READ: $c_i(=1)$ (tests that test bit is still correct). rect."

2d: WRITE: $c_i \leftarrow 0$ (restores test bit to original value).

Complexity: $2n^2 + 6n$.

Test:

Galloping 1's and 0's

Purpose: To test all possible address transitions with all possible data transitions when reading.

Test Procedure (GALPAT I): Same as for "Walking 0's and 1's" except that in Step 2b each READ: $c_j(=0)$ operation is followed by a READ: $c_i(=1)$ operation. A modified version of this test procedure, known as GALPAT II, also exists.

Complexity: $2n^2 + 8n$

REFERENCES

[1] Agrawal, V. D. and P. Agrawal, "An Automatic Test Generation System for Illiac IV Logic Boards," *IEEE Transactions on Computers,* Vol. C-21, pp. 1015–1017, September 1972.

[2] Agrawal, P. and V. D. Agrawal, "Probabilistic Analysis of Random Test Generation Method for Irredundant Combinational Logic Networks," *IEEE Transactions on Computers,* Vol. C-24, pp. 691–695, June 1975.

[3] Agrawal, P. and V. D. Agrawal, "On Improving the Efficiency of Monte Carlo Test Generation," *International Symposium on Fault Tolerant Computing,* Paris, France, pp. 205–209, June 1975.

[4] Ashkinazy, A., "Fault Detection Experiments in Asynchronous Sequential Machines," *Proc. Eleventh Annual Symposium on Switching and Automata Theory,* pp. 88–96, 1970.

[5] Bastin, D., Girard, E., Rault, J. C. and R. Tulloue, "Probabilistic Test Generation Methods," *International Symposium on Fault Tolerant Computing,* Palo Alto, p. 171, June 1973.

[6] Breuer, M. A., "A Random and an Algorithmic Technique for Fault Detection Test Generation for Sequential Circuit," *IEEE Transactions on Computers,* Vol. C-20, pp. 1364–1370, November 1971.

[7] Breuer, M. A., "Modeling Circuits for Test Generation," *International Symposium on Fault-Tolerant Computing,* pp. 3/13–3/18, June 1974.

[8] Breuer, M. A., "The Effects of Races, Delays, and Delay Faults on Test Generation," *IEEE Transactions on Computers,* Vol. C-23, pp. 1078–1092, October 1974.

[9] Breuer, M. A. and L. Harrison, "Procedures for Eliminating Static and Dynamic Hazards in Test Generation," *IEEE Transactions on Computers*, Vol. C-23, pp. 1069–1078, October 1974.

[10] Brown, J. R., "Pattern Sensitivity in MOS Memories," *Digest Symposium Testing to Integrate Semiconductor Memories into Computer Mainframes*, Cherry Hill, N. J., pp. 33–46, October 1972.

[11] Chang, H. Y., Manning, E. G. and G. Metze, *Fault Diagnosis of Digital Systems*, John Wiley & Sons, New York, 1970.

[12] Chappell, S. G., "Automatic Test Generation for Asynchronous Digital Circuits," *The Bell System Technical Journal*, Vol. 53, pp. 1477–1503, October 1974.

[13] Fischer, J. E., "Test Problems and Solutions for 4K RAMs," *Proc. Semiconductor Test Symposium*, pp. 53–71, November 1974.

[14] Friedman, A. D. and P. Menon, *Fault Detection in Digital Circuits*, Prentice Hall, N. J., 1971.

[15] Hayes, J. P., "Testing Logic Circuit by Transition Counting," *International Symposium Fault-Tolerant Computing*, pp. 215–222, June 1975.

[16] Hayes, J. P., "Detection of Pattern-sensitive Faults in Random-access Memories," *IEEE Transactions on Computers*, Vol. C-24, pp. 150–157, February 1975.

[17] Henckels, L., private communication.

[18] Hnatik, E. R., "4-Kilobit Memories Present a Challenge to Testing," *Computer Design*, pp. 118–125, May 1965.

[19] Huang, H. and M. A. Breuer, "Analysis of Detectability of Faults by Random Patterns in a Special Class of NAND Networks," *Comput. and Elect. Engng.*, Vol. 1, pp. 171–186, 1973.

[20] Johnson, D. B., "Finding All the Elementary Circuits of a Directed Graph," *SIAM J. Computing*, Vol. 4, pp. 77–84, March 1975.

[21] Mei, K. C. Y., "Bridging and Stuck-at-Faults," *IEEE Transactions on Computers*, Vol. C-23, pp. 720–727, July 1974.

[22] Moore, E. F., "Gedanken Experiments on Sequential Machines," *Automata Studies*, pp. 129–153, Princeton University Press, 1956.

[23] Parker, K. P. and E. J. McCluskey, "Probabilistic Treatment of General Combinational Networks," *IEEE Transactions on Computers*, Vol. C-24, pp. 668–670, June 1975.

[24] Parker, K. P. and E. J. McCluskey, "Analysis of Logic Circuits with Faults Using Input Signal Probabilities," *IEEE Transactions on Computers*, Vol. C-24, pp. 573–578, May 1975.

[25] Poage, J. F., "Derivation of Optimal Test to Detect Faults in Combinational Circuits," *Proc. Symposium on Mathematical Theory of Automata*, Polytechnic Institute of Brooklyn, pp. 483–528, 1963.

[26] Putzolu, G. R. and J. P. Roth, "A Heuristic Algorithm for the Testing of Asynchronous Circuits," *IEEE Transactions on Computers*, Vol. C-20, pp. 639–646, June 1971.

[27] Rault, J. C., "A Graph Theoretical and Probabilistic Approach to the Fault Detection of Digital Circuits," *International Symposium on Fault Tolerant Computing*, pp. 16–29, March 1971.

[28] Schnurmann, H. D., Lindbloom, E. and R. G. Carpenter, "The Weighted Random Test-pattern Generator," *IEEE Transactions on Computers*, Vol. C-24, pp. 695–700, July 1975.

[29] Seshu, S. and D. N. Freeman, "The Diagnosis of Asynchronous Switching Systems," *IRE Transactions on Elec. Computers*, Vol. EC-11, pp. 459–465, August 1962.

[30] Shedletsky, J. J. and E. J. McCluskey, "The Error Latency of a Fault in a Combinational Circuit," *International Symposium on Fault Tolerant Computing*, pp. 210–214, June 1975.

[31] Smith, G. W., Jr. and W. B. Walford, "The Identification of a Minimal Feedback Vertex Set of a Directed Graph," *IEEE Transactions on Circuits and Systems*, Vol. CAS-22, pp. 9–15, January 1975.

[32] Tarjan, R., "Enumeration of the Elementary Circuits of a Directed Graph," *SIAM J. Computing*, Vol. 2, pp. 211–216, September 1973.

[33] Thomas, J. J., "Automated Diagnostic Test Programs for Digital Networks," *Computer Design*, pp. 63–67, August 1971.

[34] Unger, S. H., *Asynchronous Sequential Switching Circuits*, John Wiley & Sons, New York, 1969.

[35] Younger, D. H., "Minimum Feedback Arc Sets for a Directed Graph," *IEEE Transactions on Circuit Theory*, Vol. CT-10, pp. 238–245, June 1963.

PROBLEMS

3.1 Construct a circuit S and identify a stuck-at-fault α such that

i) no test sequence $\mathbf{T}$ exists which strongly detects α,

ii) there exists a self initializing test sequence $\mathbf{X}$ which detects α.

3.2 Construct the truth table for a pseudo combinational switching function corresponding to a *JK* flip-flop.

a) Determine the primitive D-cubes for this element, assuming only one input line contains a D.

b) Determine the primitive D-cubes of the failure "line J *s-a-*1."

c) Assume a stuck-at-fault existed internal to the flip-flop such that the input $J = K = 1$ caused the flip-flop to hold its state rather than trigger. Determine the primitive D-cubes for this failure.

3.3 Develop a truth table for a pseudo combinational switching function corresponding to a master-slave *JK* flip-flop. Assume three inputs, *J,K* and

C_p, and two internal state variables, one for each latch. Assume that J and K cannot change state when $C_p = 1$.

3.4   For the synchronous circuit shown in Figure 3.44, use Procedure 3.1 to derive a test to detect the fault a s-a-1, assuming the initial state of the composite circuit is $(y_1, y_2) = (0,0)$.

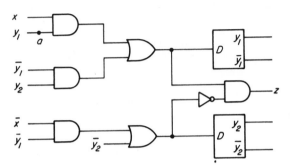

Figure 3.44

3.5   For the circuit of Figure 3.5, consider the fault z s-a-0.

a) Derive a test using Procedure 3.1 assuming initial state $(y_1, y_2) = (1,1)$.

b) Derive a test using Procedure 3.2 assuming initial state (u,u).

3.6   This problem deals with the concept of transfer sequences discussed in section 3.1.1. Consider a combinational circuit C containing one or more stuck-at-faults. Assume some of the inputs and outputs of C have been arbitrarily assigned binary values. Develop a procedure similar to the D-algorithm which will, if possible, assign binary values to the unspecified ($\times$) inputs so that the specified output values are justified. What new type of cubes, if any, are required for each primitive element? How would you solve this problem using an equation (algebraic) approach?

3.7   Given two initial states y_1 and y_2 of a synchronous sequential circuit, develop a procedure, similar to the D-algorithm, for constructing an input sequence X such that $Y(y_1, X) = Y(y_2, X)$, i.e., X drives the circuit into the same state. (Hint: Form a composite state vector y_1/y_2 having D's and $\overline{D}$'s, and note that intersecting a cube having a D or $\overline{D}$ at the input of a gate with a primitive cube suppresses the D's, i.e., the output of the gate becomes a 0 or 1. Hence by suppressing all D's in the D frontier the circuit can be driven into a state having no D's in its composite vector representation.) Discuss how this procedure can be used for circuit initialization.

3.8 For the circuit of Figure 3.10, derive self initializing tests for the following faults:

a) J_1 s-a-1

b) y_2 s-a-0, which in turn forces $\bar{y}_2$ s-a-1 due to the internal feedback in the flip-flop.

3.9 Consider the circuit shown in Figure 3.45(a). Assume x is driven by a circuit (see Figure 3.45(b)) such that its value is equal to x_0, which is a primary input, at every odd clock time, and is unknown (u) at every even clock time. Show that there is no test for the fault a s-a-1 using the six valued logic system $(0,1,\times,D,\bar{D},u)$, but there is a test for this fault using the 16 valued system shown in Figure 3.8.

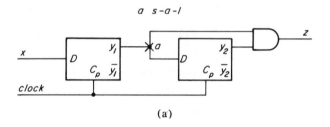

(a)

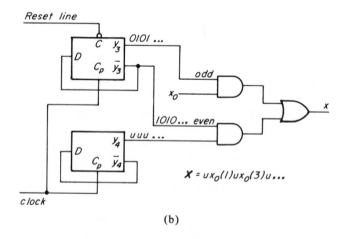

(b)

Figure 3.45

3.10 This problem is designed to illustrate several difficulties related to generating a test in an asynchronous circuit using an iterative array model designed for synchronous circuits. Consider the portion of the flow table of Figure 3.46(a) for a circuit S, and the test generation model of Figure 3.46(b). Assume the initial total state of the circuit is $(x,y_1y_2) = (0,00)$.

 a) Consider a fault which changes the output in total state $(0,01)$ from a 1 to a 0. Using Procedure 3.1 determine a test for this fault. Discuss why your solution is impractical.

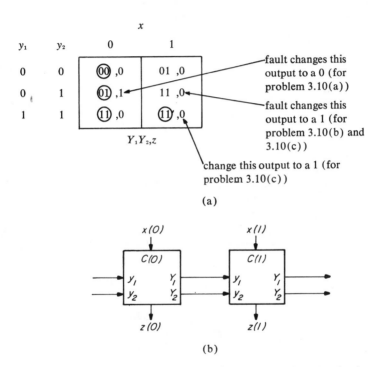

(a)

(b)

Figure 3.46   (a) Portion of a flow table for an asynchronous circuit
(b) Iterative array model applicable to synchronous circuits

 b) Consider a fault which changes the output in total state $(1,01)$ from a 0 to a 1. Using Procedure 3.1 determine a test for this fault. Discuss why this test may be invalid.

 c) Modify the table of Figure 3.46(a) such that in total state $(1,11)$ the output is a 1. Consider a fault which causes the output in total state $(1,01)$ to be a 1. Using Procedure 3.1 determine a test for this fault. Discuss why this test may be impractical to realize.

3.11 Consider the asynchronous circuit shown in Figure 3.47.

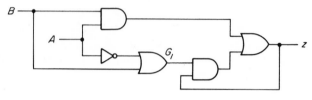

Figure 3.47

Construct a self initializing test, if one exists, for the following faults using an iterative array model.

a) z s-a-1

b) z s-a-0

c) G_1 s-a-0

d) G_1 s-a-1

Construct a self initializing test, if one exists, for the fault z s-a-1 using the circuit-time equation technique.

3.12 Construct an iterative array computational model for the circuit shown in Figure 3.48. Circuit delay exists only in the elements shown.

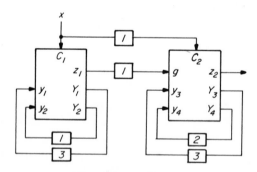

Figure 3.48

3.13 Consider the gate equivalent circuit for a *JK* master-slave flip-flop, where each internal latch is modeled by a pseudo combinational element. Assume the initial state of each latch is 0. Generate a test for the fault C_p s-a-0.

3.14 Consider the gate equivalent circuit for a *JK* master-slave flip-flop, where each internal latch is modeled functionally. Generate a test for C_p *s-a-*0 using the circuit-time equation approach.

3.15 For the circuit shown in Figure 3.49, assuming the inputs are hazard free, assign the appropriate hazard status flags and logic values to all gate inputs.

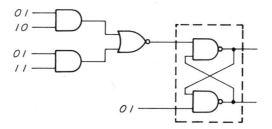

Figure 3.49

3.16 For the circuit shown in Figure 3.50, construct an iterative delay model for the delay fault indicated, and then derive a test, if one exists, for this fault.

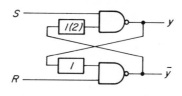

Figure 3.50

3.17 Prove that if each variable can take on the value 0, 1, or u, that

i) $AB + A\bar{B} \neq A$

ii) $A + \bar{A}B \neq A + B$

iii) $AB + \bar{A}C + BC \neq AB + \bar{A}C$

iv) $A + AB = A$

v) $\overline{A \cdot B} = \bar{A} + \bar{B}$

3.18 Verify the correctness of the equation shown in Figure 3.30 under the condition that the fault identifiers f_i^n and f_i^p have propagated around a loop in a cyclic circuit and appear in the equations for A and B.

3.19 a) Construct the circuit-time equation for the circuit shown in Figure 3.51 in terms of the input sequence $\mathbf{D} = D(0)D(1)$ and $\mathbf{C}_p = 10$.

b) Generate a test for the fault D $s\text{-}a\text{-}0$ using Procedure 3.3.

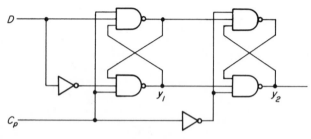

Figure 3.51

3.20 The following I/O sequence is generated by a 3 state machine. The outputs indicated by a_1, a_2, a_3, a_4 are not known. Determine these outputs if possible, and add a minimal number of additional inputs to uniquely determine the machine. If the minimal additional input sequence depends on the output response specify all contingencies.

$$\mathbf{X} = 0 \ \ 0 \ \ 0 \ \ 0 \ \ 0 \ \ 0 \ \ 1 \ \ 0 \ \ 0 \ \ 1 \ \ 0 \ \ 0 \ \ 0$$

$$\mathbf{Z} = 0 \ \ 0 \ \ 1 \ \ 0 \ \ a_1 \ \ 1 \ \ 0 \ \ 1 \ \ a_2 \ \ 0 \ \ 1 \ \ a_3 \ \ a_4$$

3.21 Consider a JK flip-flop, neglecting the clock input.

a) Construct "heuristically" what you consider to be a good functional test for this device.

b) Construct a checking sequence for this device. Compare this result with that of part (a) and explain any differences in these two results.

3.22 Consider an 8×8 array of cells (RAM) arranged such that the right edge is adjacent to the left edge, and the top is adjacent to the bottom. (Hence, there are no edges or corners as in a Karnaugh graph.) It is desired to test M_{64} by setting $c_i = \delta, \delta \in \{0,1\}$, and then placing all 2^4 patterns in its 4 adjacent neighbors. Every time a new 4-tuple pattern is set up about c_i, c_i should be read. Note that while setting up patterns for cell c_i, other cells can also be tested. Devise an efficient scheme for testing this memory. What is the complexity of your test?

3.23 Determine a "short" test sequence which would prove that there are at least two distinct cells in the RAM M_n capable of storing a 0 and a 1. What other properties can be deduced from your test concerning M_n?

3.24 Construct a checking sequence for the RAM M_2.

3.25 Often adjacent physical cells in a RAM memory do not have consecutive (adjacent) addresses. How does this situation effect the test procedure?

3.26 Consider the fanout free NAND network having L logic levels, as shown in Figure 3.52, where each 'gate has n inputs. Let the probability of a logical 0 and 1 value occuring at the output of a gate at level ℓ be p_ℓ^0 and p_ℓ^1, respectively.

a) Show that

$$p_\ell^0 = (p_{\ell-1}^1)^n = (1 - p_{\ell-1}^0)^n$$

and

$$p_\ell^1 = 1 - (p_{\ell-1}^1)^n.$$

b) Let $P(L)$ be the probability that a random input pattern would detect the fault a s-a-0.
Show that

$$P(L) = \prod_{k=0}^{L-1} (p_k^1)^{n-1}.$$

c) Let $P(L,M)$ be the probability that at least one test out of M random test vectors will detect the fault a s-a-0.
Show that

$$M = \frac{\log_2 (1 - P(L,M))}{\log_2 (1 - P(L))}.$$

d) Calculate the value of M for $p_0^0 = p_0^1 = 0.5$, $L = 6$, $P(L,M) = 0.9$ and for $P(L,M) = 0.99$.

e) For $L = 6$ and $n = 2$, determine the value of $p_0^0 = (1 - p_0^1)$ which maximizes $P(L,M)$.

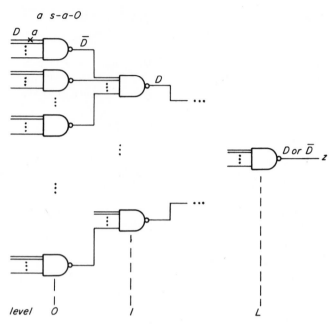

Figure 3.52   Fanout free NAND network

3.27 Let A be a signal in a network, and a be the probability that $A = 1$, i.e., $a = P(A = 1)$, given a random input vector. (We will use the convention that upper case letters correspond to signal names and lower case letters correspond to probabilities.)

   a) For the basic functions of AND, OR and NOT, verify that the output probability can be expressed in terms of the input probabilities, as shown below.

Function	Output Probability	Assumptions
A	a	
$\overline{A}$	$1 - a$	
$X_1 X_2 \ldots X_n$	$x_1 x_2 \ldots x_n$	all X_i are independent
$X_1 + X_2 + \ldots + X_n$	$1 - \displaystyle\prod_{i=1}^{n} (1 - x_i)$	all X_i are independent
$X_1 + X_2 + \ldots + X_n$	$\displaystyle\sum_{i=1}^{n} x_i$	$X_i \cdot X_j = 0$ for all $i \neq j$

b) Let Z be the output of a combinational circuit realizing the function f. Now f can be expressed as a sum of minterms, i.e., $f = \sum\limits_{i=1}^{k} T_i$. If $t_i = P(T_i = 1)$, show that

$$z = \sum_{i=1}^{k} t_i.$$

c) Consider the circuit shown in Figure 3.53. Determine the value of $z = P(Z = 1)$ in terms of a, b and c.

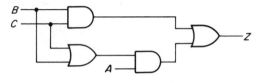

Figure 3.53

d) Evaluate z for the case $a = b = c = q$, and plot z as a function of q.

e) Show that if each input to a combinational circuit has the value 1 with probability q, then the output probability is a polynomial over q.

3.28 To test the decoder referred to in Problem 2.18 requires all 2^n input patterns be applied. Determine the expected member of input/output (pin) stuck-at-faults detected by a random test sequence as a function of its length for this decoder circuit.

3.29 Consider an n-input NAND gate, denoted by G_n. All (single and multiple) stuck type faults associated with G_n can be detected by the unique, minimal test set T consisting of $n + 1$ test vectors shown below:

$$u = (1,1, \ldots,1)$$
$$e_1 = (0,1,1, \ldots,1,1)$$
$$e_2 = (1,0,1, \ldots,1,1)$$
$$\vdots$$
$$e_n = (1,1,1, \ldots,1,0).$$

The correct response to u and e_i is 0 and 1 respectively. Every complete TC test sequence $\mathbf{X}_n$ for G_n must include every test pattern in T, hence $|\mathbf{X}_n| \geq n + 1$.

a) Show that $X_1 = ue_1$ and $X_2 = e_1ue_2$ are minimal TC tests for $n = 1$, and 2 respectively.

b) For $n > 2$, the minimal value of $|X_n|$ is $n + 2$, as shown in the following theorem.

Theorem [15]: $X_n = ue_1e_2 \ldots e_{n-1}e_ne_1$ is a minimal TC test of length $n + 2$ for both single and multiple stuck-type faults for an n-input NAND gate G_n.

Prove this theorem.

3.30 For an n-input NAND gate G_n, how many single and multiple stuck-type faults are locatable and how many are TC locatable?

3.31 Prove the following theorem:

Theorem [15]: Let T be any test set for a two-level circuit C. Let Z_0 denote the fault free response of C to any sequence X containing every member of T. No single or multiple fault can change the response of C to X from Z_0 to $\overline{Z}_0$.

3.32 Let $T = [T^0, T^1]$ be an arbitrary single fault test set for a two-level sum of product irredundant circuit C containing $r = p + q$ vectors, where $T^0 = \{t_1^0, t_2^0, \ldots, t_p^0\}$, and $T^1 = \{t_1^1, t_2^1, \ldots, t_q^1\}$. It is well known that T also detects all multiple stuck-type faults.

a) Show that the sequence

$$X^2 = t_q^1 t_1^1 t_2^1 \ldots t_q^1 t_p^0 t_1^0 t_2^0 \ldots t_p^0$$

of length $r + 2$ is a TC test for C with respect to both single and multiple faults.

b) Assume T is a minimal test set. Show that (1) if $D = 0$ or 1, the sequence X^* defined by Theorem 3.5 is a minimal length TC test; (2) for $D = 2$, both X^* and X^2 are of the same length; and (3) for $D > 2$, X^2 is shorter than X^*.

3.33 Consider the circuit shown in Figure 3.54. Construct a minimal length test set T for all stuck-at-faults. Construct X^* and X^2 (defined in Problem 3.32). Is X^* a TC test for all multiple faults?

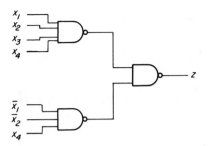

Figure 3.54

Chapter 4

LOGIC LEVEL SIMULATION

Logic simulation is the process of building and exercising a model of a digital circuit on a digital computer. By exercising we mean the evaluation of signal values in the modeled circuit as a function of time for some applied input sequence.

There are two main applications for a logic simulator. The first is in the evaluation of a new design. Here, the logic designer is interested in testing for logical correctness, as well as timing and signal propagation characteristics. He may desire information related to race, hazard and oscillatory circuit conditions. For LSI circuits, where design errors are very costly and breadboarding is impractical, logic simulation is an invaluable aid.

A second application for logic simulation exists in the area of fault analysis. Here, the test engineer or logic designer may desire information related to what faults are detected by a proposed test sequence, what is the operational characteristic of the circuit under specific fault conditions, or what degree of fault resolution is obtainable with a given test sequence? These and other questions can be dealt with effectively by the process of fault simulation. The table of Figure 4.1 gives a detailed list of potential applications for a logic simulation system.

The usefulness of a logic simulation system can be evaluated with respect to the attributes of accuracy, efficiency, and generality. By accuracy we mean that there must be a close correspondence between predicted signal values vs. time as calculated by the simulator, and that which occurs in the actual circuit. By efficiency we mean that the process of simulation must be cost effective. Generality implies that the simulator should be able to handle a broad class of circuits including the following cases: (1) many different circuit types such as combinational, synchronous, and asynchronous circuits; (2) a wide selection of element types such as gate types (NAND, NOR,

174

1. Hardware Design Verification
   a. Verify logical correctness
   b. Timing analysis
      Delay models
      Race and hazard analysis
   c. Initialization analysis

2. Fault Analysis
   a. Fault coverage
   b. Timing analysis under fault conditions
   c. Initialization under fault conditions
   d. Fault induced hazards and races
   e. Evaluation of test point effectiveness
   f. Evaluation of self checking circuitry
   g. Evaluation of fail-safe circuitry
   h. Evaluation of roll back hardware-software

3. Software Development
   a. Debugging software to run on hardware not yet implemented
   b. Development of diagnostic software programs and microcode for computer systems.

Figure 4.1   Applications of simulation

AND, OR, . . .), flip-flop types (latches, master-slave, edge triggered, . . .), special elements such as RAM's, ROM's, one shots, and multi-vibrators; (3) multi-valued logic systems; (4) a suitable assortment of delay specifications; (5) race and hazard conditions; (6) unknown signal values which may occur, e.g., during initialization or "power-up" of a circuit; and (7) various types of fault modes. It should be noted that a logic simulation system may include many different simulators, some having different capabilities than others.

This chapter deals with the major concepts related to the design of logic level simulators. The primitives in such a simulator are elements whose inputs and outputs are binary valued, and for which the signal propagational delay characteristics through the device can be specified. Each element is assumed to model a physical device in the circuit being simulated. Most of the techniques discussed here are applicable to higher level simulators, such as for register transfer languages or functional level models, but not for circuit level simulators.

4.1 AN OVERVIEW OF A LOGIC SIMULATION SYSTEM

The input information to a logic simulator usually consists of the following:
  (1) Description of the circuit to be simulated.
  (2) Input data to be simulated.
  (3) Initial value of memory states.
  (4) Faults to be simulated, if any.
  (5) Signals to be monitored.

The circuit description (1) consists of the topology of the circuit and the circuit element types, along with a list of primary inputs (pi's), and primary outputs (po's) including test points. The specification of delay parameters, as well as circuit restrictions such as fanin, and fanout restrictions may also be included (frequently on an optional basis). If the initial state of some devices is not known, or some input lines are not controllable, a don't know or unknown value, denoted by u, can be used. Faults may consist of lines being open, shorted to ground or power, signal lines shorted, adjacent pin shorts, etc. Permanent and intermittent faults may also be simulated. A high level language is often used for describing input sequences, desired output format, circuit description, etc.

4.1.1 Input Circuit Description

Figure 4.2 illustrates one possible method by which a circuit consisting of IC's may be described to a simulator. Under the input/output (I/O) header, signal A is defined as a primary input which is connected to pin 1 of the connector, and B is defined as a primary output connected to pin 2. Under the parts list, the chip type corresponding to each unit Ui is specified. The interconnection list indicates every pin associated with each signal. For example, signal C connects pin 2 of $U1$ to pin 1 of $U2$. The input description illustrated here is net oriented, i.e., all pins associated with each net are specified.

Another form of description is element oriented. Here, each element is associated with all of its signals. For example, we may write

$$U1 \quad A.1/C.2/D.3/D.4/\text{etc.}$$

For describing circuits in terms of logic elements, usually the latter form is used, for example an AND gate having input A and B and output C may be specified as

$$\text{AND} \quad A/B,C.$$

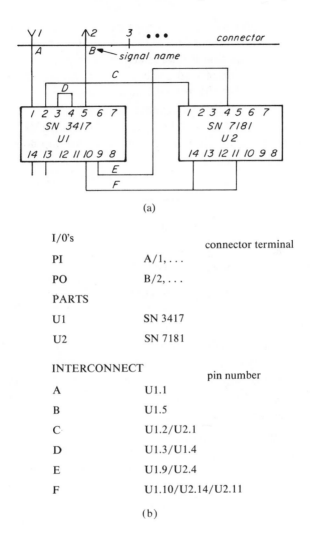

(a)

I/0's		connector terminal
PI	A/1, . . .	
PO	B/2, . . .	

PARTS	
U1	SN 3417
U2	SN 7181

INTERCONNECT	pin number
A	U1.1
B	U1.5
C	U1.2/U2.1
D	U1.3/U1.4
E	U1.9/U2.4
F	U1.10/U2.14/U2.11

(b)

Figure 4.2 (a) Portion of a circuit schematic (b) Input circuit
description to the simulation system

When elements are described by part type, such as *SN* **XXXX**, it is
assumed that the description of this part in terms of the primitives of the
system are available to the system. These descriptions are stored in the
system Parts Type Library. Figure 4.3(b) shows the library entry for an
element *SN* **XXXX** whose circuit diagram is shown in Figure 4.3(a). The

format shown in Figure 4.3(b) is that used by a designer to describe a new part type to the library. Other information which may be kept along with the description of an element is data related to maximum allowable fanout, circuit delay as a function of load, logic voltage levels, etc. In this example we have assumed that NAND and DEL (delay) are primitives. Usually, the primitive elements to a logic level simulator are as follows:

(1) gate elements such as NAND, NOR, AND, OR, INVERTER, etc.
(2) memory elements such as latches, master-slave flip-flops, edge triggered flip-flops, etc.

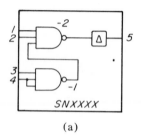

(a)

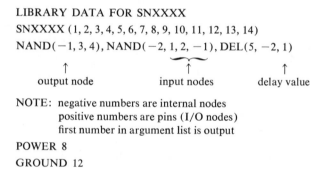

LIBRARY DATA FOR SNXXXX
SNXXXX (1, 2, 3, 4, 5, 6, 7, 8, 9, 10, 11, 12, 13, 14)
NAND($-1, 3, 4$), NAND($-2, 1, 2, -1$), DEL($5, -2, 1$)

    ↑   ↑   ↑
output node   input nodes   delay value

NOTE: negative numbers are internal nodes
           positive numbers are pins (I/O nodes)
           first number in argument list is output
POWER 8
GROUND 12

(b)

Figure 4.3   (a) Circuit element (b) Library description

Some systems employ relatively few primitives. For example, the only primitive in the LASAR system [16] is NAND, hence a master-slave *SR* flip-flop is usually modeled by nine NAND gates. Future logic level simulators will probably have higher level primitives such as decoders, multiplexers, ROM's, RAM's, counters and shift registers.

Often the input language has several features to facilitate the description of the circuit to the system. Examples of such features are macros, nesting of macros, and subscripting. For example, the statement

REPEAT FOR $I = 1,32$ "AND $A[I]/B[I],C[I]$"

could be used to describe an array of 32 AND gates.

4.1.2 Modeling

Modeling is the process of describing a circuit (schematic) in terms of the primitives of the processing system. The objective is to model the circuit such that the results from the simulator will correspond to the signal values in the actual circuit. Often, modeling is quite straightforward; however, in some cases it can be quite complex. Modeling is a function of three factors:

(a) the element types in the original circuits
(b) the primitives in the processing system
(c) the basic processing algorithm

Since modeling can be a function of how the simulator operates, we will defer this subject until Section 4.8.

4.1.3 Input Data Language

There are two common ways of describing the input sequence data to be simulated. The first is by an $n \times m$ array $A = [a_{ij}]$, $a_{ij} \in \{0,1\}$, where each row of A corresponds to an input vector. The value a_{ij} is applied to the i-th input line at time t_j. If the t_j are prescribed, then A is called a *real time input*. Otherwise the vector $\mathbf{a}_j = (a_{1j}, \ldots, a_{nj})$ is applied after the circuit has stabilized in response to $\mathbf{a}_{j-1}$, and the inputs are called *static*.

The second way to specify the input sequence is via a high level language. For example, to generate a periodic pulse on input line ALPHA, which is to be on for 5 units of time and off for 7, one could write

PERIODIC PULSE(5,7) ALPHA.

In general, there exists a set of operators which can be used to define binary signal sequences.

In addition to describing the circuit and input data, a simulation system typically has a high level simulation control language useful to specify data such as:

(a) initial state of elements;
(b) type of simulation to be carried out;

(c) output format and data desired;

(d) duration of real circuit time to be simulated.

The basic structure of a logic level simulation system is shown in Figure 4.4.

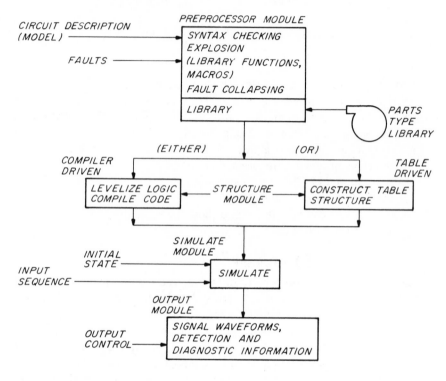

Figure 4.4   Basic structure of a logic level simulation system

4.1.4   Preprocessor Module

The major function of the preprocessor module is to read in the users description of a circuit and replace it by an equivalent circuit consisting entirely of the primitives in the system. This process involves replacing macro calls by their macro definitions, and library elements by their library definitions. The preprocessor module should detect errors in the syntax of the input language, as well as simple errors in interconnecting circuit elements, e.g., an AND gate driving no load. If fault simulation is required some form of fault collapsing is usually required (see Section 2.5). This module should also identify unused elements or inputs, and either remove them from the circuit or flag them accordingly. For example, a user may call a library element containing four NAND gates, though in his actual circuit only three are used. The fourth gate is untestable and should not be simulated.

4.1.5   Structure Module

There are two classical ways of representing a circuit during simulation. The earliest systems used compiled code, i.e., the behavior of the simulated circuit was represented by a sequence of computer instructions. Due to several factors, such as multi-valued logic, timing considerations and efficiency, most modern simulators operate off of a table structure which describes the topology (element interconnection) of the circuit as well as such data as element type, delay, etc. The function of the structure module is to prepare the internal data structure required for efficient simulation. For compiler driven simulators it produces a sequence of machine executable instructions, for table driven simulators it produces a series of tables describing the circuit to be simulated.

4.1.6   Simulate Module

In a simulation system time in quantized into units, e.g., a unit may be 5 ns. We will consider a table driven *activity directed* simulator. By *activity directed* we mean that an element is not simulated unless there is a signal change in at least one of its inputs. This follows from the fact that for the type of elements we are considering, all output value changes occur in response to some input value change.

Figure 4.5 shows the essential behavior of the Simulate Module for such a simulator. Block A deals with setting up the initial state of the circuit. In Block B a new input vector is read. Only line *changes* need be processed since only they define activity. Skipping over Block C temporarily, in Block D all changed line values caused by the new input are updated and in Block E elements affected by current activity are simulated. If any of these elements change states they are scheduled to change at some future time. All such activities are sequentially processed, after which the simulated time is incremented by one unit, and race and oscillation analysis is performed and processed accordingly (Block C). Simulators allowing for real time dynamic inputs would branch from Block G to B. For static simulation, the computation loop consisting of Blocks C, D, E, F, G is usually repeated until the circuit stabilizes, at which time a new input vector is processed.

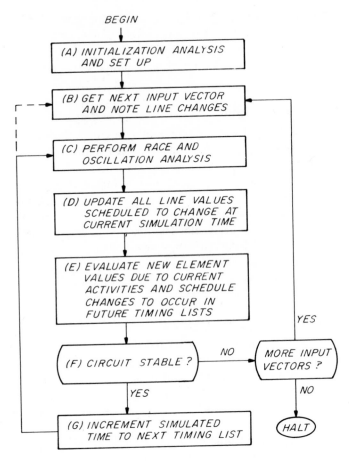

BEGIN

(A) INITIALIZATION ANALYSIS AND SET UP

(B) GET NEXT INPUT VECTOR AND NOTE LINE CHANGES

(C) PERFORM RACE AND OSCILLATION ANALYSIS

(D) UPDATE ALL LINE VALUES SCHEDULED TO CHANGE AT CURRENT SIMULATION TIME

(E) EVALUATE NEW ELEMENT VALUES DUE TO CURRENT ACTIVITIES AND SCHEDULE CHANGES TO OCCUR IN FUTURE TIMING LISTS

(F) CIRCUIT STABLE ?   NO   MORE INPUT VECTORS ?   YES

YES   NO

(G) INCREMENT SIMULATED TIME TO NEXT TIMING LIST   HALT

Figure 4.5   Basic structure of simulation module

4.1.7 Output Module

The output module produces a multitude of information. Prior to simulation, it can produce a simple analysis of the logic circuit showing all fanin and fanout information, the results from fault collapsing, the results from macro expansion and library function substitutions, etc. Upon simulating the fault free and/or a faulty circuit, the output module can produce a plot of the output waveform for any line specified by the output control information. The output module can also produce tables summarizing fault detection and fault location data.

4.1.8   CPU Simulation Time

Logic simulation is inherently a slow process. The primary reason for this is that a simulator processes elements sequentially, while in the actual circuit signals propagate along numerous paths simultaneously. Consider a synchronous circuit containing N elements and operating at a 1 MHz clock rate. If t seconds are required to simulate each element then we require $t \cdot N$ seconds to simulate the entire circuit for one input vector. Typically there are about 2-3 nonequivalent stuck-at faults per element (gate). Hence, to simulate this circuit under each fault condition would require at least $2tN^2$ seconds. Assuming that the length L of a test sequence for a circuit is proportional to N, i.e., $L = kN$, then to simulate the circuit for a given input test sequence for each fault would require $2tkN^3$ seconds. The table of Figure 4.6 indicates some representative calculations for $t = 10^{-5}$ seconds and $N = 10^4$. Since 10^{-1} seconds are required to simulate one clock cycle of this circuit ($1\mu s$ of actual operation), there is a "slow-up" of $10^{-1}/10^{-6} = 10^5$ in simulation with respect to real time operation.

	One Input Vector	$L = N$ Input Vectors $(k = 1)$
Good machine simulation	$tN = 10^{-1}$	$tN^2 = 10^3$
Faulty machine simulation	$2tN^2 = 2 \times 10^3$	$2tN^3 = 2 \times 10^7$

$t = 10\mu s = 10^{-5}$ sec.

$N = 10^4$

Figure 4.6   Simulation time

Because of this situation, much of the research in the area of simulation has been directed toward developing techniques to reduce simulation time. An example of such a technique is the process of activity directed simulation.

4.2   CIRCUIT DELAY

Simulation deals with calculating the logic value of each signal line as a function of time. In order to do this correctly, delays within the circuit must be considered. Delay is an important attribute to the correct functional operation of many circuits. For some elements, such as delay lines, multivibrators and one-shots, delay is the essential characteristic of their operation. It is therefore important to develop careful simulation techniques and component models to insure the integrity of the simulation process. We can categorize most techniques as being either pessimistic or optimistic models of the real circuit. Usually a more detailed timing model is used for design verification than is used for test verification. The problem of accurately modeling the timing behavior of a circuit for purposes of simulation requires further research. The problem of modeling delay in complex function elements, such as an MSI device, is particularly difficult. In general, circuit delays can be characterized by one or more of the delay models which we shall now consider.

4.2.1   Transport Delay (Δ_T)

Every element and wire introduces delay to the signals propagating through it. We denote this *transport (pure) delay* by the symbol Δ_T. The delay through an etched conductor is typically 1 ns/foot, while that through a gate is from 1-3 ns for high speed logic. If an input change to an element occurs at time t, then the effect of this change on the output will not occur until time $t + \Delta_T$. An element and its transport delay is modeled as shown in Figure 4.7. Note that the delay is added to the output of the functional element.

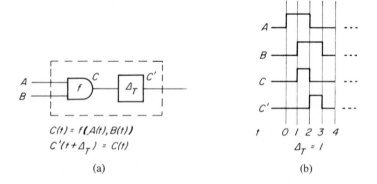

$$C(t) = f(A(t), B(t))$$
$$C'(t + \Delta_T) = C(t)$$

(a)

$t \quad 0\ 1\ 2\ 3\ 4$

$\Delta_T = 1$

(b)

Figure 4.7   (a) Model of a logic element (AND gate) showing its functional and transport delay components (b) Example input/output timing diagram

Typically the transport delay values assigned are multiples of some common unit. For example, if the delay through a NAND gate is 5 ns, and the delay through a flip-flop is 15 ns, we may set Δ_T (NAND) $= 1$, Δ_T (flip-flop) $= 3$, where one unit of delay represents 5 ns.

4.2.2 Ambiguity Delay $(\Delta_M - \Delta_m)$

Often the exact transport delay through a device is not known. For example, the delay through a specific type of NAND gate may vary from 5 ns to 10 ns, as specified by the circuit manufacturer. The delay through an element may not even be specified by the manufacturer. For example, in an MSI device, the delay is usually specified between input pins and output pins. The delay through each internal gate and flip-flop is not specified. One can model this situation by assigning a pair of delay values to the element. Let Δ_m and Δ_M be the minimum and maximum delay through an element. Then these delays define an ambiguity region of duration $(\Delta_M - \Delta_m)$. We illustrate this situation in Figure 4.8. R_1 and R_2 represent the ambiguity region, i.e., the signal changes value sometime within these regions.

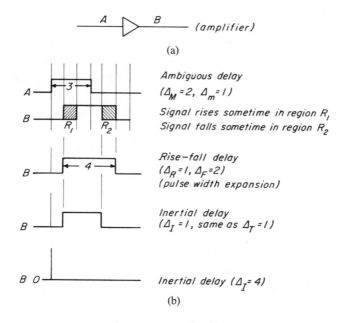

Figure 4.8 (a) Circuit element (b) Input/output timing diagrams for various delay models

This example illustrates the necessity for more than two logic values, namely logic 0, 1, and some symbol(s) to specify the value of signal B in regions R_1 and R_2.

Logic simulators can process delay in two ways, referred to as *delay propagation* and *min/max path analysis*. Most simulators use the former, though the latter can be more accurate. For delay propagation, signals through an element are propagated based upon their current inputs and their delay values, as illustrated in Figures 4.7 and 4.8. For the min/max path analysis techniques, signals are first propagated using the delay propagation approach, though simplified delay parameters are frequently used. For example, Δ_M and Δ_m may be replaced by $\Delta_T = (\Delta_m + \Delta_M)/2$. Once this process is completed, critical circuit areas, such as a 0 to 1 and 1 to 0 transition on the inputs to a gate, are investigated in detail. This involves calculating the exact minimum and maximum delay between a signal change at some node i and the source of this signal change. If two nodes i and j have a common source, then this calculation can be quite valuable because an ambiguity element delay model can often lead to overly pessimistic results. There are two reasons for this. First the actual delay through a specific gate is usually constant, fixed between Δ_m and Δ_M. Every signal change propagating through this gate is delayed by the same amount. However, the model allows for the delay to change between Δ_m and Δ_M for each propagating signal change, i.e., the delay per element is a random variable. The second problem area deals with reconvergent fanout. Consider the circuit shown in Figure 4.9(a), where $\Delta_m = 2$ and $\Delta_M = 3$. For the 0 to 1 signal change on line 1, we obtain the signal values shown in Figure 4.9(b). Note that a potential hazard is predicted for line 7. This hazard is due to a momentary (11) input to gate 7 which may occur sometime between time 9 and 10. We will now apply the concept of min/max path analysis. When node 3 goes from 0 to 1, the earliest line 5 can go to a 1 is the minimum delay between nodes 3 and 5 which is $2 + 2 = 4$; the longest time the 1 can persist at node 6 after the transition at node 3 is $\Delta_M = 3$. Hence gate 7 can never have a (11) input and no hazard can exist.

The major problem associated with using min/max path analysis is that it is based upon the results of a first pass delay propagation type simulation. It is not known exactly what delay values should be used in this first pass in order that during the second pass all critical circuit areas requiring min/max path analysis can be correctly identified.

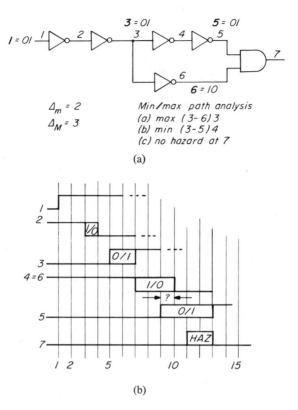

(a)

(b)

Figure 4.9 (a) Circuit with ambiguity delay (b) Results using ambiguity
delay propagation indicating a potential hazard which,
in actuality, cannot exist

4.2.3 Rise-fall Delay (Δ_R, Δ_F)

For some devices the output response rise (0 to 1) and fall (1 to 0) time
are different due to various electrical parameters such as capacitance. For
some MOS devices these delays can differ by a ratio of 3 to 1. Such devices
can be modeled by assigning two delays Δ_R and Δ_F to the output of the
element as shown in Figure 4.8(b). Note that the result of having $\Delta_R \neq \Delta_F$
is to modify the width of the pulse propagating through the element.

4.2.4 Inertial Delay (Δ_I)

All circuit devices require energy in order to switch state. The energy in
a signal is a function of its amplitude and duration. If its duration is too

small, the signal will not force the device to switch. The minimum duration for which an input change must persist in order for the device to switch states is called the *inertial delay* of an element and is denoted by Δ_I. Unlike the preceding types of delay, inertial delay is usually modeled at the inputs to elements. Note that if the input pulse duration is equal to or exceeds Δ_I, then the element appears to have a pure transport delay of value Δ_I (see Figure 4.8).

Simulation of elements having inertial delay can lead to some complications, as shown in Figure 4.10. Here we see that each input pulse is of unit duration, and the combined inputs to the OR gate represent a 1 signal value of duration 3. However the value of the output may be dependent on the circuit technology. If the inertial delay is due to the input part of the circuit, then the output may not switch. If the delay is due to the output circuitry in the OR gate, then the combined input pulses may force the output to switch. Hence, the simulator must be constructed to model what is predicted by the analysis of the circuit.

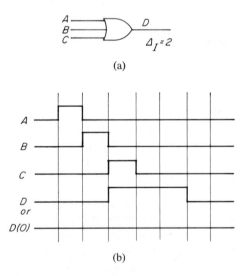

(a)

(b)

Figure 4.10   (a) OR gate (b) Unit pulse inputs

In general, combinations of the delay types presented can be used. For example, each element can be assigned an inertial delay, Δ_I. In addition they can have a Δ_R and a Δ_F. Finally, each of these values can be assigned minimum and maximum values. Of course, such a situation is seldom if ever used since it would drastically slow up the simulator. The easiest delay to simulate is transport delay, sometimes called *nominal delay*. If every element is assigned the same value of Δ_T, then we can set $\Delta_T = 1$ and thus have a *unit delay simulator*. A simulator which evaluates elements as if they had no delay is said to employ a 0-delay model. Such a simulator deals primarily with only static logic values.

Simulation of rise and fall delay is slightly more complex than simulation of pure transport delay, while simulation of ambiguity delay is still more difficult, due in part to the need for more state values. Finally, inertial delay is the most complex to simulate, since, if an input pulse is less than the inertial delay Δ_I, a complex unscheduling of a scheduled output change is required.

Besides associating delay with each circuit element, there are other areas where delay may be introduced. In forming the circuit model to be simulated, it is often as important to correctly model the delay as it is to model the Boolean function of each element. For example, if the delay in signal paths is important, they can be modeled as shown in Figure 4.11. In addition, delay may be a function of loading. Thus in the circuit of Figure 4.11, the "apparent delay" in a change in line A may be a function of whether or not it is to change the state of lines B or C or both.

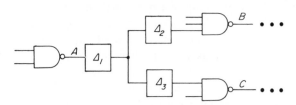

Figure 4.11 Inserting delays in signal branches

One important area where ambiguous delay elements should often be inserted is at the input and output of the circuit. This is required because when the circuit is actually tested by a piece of automatic test equipment, tester skew is often present. For example, even though a test sequence may designate that two input bits change for a given new input vector, the test hardware may not be able to change these two inputs simultaneously— hence we have input *skew*. This skew can vary from a few nanoseconds to milliseconds, depending on the ATE.

The selection of delay parameters to be used in a simulation run is dependent on the function of the run. For example, in attempting to verify the logical correctness of a design one may first employ a nominal delay value of $\Delta_T = 1$. Once the logical correctness has been established, one may then test the timing aspects of the circuit by employing ambiguity and/or rise-fall time delays. Since these delay values often lead to worst-case analysis, and hence are pessimistic, often a Monte Carlo approach is employed. In this approach the delay of each element is randomly selected as a fixed value between its minimum and maximum values using some probabilistic model, such as a uniform or Gaussian distribution. Once each element is assigned a delay, the simulation is carried out. This process is then repeated for another set of randomly selected delay values. The best distribution to use in selecting the delay value can sometimes be established from the vendor's data sheets.

When faults are simulated, nominal delay values are typically used under the assumption that detailed race and hazard analysis has already been carried out for the fault free circuit. However, since faults may introduce new race and/or hazard situations into a circuit, this assumption can lead to some errors.

4.3 MULTI-VALUED LOGIC SYSTEMS

For many simulation applications two logic values (0, 1) are not sufficient. In the previous section, for example, we saw that ambiguity delay introduced a region of time during which a signal was in transition, denoted by 0/1 and 1/0. Also, due to a race or hazard in the circuit, the value of a signal may not be known. This situation also occurs when a circuit is initially powered-up. For these reasons and others most logic simulators employ a multi-valued logic system. Consider the circuit shown in Figure 4.12. Assume the initial state of the flip-flop is $y = 0$, and let the input sequence consist of the initial input vector $x(1) = (0,0,1)$ followed by the vector $x(2) = (1,1,0)$. We wish to determine if this test detects the fault x_1 s-a-0. The answer is positive if y remains in the state 0. However, there is a chance that the race at the input to the NOR gate creates a hazard which sets the flip-flop, resulting in the state $y = 1$. In this case the sequence $x(1)x(2)$ does not detect the fault x_1 s-a-0.

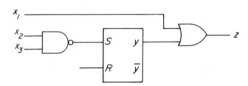

Figure 4.12   Circuit exhibiting race and hazard problems

In this section we will discuss multi-valued logic systems which can be used to handle simulation problems due to races and hazards. We will also develop other applications for multi-valued logic systems such as testing the reset capability of a circuit.

4.3.1 Application of Three Valued Logic to Hazard Detection

One of the first procedures to consider the detection of static hazards in a circuit is due to Eichelberger [10], who noted that when a signal line changes values, it goes through a transition period where its value may be interpreted by each of its loads, independently, as either a 0 or 1. We denote this "indeterminate" value by the symbol "u" representing the fact that the value is unknown. (Eichelberger used the symbol "1/2" rather than "u".)

We can now develop a three valued algebra for switching elements. The ternary truth tables for AND, OR and NOT are shown below. Note that $(\bar{u}) = u$ since this is a three valued algebra.

AND	0	1	u
0	0	0	0
1	0	1	u
u	0	u	u

OR	0	1	u
0	0	1	u
1	1	1	1
u	u	1	u

NOT	0	1	u
	1	0	u

Consider a combinational circuit C having input signals $\mathbf{x} = (x_1, x_2, \ldots, x_n)$. Let the current input vector be $\mathbf{x}(t) = (a_1, a_2, \ldots, a_n)$ and the next input vector be $\mathbf{x}(t + 1) = (c_1, c_2, \ldots, c_n)$, where $a_i, c_i \in \{0,1\}$. Now we can construct a pseudo input vector $\mathbf{x}(t+) = (b_1, b_2, \ldots, b_n)$ where $b_i = a_i$ if $a_i = c_i$, otherwise $b_i = u$. Let the response on line z in C to the input sequence $\mathbf{x}(t)\mathbf{x}(t+)\mathbf{x}(t + 1)$ be $z(t)z(t+)z(t + 1)$. The following procedure can be used to determine this response, from which static hazards can be identified.

Procedure 4.1 *(Generation of data for static hazard analysis):*
Using in turn, $\mathbf{x}(t)$, $\mathbf{x}(t+)$, and $\mathbf{x}(t + 1)$ as inputs, simulate C and determine the corresponding output values $z(t)$, $z(t+)$, and $z(t + 1)$.   □

Theorem 4.1: A necessary and sufficient condition for the existence of a static hazard on line z when the input sequence $\mathbf{x}(t)\mathbf{x}(t + 1)$ is applied to a combinational circuit C is that the response obtained from Procedure 4.1 be of the form $0u0$ or $1u1$.   □

The following results can be readily verified.

Corollary 4.1:   a) When $x(t+)$ is applied, the output of a gate either remains unchanged or else takes the value u.

b) When $x(t + 1)$ is applied the output of those gates at u will change to a 0 or 1, all other gate outputs will remain at their binary value.   □

Thus if C is a combinational circuit, then $z(t + 1)$ will be either 0 or 1.

Example 4.1:   We illustrate the application of this theorem on the circuit shown in Figure 4.13. The u in the output sequence $1u1$ indicates the possibility of a static 1-hazard on z.   □

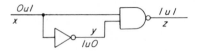

Figure 4.13   Prediction of static hazard via three-valued simulation

Note that Procedure 4.1 actually constitutes a two pass simulation process. That is, starting with the present state (value of inputs and internal signals) $x(t)$, called the *basis*, one carries out a simulation "*u-pass*" using the pseudo input vector $x(t+)$, and then a second simulation pass using the input $x(t + 1)$ present at time $t + 1$. These results become the basis for the next input to be processed. The net effect of this procedure is that the delay of each element is ignored. The result is a worse-case delay analysis of the circuit, independent of the delay model used to drive the simulator. Hence, we say that this procedure uses an *arbitrary* delay model and produces pessimistic results.

We now illustrate the difference between a 0-delay, unit delay and Eichelberger's arbitrary delay simulation model with a u pass.

Example 4.2:   We again consider the circuit of Figure 4.13 with the input sequence 010. For the 0-delay model we obtain the signal sequences $X = 010$, $Y = 101$, $Z = 111$. Thus no hazard is predicted. This is because a 0-delay model actually deals only with the static behavior of a circuit, not its dynamic behavior.

For the unit delay model, we obtain the signal sequences $X = 0100 \ldots$, $Y = 1101 \ldots$, $Z = 11011 \ldots$. Thus a hazard is predicted in response to the 0 to 1 transition on x. However, for the 1 to 0 transition no hazard is predicted.

For the arbitrary delay model we obtain the signal sequences $\mathbf{X} = 0u1u0$, $\mathbf{Y} = 1u0u1$, $\mathbf{Z} = 1u1u1$. Thus a hazard is predicted in response to both the 0 to 1 and 1 to 0 input transitions.

This is an overly pessimistic result, since in general either the direct path from x to z or the path through the inverter has the most delay, in which case only one of the input transitions should lead to a hazard. However, if it is not known which path has the most delay, a hazard for both transitions is predicted. Note that the direct path from x to z could contain a very long interconnection path such that its delay exceeds the delay through the inverter.   □

In asynchronous sequential circuits we are also concerned with the problems of hazards, races and oscillation. Assuming an arbitrary delay model, the three valued logic can also be used to predict some forms of malfunction in sequential circuits. Let us consider a circuit model in which each cyclic path and/or memory element is represented as a feedback line, as shown in Figure 4.14*. The y_i's represent the current state of the circuit, and the Y_i's the next state.

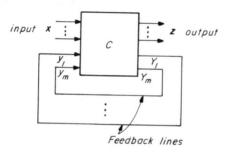

Figure 4.14   General form for an asynchronous circuit

The following procedure is used to construct the data required to identify races and hazard conditions in an asynchronous circuit.

Procedure 4.2 *(Sequential hazard analysis without delay elements):*
 (1) If the input x changes from $\mathbf{x}(t) = \mathbf{a}$ to $\mathbf{x}(t + 1) = \mathbf{c}$, simulate C for the pseudo input vector $\mathbf{x}(t+) = \mathbf{b}$. For each Y_i which takes the value u, set $y_i = u$. Repeat step 1 until no new Y_i takes the value u, while keeping the primary input lines at value $\mathbf{b}$. Note that from

---

*In the next section we will indicate how explicit delays can be introduced into this model.

Corollary 1 no Y_i which takes the value u will subsequently take the value 0 or 1.
(2) Simulate C for the input c. For each Y_i which takes on a new value, i.e., a u changing to an e, $e \in \{0,1\}$, set $y_i = e$. Repeat step 2 until no new y_i changes value. □

In the first step of the procedure all feedback lines which either contain a static hazard, or which change state (i.e., 0 to 1 or 1 to 0 transitions) are set to u. Note that these lines will include all lines which either may oscillate or are involved in a critical race. The steady state value of all lines in the circuit is determined in the second step of the procedure.

Theorem 4.2: If in applying Procedure 4.2 the final value of Y_i is 0 or 1, then the feedback line Y_i stabilizes in this state under the input transition **a** to **c**, regardless of the value of the line and gate delays in the circuit. If the final value of Y_i is u, then the circuit may have a critical race, an oscillation, or a hazard. □

Example 4.3: We will now illustrate the application of Procedure 4.2. The circuit of Figure 4.15 is a NAND latch. If we apply the input sequence 01

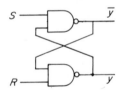

Figure 4.15 Use of Eichelberger simulation in predicting a critical race or oscillation

to both S and R, we find that $y = \bar{y} = u$ is the final state. Depending on the actual delays in the circuit, the final state may actually be $y = 0$, $\bar{y} = 1$ or $y = 1$, $\bar{y} = 0$ or the circuit may oscillate. □

Procedure 4.2 may sometimes generate overly pessimistic results since it may predict the final value of a line to be u when it should be 0 or 1. Consider a circuit having feedback equations of the form

$$Y_1 = x_3(\ldots)$$
$$Y_2 = x_1\bar{y}_1 + x_2y_1$$
$$Y_3 = \ldots$$

If $x = (x_1, x_2, x_3)$, and $a = (1,1,1)$, $c = (1,1,0)$, then $b = (1,1,u)$. Assume Y_1 is involved in a critical race such that the final value of Y_1, denoted by Y_1^*, is 0 or 1, but no oscillation occurs. For this case $Y_1^* = u$, and hence $Y_2^* = x_1 u + x_2 u = u$. But in the actual circuit $y_1^* = 0$ or 1, hence

$$Y_2 = x_1 \cdot 1 + x_2 \cdot 0 = 1 \text{ (for } y_1^* = 0)$$

or

$$Y_2 = x_1 \cdot 0 + x_2 \cdot 1 = 1 \text{ (for } y_1^* = 1),$$

and $Y_2 = 1$ regardless of the final state of Y_1.   □

We will subsequently see that Procedure 4.2 may also fail to initialize the gate equivalent circuit for a *JK* flip-flop. Though this procedure assumes an overly pessimistic model, it is relatively easy to implement. Note that while executing step 1 any element whose value is currently u need not be reevaluated. Also, in step 2, any element whose value is currently 0 or 1 need not be reevaluated. The table-driven event-directed procedure outlined previously can efficiently implement this two pass simulation process. In fact, feedback lines need not be identified. That is, since this is a worse-case delay model, the order of simulating the elements is not important. All that is necessary is to apply the b vector and simulate the circuit until it stabilizes, and then apply the c vector and again simulate until the circuit stabilizes. Note that the symbol u now has taken on several meanings, namely

(a) on a primary input it symbolizes a transition

(b) in the sequence $0u0$ or $1u1$ it symbolizes a hazard

(c) in the sequence $0u1$ or $1u0$ it symbolizes either a transition or a dynamic hazard

(d) in the sequence $0uu$ or $1uu$ the last u symbolizes either that the final value of the line is 0 or 1 or that the line oscillates.

Since there are no bounds on specified delay values, Procedure 4.2 tends to be overly pessimistic. We will now illustrate how delay elements can be introduced into the simulation procedure.

Let us reconsider the basic circut model of Figure 4.14 and assume that each feedback line y_i contains a pure delay element of magnitude Δ_i. The combinational circuit C has two input vectors, the primary input x and the state input y, and two output vectors, z and Y. Let the maximum (stray) delay between any input line x_j and any line in Y be Δ. We assume that $\Delta_i > \Delta$ for all i. That is, we assume that the effect of a primary input change to C will propagate to all elements in C before its effect can be seen on any feedback line y_i. Under this condition, the circuit can be simulated as specified in the following procedure.

Procedure 4.3 *(Three valued simulation with delays):*
Consider an input transition from **a** to **c** in initial state **y**.
(1) Simulate C for the input pair (**b,y**), where **y** is the current state of the feedback lines, and **b** is the pseudo input defined by **a** and **c**. Determine the value **Y** of all feedback lines, and place **Y** onto a first in first out queue, denoted by $Q^†$.
(2) Simulate C for the input pair (**c,y**), and determine the value **Y** of all feedback lines. Place **Y** onto Q as long as it is different from the last element in this queue.
(3) If Q is empty, then halt. Otherwise remove the first element from Q, and label it **y**. Simulate C for the input pair (**c,y**). Place the value **Y** of the state vector on the queue Q as long as it is different than the last element on Q. Repeat step 3 until Q is empty.   □

Since many common circuits contain essential hazards, and are made to operate correctly by employing delay elements, this procedure is adequate for their simulation. Circuit oscillations can be detected in one of two ways. If the queue becomes empty but some feedback lines remain at u, then either a race or oscillation is present.

Unfortunately, some forms of circuit oscillation will produce an oscillating (cyclic) sequence of state vectors on Q. For this case, some form of simulation oscillation detection is required so that the simulation does not continue indefinitely (see Section 4.7). We illustrate this situation in the circuit shown in Figure 4.16. For the initial state $y = 1$, when the input x

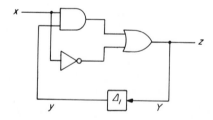

Figure 4.16   Oscillation in the circuit and simulator

---

†A first in, first out queue is a data storage structure where elements are inserted (stored) via a push operation and removed via a pop operation, and where the element removed is the one in the queue the longest.

changes from 0 to 1, a momentary 0-pulse may be generated at z and Y. This pulse propagates through the delay element and then propagates through C. The simulator processes this behavior by producing the sequence $1u1u1u\ldots$ on the line Y. In practice this situation would be avoided by using inertial delay to filter out the 0-pulse. If the simulator could handle inertial delay this oscillation situation would not occur.

Using the concepts of pseudo input vectors and delay elements is analogous to assuming that the non delay elements have 0 delay, i.e., we analyze them statically. Therefore, in modeling a circuit, it may be necessary to add delay elements so that the simulation algorithm being employed produces the desired results. We illustrate this concept in Figure 4.17. A simple circuit with no delay elements is shown in Figure 4.17(a). The response to the input sequence 010 contains two hazards, as shown in Figure 4.17(b). If we assume the delay through the path 1-2-3-4-7 is longer than that through the path 1-7, then we can add a delay element to this path. In Figure 4.17(c) we show the revised circuit, and in Figure 4.17(d) the simulation results. The hazard due to the 0 to 1 transition on

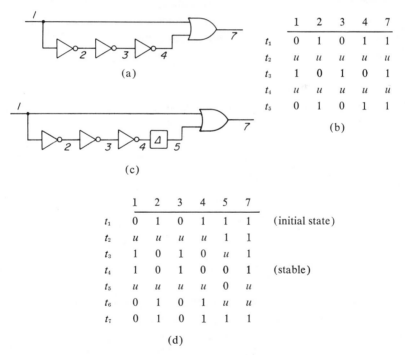

Figure 4.17 Eichelberger simulation with delay elements

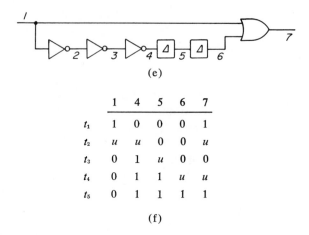

(e)

	1	4	5	6	7
t_1	1	0	0	0	1
t_2	u	u	0	0	u
t_3	0	1	u	0	0
t_4	0	1	1	u	u
t_5	0	1	1	1	1

(f)

Figure 4.17   (*continued*)

line 1 has been eliminated. If the original circuit of Figure 4.17(a) is a model of a one-shot, i.e., for the input sequence 10 a 0 pulse should be produced on line 7, the simulator will produce this effect only if two units of delay are used, as shown in Figure 4.17(e) and (f).

4.3.2   Five Value Logic Systems

Earlier we saw that when ambiguous delay values existed a five valued logic system was useful. These five values are summarized below

Logic Value	Symbol
0	0
1	1
0 to 1 transition	0/1
1 to 0 transition	1/0
Unknown	u

If a line has the value 0/1 from t_1 to t_2, then all that is known is that during this period a transition from 0 to 1 is to take place. For any specific value of t, $t_1 < t < t_2$, the actual value of the line may be 0, 1 or in transition from 0 to 1. The truth table for a two-input NAND gate whose inputs can be any of these five values is shown in Figure 4.18.

NAND	0	1	0/1	1/0	u
0	1	1	1	1	1
1	1	0	1/0	0/1	u
0/1	1	1/0	1/0	u	u
1/0	1	0/1	u	0/1	u
u	1	u	u	u	u

Figure 4.18   Truth table for five valued logic

When using this five valued logic and ambiguity delay, care must be taken in scheduling line changes. For simulation purposes, the five values can be ordered as follows

$$u \geq 1/0 = 0/1 \geq 0 = 1.$$

Now, if $a,b\epsilon\{u,1/0,0/1,0,1\}$, b *dominates* a if and only if $b \geq a$, i.e., the more pessimistic value always dominates. During simulation, if a line makes a transition from a to b, then if b dominates a this change is scheduled to occur as soon as possible, i.e., using delay Δ_m. Otherwise it is scheduled to occur as late as possible, i.e., using delay Δ_M. By this process the most pessimistic case is always scheduled to occur.

Example 4.4.:   Consider the circuit of Figure 4.19. The simulation procedure operates as follows. At time t_1 there is a change on line 1 from 0 to 0/1. Simulation of the gate determines that line 2 should change from 0

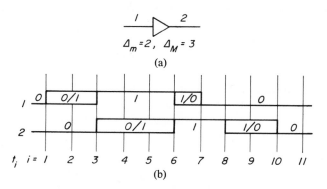

(a)

(b)

Figure 4.19   Scheduling changes in line 2 due to input changes on line 1

to 0/1. Since 0/1 dominates 0, this change is scheduled to occur at time $t_{1+\Delta_m} = t_3$. At t_3 this scheduled change is made on line 2. Note that line 1 has changed from 0/1 to 1 causing line 2 to change from 0/1 to 1. Since 1 does not dominate 0/1, this change is scheduled for $t_{3+\Delta_M} = t_6$. In similar fashion the signals shown in Figure 4.19(b) are obtained. □

Note that by adding a pseudo gate having ambiguity delay to every primary input line, we can use binary input values and have the simulator automatically produce the values 0/1 and 1/0. These transition values can then be propagated through the circuit, even if every gate only has a nominal delay value. Hence input skew can be effectively handled.

Some systems differentiate the use of a u for both hazards and steady state errors by adding a sixth logic value, h, to denote a hazard. For example, a 0/1 and 1/0 input to a NAND gate would produce an h output rather than a u.

4.3.3 Eight Valued Logic Simulation*

One of the deficiencies of the three-valued logic simulation is that it can not predict the existence of a dynamic hazard in combinational logic. To solve this problem 8-valued [5] and 9-valued [11] logic systems have been devised.

The logic values in the 8-valued system are shown in the table of Figure 4.20.

Note that each of the 8 logic symbols represents the value of a signal line over an interval of time t_1 to t_2. The symbol ab indicates that the steady value of the line at t_1 is a, and that the steady state value at t_2 is b. A hazard which occurs from t_1 to t_2 is denoted by $ab*$. If $a = b$, then the hazard is static, otherwise it is dynamic. Truth tables for the various gates can be defined for these 8 values and used to detect static and dynamic hazards.

Procedure 4.4 (*Detection of static and dynamic hazards in combinational logic functions*):
   (1) To each input in the circuit assign a value 00, 11, 01 or 10 based on the current input vector **a** and the next input vector **c**.
   (2) Process the gates in the circuit, from input to output. For each gate, determine its output from its input values and the 8 valued truth table associated with the gate type. □

---

*This section contains material similar to that in Section 3.2.2, and is repeated here for completeness.

Logic Value	Explanation	Example Wave Form (and logic sequence)
00	static zero value	(0)
11	static one value	(1)
01	hazard free 0 to 1 transition	(01)
10	hazard free 1 to 0 transition	(10)
00*	static zero hazard	(010)
11*	static 1 hazard	(101)
01*	dynamic hazard	(0101)
10*	dynamic hazard	(1010)

Figure 4.20   Eight logic values

This procedure can be extended to some forms of sequential circuits. Namely, truth tables can be developed for sequential devices such as flip-flops and latches. For this case, a ninth logic value "u" is useful to represent an unknown line value. Procedure 4.4 can then be extended to apply to acyclic networks which include flip-flops as primitive elements [5].

The extension of this procedure to cyclic circuits has not yet been developed. The problem here is that the assignment of the flag (*) which indicates the existence of a hazard is dependent on the present and next steady state values of the circuit, but the next steady state value may be dependent on whether or not there is a hazard.

4.3.4   Initialization of Circuits

When simulating a circuit it is necessary to specify the initial value of those lines which determine the state of the circuit. Often, this initial state information is not known. For example, when a circuit is initially powered-up, the initial state of flip-flops and latches are often unpredictable. The most common way to deal with this problem is to set the initial value of each line to an unknown value, again denoted by u. Then, if an initialization sequence or homing sequence is applied, the simulator should calculate the correct final state of the circuit.

For example consider the SR latch shown in Figure 4.15. Let the initial state of every line be u. When $(R,S) = (1,0)$ is applied, then $(y,\bar{y}) = (0,1)$. Unfortunately, it is not always easy to initialize simple elements, such as flip-flops. Consider the circuit shown in Figure 4.21. If we simulate the flip-flop with initial state $(y,\bar{y}) = (u,u)$, $(R,S) = (u,0)$ and the sequence $C_p = 10$, the state of the flip-flop remains at u. However, simple circuit analysis indicates that this flip-flop will be reset by this process.

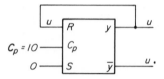

Figure 4.21   A simple circuit not correctly initialized via three valued simulation

The initialization of circuits via simulation is a most difficult problem, which has not been completely solved. The problem of driving lines to known states given that their present state is unknown does not only arise during power-on or circuit initialization. Often an input sequence will cause a critical race, or a hazard may set or reset a flip-flop. In either case, the result is that some lines will be set to an unknown value, and it is desired that subsequent input vectors drive these lines to a known value.

Before we study this problem in more depth, we must note that employing the complementary unknown values of u and $\bar{u}$ does solve some problems, but unfortunately leads to others. Thus for the situation shown in Figure 4.22, if we use the identities $u + \bar{u} = 1$ and $u \cdot \bar{u} = 0$, then we can come to the erroneous conclusion that $z = 0$. Since it is better to be pessimistic than incorrect, using u and $\bar{u}$ is not a satisfactory solution.

Order of Indeterminate Initialization

One approach to the initialization problem is to use several distinct unknown signals $u_1, u_2, \ldots, u_k$. The output of a gate may be a logical function of these unknowns. If some gate output is a nontrivial function of m unknowns, m is called the *order of indeterminant initialization*. To initialize

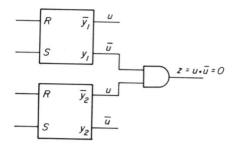

Figure 4.22 Erroneous result from using u and $\bar{u}$ for complementary unknown states

a JK master-slave flip-flop requires indeterminant initialization of order two.

One problem of practical importance is to verify that a given input sequence initializes a circuit to a specific state. The most common example of this situation is that of a reset line used to set all flip-flops to their zero state. If there are n flip-flops, there are 2^n possible states in which the circuit can be when the initialization sequence is applied. Simulating all possible cases is usually infeasible. Alternatively, one could set all flip-flops to the unknown state and simulate the initialization sequence. If all flip-flops end up in the desired known state then the circuit does initialize correctly. If not, either the design has an error, or the initialization sequence was incorrect, or the simulation algorithm and/or level of modeling are not capable of predicting the exact operation of the circuit.

4.4 BASIC SIMULATOR STRUCTURES

In this section we consider the basic design of the structure and simulate modules of a digital simulator (Figure 4.4). Recall that there are two basic classes of simulators, compiler driven and table-driven event-directed. The earliest simulators were of the former type, but most modern ones are of the latter type since they allow for more versatility in handling delays as well as a reduction in simulation time.

4.4.1 Compiler Driven Simulation

The first step in compiler driven simulation is carried out by the structure module, which translates the description of the circuit into machine executable code, such as an assembly language program. The circuit is first represented in a canonical form such as that of Figure 4.14. If the circuit is cyclic, circuit loops are identified, and feedback paths defined. All flip-flops are normally placed in the feedback paths.

Before code is generated, the elements in C are ordered. The first step in ordering is called *levelizing*. Levelizing consists of assigning a level number (non-negative integer) to each element and signal line. The output signal of an element is assigned the same level number as the element itself. If k_i is the logic level of element i, and if element β has inputs from elements $i_1, i_2, \ldots, i_\alpha$ then

$$k_\beta = 1 + \max\left(k_{i_1}, k_{i_2}, \ldots, k_{i_\alpha}\right). \tag{1}$$

Logic level values are assigned according to the following procedure.

Procedure 4.5 (*Circuit levelizing*):
(1) Assign all primary input lines (**x**) and feedback lines (**y**) the logic level 0.
(2) For any element not yet assigned a logic level, and such that all its input lines have been assigned a logic level, assign this element and its output lines a level value as defined by equation (1).   □

Figure 4.23 shows a simple circuit and the logic levels associated with each element. Once logic levels have been assigned the elements can be

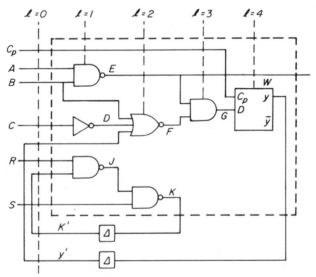

Figure 4.23   Simple circuit showing logic level for each element

sorted in ascending order, i.e., all i-th level elements are grouped together, followed by all $i + 1$-st level gates, for $i = 1,2,\ldots$. For the circuit of Figure 4.23 the following levels are determined:

level 1: E,D,J

level 2: F,K

level 3: G

level 4: W

If elements are simulated in the order of ascending value of logic level, then whenever an element at logic level k is evaluated, the logic value of each of its inputs has already been evaluated, and hence is known since C is acyclic. This process of ordering elements to be simulated is called *static ordering*.

Once the elements have been ordered, code can be generated. Usually one computer word is used to specify the value of each signal in the circuit even though only one bit is sufficient to store the binary value of the signal. Assume the logic value of a signal α is stored in bit 1 of word α in the host computer. Then, for an AND gate having inputs A, B, and C and output D, the code generator might produce the following sequence of instructions:

Code	Comments
CAL A	Place word A in the accumulator
ANA B	Form A AND B in the accumulator
ANA C	Form A AND B AND C in the accumulator
SLW D	Store this result in word D.

Similarly code for other elements, such as NAND's, NOR's, latches, and master-slave flip-flop can be easily generated. The resulting code is typically stored as a sequential file, with the beginning of logic level i labeled by Li. The simulate module can now process this code as specified in the following procedure.

Procedure 4.6 (*Execution of compiled code*):
(1) Read in the initial value of each line.
(2) Read in new (next) input vector and update values. If no new input data, then halt.

(3) Execute the compiled code, i.e., simulate the logic in C. This is called a *scan*. If $y = Y$ go to step 4, otherwise set $y \leftarrow Y$ and repeat step 3.

(4) Output results and go to step 2. □

In general, the simulate module must also handle race and oscillation conditions, problems which we will not consider in this chapter.

Compiler driven simulators usually imply a 0-delay model. Consider the circuit shown in Figure 4.24(a) and the compiled code shown in Figure 4.24(b). For $A = 0$ or 1 the value $C = 1$ is always generated. Hence no hazard or signal propagation is predicted. For this reason, compiler driven simulators are usually employed for simulating synchronous logic where race and hazard conditions can often be ignored. This problem can be partially rectified by employing a pseudo delay element Δ in the line between gates B and C. If we assume each delay element is in a feedback path, then we obtain the circuit shown in Figure 4.24(c). Now when A changes from 1 to 0 gate C will be simulated twice, and the 1-hazard will be detected. This example illustrates that simulation systems have inherent deficiencies or make certain assumptions concerning the properties of a circuit (in this case delay). If these assumptions are not applicable, then often remodeling the circuit can compensate for the deficiency.

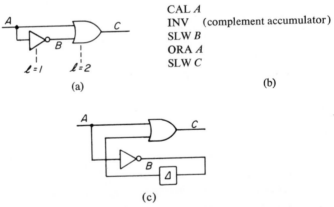

CAL A
INV　(complement accumulator)
SLW B
ORA A
SLW C

(a)　　　　　　　　　　　　　　　　　(b)

(c)

Figure 4.24　(a) Simple circuit with hazard (b) Compiled code
(c) Circuit with delay element

The simulation time for a compiler driven simulator is proportional to tN where t is the time to simulate an element and N is the number of elements. There are several ways the time t to simulate an element can be reduced. One way is by employing the concept of *stimulus bypass*. For example, consider an AND gate realizing the function $D = A \cdot B \cdot C$. If any of the input variables is 0, then $D = 0$ independent of the other variables. Hence this gate can be simulated by the following code.

```
CAL A

BZE * + 4  (skip next 3 instructions if accumulator is 0)

CAL B

BZE * + 2

CAL C

SLW D
```

By judiciously placing branch instructions (BZE) the average execution time for elements can be reduced. The penalty is that the length of the compiled code is usually increased. (Also, most of the advantages of this technique are lost when one employs the concept of parallel simulation, which will be discussed in a later section.)

Although the number of elements N in the circuit cannot be reduced, the average number of elements simulated per scan can be reduced, thus speeding up simulation.

4.4.2 Event (Activity) Directed Simulation

During a single simulation computation scan frequently only a small percentage of the signal lines change values. The ratio of lines which change values to the total number of lines in the circuit is called the *activity* and is denoted by A. Usually A is between 2-10%. Because of this fact it appears wasteful to simulate all the logic when only a small portion of the circuit is going to change. This observation has led to the concept of *event (activity) directed simulation (selective trace)*.

An *event* is a change in value of a signal line. The output of a stable element i will only change value when one or more of its inputs change value. Hence element i need only be simulated when an event occurs at one of its inputs. When an event does occur, then every element to which this line fans-out is called *potentially active*. If we simulate these potentially active elements, we will find that some are active while others are not. A significant reduction in computation can often be achieved by simulating only potentially active elements rather than all the elements.

A table-driven event-directed simulator has two other advantages over a compiler-driven simulator, namely it handles combinational, synchronous and asynchronous circuits with equal ease, and delays can be processed in a very simple fashion. In the next section we will describe the operation of a simple table-driven event-directed simulator, and in subsequent sections we will consider several factors related to the design and operation of this class of simulators.

Table-Driven Event-Directed Unit Delay Simulator

We will describe a simulator in which each element is assumed to be a single output combinational circuit with unit delay. Two lists, L_0 and L_1 (referred to in the algorithm as L_a and L_b; $a,b \in \{0,1\}$), are used to schedule lines (elements) which contain activity and which must be processed during the present or next unit of simulation time. We denote by $v(i)$ the present value of signal i, and by $v'(i)$ the next value of signal i one unit of time later. List L_a contains all active elements i and their new (next) value which they should take on at simulated time t. List L_b is used for all elements which become active due to the events represented in L_a. These elements will take on their new values at simulated time $t + 1$.

The basic structure of the simulator is shown in Figure 4.25. $U(i)$ represents the set of elements to which element i fans-out. If a and b are interchanged more than K times between processing any two consecutive input vectors, oscillation is assumed.

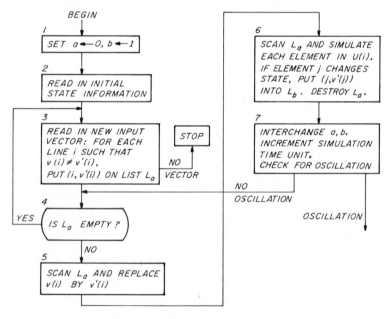

Figure 4.25   Basic structure of a unit delay (dual list)
event directed simulator

Figure 4.26(b) indicates the computations which the simulator of Figure 4.25 would execute on the circuit of Figure 4.26(a). First the initial value of each line is set to u. Then the new input vector $(0,1)$ is read and the list L_0 is created. Since events occur on lines 1 and 2, both gates 3 and 4 are potentially active and are simulated, but only gate 3 is active. Gate 4 is then simulated a second time since line 3 has an event on it. We now find that line 4 takes the value 0. In step 6.3 gate 3 is simulated but no new activity is found and therefore nothing is added to list L_a. Since L_a is now empty the circuit has stabilized. The resulting timing diagram is shown in Figure 4.26(c).

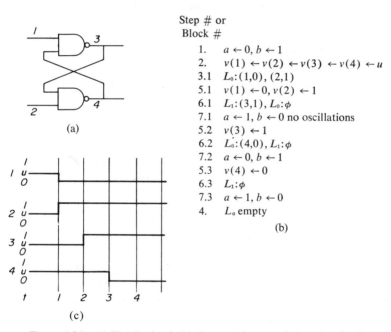

Step # or
Block #

1. $a \leftarrow 0, b \leftarrow 1$
2. $v(1) \leftarrow v(2) \leftarrow v(3) \leftarrow v(4) \leftarrow u$
3.1 $L_0 : (1,0), (2,1)$
5.1 $v(1) \leftarrow 0, v(2) \leftarrow 1$
6.1 $L_1 : (3,1), L_0 : \phi$
7.1 $a \leftarrow 1, b \leftarrow 0$ no oscillations
5.2 $v(3) \leftarrow 1$
6.2 $L_0 : (4,0), L_1 : \phi$
7.2 $a \leftarrow 0, b \leftarrow 1$
5.3 $v(4) \leftarrow 0$
6.3 $L_1 : \phi$
7.3 $a \leftarrow 1, b \leftarrow 0$
4. L_a empty

(b)

(a)

(c)

Figure 4.26   (a) Simple circuit (b) Computations carried out by simple event-directed simulator (c) Resulting timing diagram

It is important not to update the value of each element simulated in block 6 until after all elements have been simulated. For example, in step 6.1 (Figure 4.26(b)) both gates 3 and 4 must be simulated. If we simulate gate 3 first and set its new value to 1, then when we simulate gate 4 we will find its value is 0. Hence we have lost track of the delay through gate 3. Because of this situation one must first simulate gates using their present input values (pass 1), calculate their new values, and then update these new values (pass 2).

Note that no logic levelizing is required, and signals are simulated in the same order as they propagate through the circuit, assuming a unit delay model is appropriate. This process is called *dynamic levelizing*. Storage for the lists L_0 and L_1 may require dynamic allocation since, in general, their size cannot be predetermined.

This form of simulation requires a special type of data structure. For example, we made use of the fanout of element i. Also, to simulate element j we need to know its inputs or fanin. Hence event directed simulators employ a special data or table structure, and are called *table-driven*. Also, in order to handle more complex timing conditions than unit delay, a time-flow mechanism is necessary. These two concepts will be discussed in the next sections.

4.4.3   Data Structure

In a table-driven simulator the circuit is represented by a set of tables (vectors or matrices) indicating the important attributes of each element, such as:

(1) the logic value of the output lines.
(2) the type of element, e.g., AND, OR, etc.
(3) the delay associated with this element.
(4) the name of the inputs to this element (the fanin list).
(5) the name of each element which is a load to this element, (the fan-out list).
(6) the state of the element, if it has memory.

Simple Data Structures

Numerous data structures exist for representing a circuit within a computer. We shall consider two representative structures. Figure 4.27(b) represents a portion of a simple data structure associated with the circuit shown in Figure 4.27(a). In this data structure we assume each element has a single output, hence the name of the element and the name of its output signal are the same. Also each element and signal has both an alphanumeric user's name, denoted by NAME, and an internal name, called its INDEX, which is a positive integer. This INDEX is used as the argument in vector arrays to address the piece of information desired. Gate C (INDEX = 3) has a fanin of two (lines A and F) and a fanout of three (gates F, EP, and DD). The structure shown consists of two tables, ELEMENT and IOLIST (input-output list). The ELEMENT i table has the following columns:

(1) NAME(i) indicates the users name for the i-th element.
(2) VALUE(i) is the current logic value for the i-th element or line.
(3) NFO(i) is the fanout of line i.
(4) NFI(i) is the fanin of element i.

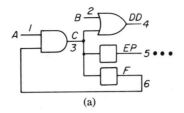

(a)

ELEMENT TABLE

INDEX	NAME	VALUE	NFO	NFI	FIL	FOL	TYPE	DELAY	INTERNAL STATE	IOLIST TABLE
1	A									
2	B									4
3	C	0	3	2			AND			5
4	DD						OR	2,3		6
5	EP									
6	F									
7	•									1
8	•									6

(b)

Figure 4.27   (a) Portion of a circuit (b) Data structure for table driven simulation

(5) FOL(i) is a pointer to the IOLIST indicating the first element to which element i fans-out. The remaining NFO(i) − 1 elements are found in the next NFO(i) − 1 cells in this list.

Similarly there are fields specifying the fanin lines, type, delay characteristics, etc. of each element. Most simulation systems are limited by the number of elements and/or the size of IOLIST. The last factor is the most critical. Usually such factors as number of feedback lines, number of flip-flops, etc., are immaterial.

This data structure is quite versatile and we shall now indicate how it is used by the simulate module. Assume we desire to simulate gate i. Then TYPE(i) gives us its type. FIL(i) points to its first input, hence VALUE(FIL(i)) is the value of this input. By carrying out the same process on FIL(i) + 1, . . . ,FIL(i) + (NFI(i) − 1) all input values to i can be found. From this, the output value of i can be calculated. If an event has occurred the elements FOL(i),FOL(i) + 1, . . . ,FOL(i) + (NFO(i) − 1) can be placed onto the appropriate list or the schedulor.

This data structure can be extended to include more complex situations and additional data, such as: multi-output elements; *IC* pin number information; and internal state information if the element has memory.

Descriptor Based Data Structure

We shall now describe another efficient data base structure in which each element is associated with its own complete data structure, called an *element descriptor,* the general form of which is shown in Figure 4.28.

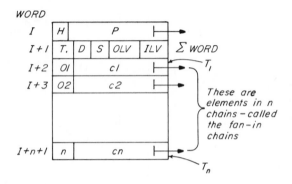

Figure 4.28   Data descriptor for an element

The first word in the descriptor for an element e is called the header, and is denoted by the flag H, and the P field whose entry points to the first element in the fanout list of element e. If P points to word J, then the contents of word J will point to the second element in the fanout list of e. This chaining effect continues until the last element in the fanout list of e is reached. This element then points back to the header word I. The second word in the data structure for e is denoted by Σ and contains the following subfields.

(1) T — the element type of e
(2) D — the element delay of e
(3) S — a flag used to indicate if e is in the future events schedulor
(4) OLV — the logic value of the output of the element, e.g., $0,1,u$
(5) ILV — the logic values of all the input lines to e (in the fault-free circuit). Note that this information is logically redundant but will prove useful when simulating element e.

The remaining n words consist of elements in the fanin chains associated with each input to e, where e has n inputs. Each entry T_i is of the form $[i,ci]$, $i = 1,2, \ldots,n$ where ci is a pointer to the next element in the chain of the i-th input to the element. The contents of the "c" field of word $K = T_i$ is denoted by $c(K)$. The value i is used for two important keys.

Namely (1) i words preceding the word T_i is the Σ word, and (2) the i-th subfield of the *ILV* field of Σ contains the value of the i-th input to this element. If the maximum value of n is $n_{\max}$, and if three valued logic which requires two bits per logic value is being employed, then the *ILV* field must have $2 \cdot n_{\max}$ bits.

For example consider the simple circuit shown in Figure 4.29(a) and its associated data structure shown in Figure 4.29(b). Elements A and B are primary inputs and hence have no fanin, and element E is a primary output and hence has no fanout. Each element has its associated data descriptor beginning with a header word. For element C, the first word points to 15, which is the first input to element E as well as the first fanout element of C. Now $c(15) = 11$, and word 11 is the entry for the second

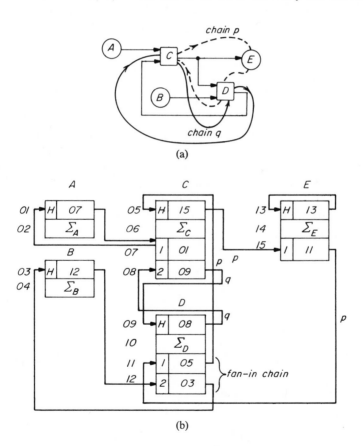

(a)

(b)

Figure 4.29 (a) Simple circuit (b) Corresponding descriptor oriented data structure

element in the fanout of C, as well as the first input to element D. Finally $c(11) = 5$, and word 5 is our original header word in the chain.

We now illustrate how this data structure can be efficiently used. Assume element C changes state. All elements on C's fanout list must be reevaluated. The entry $i = 1$ in word 15 points to word $15 - i = 14$ which is Σ_E. This word specifies the element type. Subfield i of ILV is set to the new value of C. From these two pieces of information, namely type and input, the new value of E can be computed. The simulation proceeds to word $c(15) = 11$ and this process is repeated on element D.

The ILV is redundant in the sense that having the fanin chains, one could trace back to each header and find the value of each input line. However, it is much more efficient to store these values in the ILV field. In general only one input to an element changes during simulation time t_k, hence tracing back to look up line values which are static is quite inefficient and becomes unnecessary because of the use of the ILV field.

4.4.4   Time Flow Mechanism and Event Scheduling

When an element i is simulated, and it is determined that its output line j has changed state, i.e., $v(j) \neq v'(j)$, then line j must be scheduled to change to $v'(j)$ at time $t_0 + \Delta$, where t_0 is the current simulated time, and Δ is some appropriate delay value. In this case j is said to be a scheduled event element, and the event $(j, v'(j), t = t_0 + \Delta)$ must be scheduled in the space for future events. The technique used to schedule and unschedule events is called the *time-flow* mechanism.

One way to mechanize the scheduling of events is to use a list structure, as shown in Figure 4.30, where events occurring during the same event

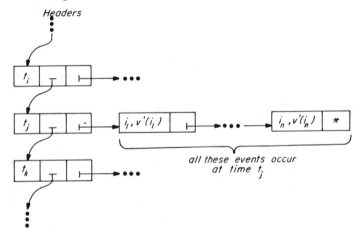

Figure 4.30   Future events scheduler implemented as a list structure

time t are stored in the same list. Here the headers are ordered, i.e., $t_i < t_j < t_k$. One problem with this mechanism is that scheduling an event to occur at time t requires a scan through the headers, which can be a slow process. In general, the headers are dense. Hence a timing wheel scheduler (Figure 4.31) is more efficient. Here the headers are stored in sequential words, and to schedule an event for time $t + \Delta$ the header for this list can easily be found Δ units ahead of the current header. In the event that $\Delta \geq M$, where M is the number of headers in the timing wheel, then an entry can be made in an overflow events scheduler of the list structured variety. Whenever one full rotation of the timing wheel is made, the overflow schedule must be scanned and any entries there which can now be placed onto the timing wheel must be removed.

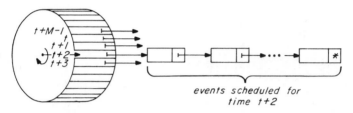

Figure 4.31   Future events scheduler implemented as a timing wheel

Assume the headers in the timing wheel represent times t to $t + M - 1$. Once a value of t' is processed, the headers from t to t' are not needed. Note that as t' approaches $t + M$, more and more events must be scheduled in the overflow list. To avoid this inefficiency, the time associated with the entries of the wheel can be re-scaled each half revolution around the wheel. For example, when t' reaches $(t + M/2)$, the time associated with the half of the timing wheel just processed $(t$ to $(t + (M/2) - 1))$ can be rescaled to correspond to $(t + M)$ to $(t + (3M/2) - 1)$.

Another minor disadvantage of the timing wheel is that some event lists may be empty. The number of empty lists increases with the average value of element delay, and decreases with the level of activity. Not that the simple simulator presented earlier corresponds to the case $M = 2$, and no overflow scheduler was required.

The mechanisms presented here for scheduling events allows for the processing of *real time inputs*. That is, assume that at time t_j, input line i is to take the value $v'_{t_j}(i)$, for $j = 1,2, \ldots,k$. Now, before simulation is begun these events can be scheduled to occur at the correct time. During simulation these input changes will occur at the appropriate time. Hence it is not necessary to wait for the circuit to stabilize before a new input vector is read.

Figure 4.32 shows a revised version of the simulation algorithm where the value of Δ_T is arbitrary. The only item requiring explanation is step 4(a). Here it is possible that the new value $v'(i)$ of a signal can equal its current value For instance consider a two input OR gate, having delay $\Delta_T = 2$, output label 3, and let input 1 become 1 at time t and input 2 become 1 at time $t + 1$. The simulator would process these events as follows. At time t line 1 goes to a 1, hence the event $(3,1,t + 2)$ is scheduled. When line 2 goes to 1 at time $t + 1$, $(3,1,t + 3)$ is scheduled. At

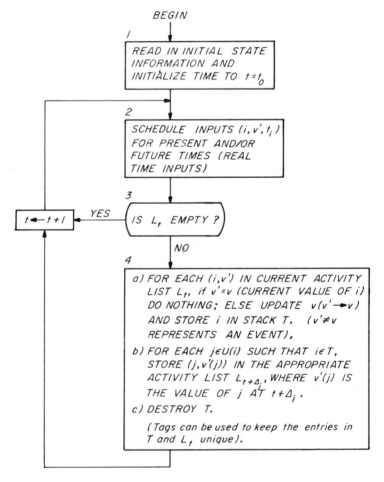

BEGIN

1 — READ IN INITIAL STATE INFORMATION AND INITIALIZE TIME TO $t = t_0$

2 — SCHEDULE INPUTS (i, v', t_i) FOR PRESENT AND/OR FUTURE TIMES (REAL TIME INPUTS)

3 — IS L_t EMPTY ?

YES → $t \leftarrow t + 1$

NO

4 —
a) FOR EACH (i,v') IN CURRENT ACTIVITY LIST L_t, if $v'=v$ (CURRENT VALUE OF i) DO NOTHING; ELSE UPDATE $v(v' \rightarrow v)$ AND STORE i IN STACK T. ($v' \neq v$ REPRESENTS AN EVENT).

b) FOR EACH $j \epsilon U(i)$ SUCH THAT $i \epsilon T$, STORE $(j, v'(j))$ IN THE APPROPRIATE ACTIVITY LIST $L_{t+\Delta_j}$, WHERE $v'(j)$ IS THE VALUE OF j AT $t+\Delta_j$.

c) DESTROY T.

(Tags can be used to keep the entries in T and L_t unique).

Figure 4.32   Event directed simulator algorithm for arbitrary value of transport delay

time $t + 2$ line 3 is set to 1. At time $t + 3$, when attempting to set line 3 to 1 it is discovered that it already has this value.

This simulation scheduling procedure is quite general, and can be employed for nominal delays, ambiguous delays, inertial delays, and when multi-valued logic is employed. Unfortunately, inertial delays lead to several complexities, the principal one being that if an input pulse to an element is shorter than the inertial delay, then a scheduled change caused by the initial transition of the pulse must be unscheduled.

Processing Inertial Delays

Assume an element has an output inertial delay Δ_I equal to its transport delay value. In simulating such an element we must have the capability of handling the concept of *high frequency rejection*, i.e., of filtering out short spikes of width Δ_I or less. Assuming a data structure similar to the one shown in Figure 4.28, with a field S which indicates the current number of times this element exists on the future events schedulor, the following procedure can be used to simulate inertial delays.

Procedure 4.7 *(Inertial delay simulation):*
Part 1: Begin here when an input event has occurred at element E.
(1) Evaluate the expected future output of E based upon its present input values.
(2) If there is an output event, schedule this event, increment S and exit. If there is no output event but $S > 0$, unschedule all future events associated with this element, set $S \leftarrow 0$, and exit. If there is no output event and $S = 0$, exit.
Part 2: Begin here when the scheduler processes an event for element E.
(1) Decrement the S field of E by 1 and exit. □

Example 4.5: Consider the inverter of Figure 4.33(a) and the input signal A shown in Figure 4.33(b).

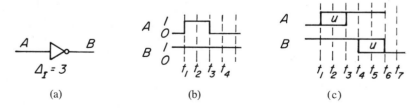

(a)　　　　(b)　　　　(c)

Figure 4.33 Processing inertial delays

At time t_1 since $A = 1$ the future value of B is 0, which is not equal to the present value of B, which is 1. Therefore S is set to 1 and B is scheduled to change to a 0 at time $T_{1+\Delta_I} = t_4$. At t_3 A becomes 0 and now the future value of B equals the present value of B, namely 1. Hence the scheduling of B to 0 at t_4 is deleted. For the input A shown in Figure 4.33(c), at time t_1 B is scheduled to go to a u at time t_4. At time t_3 B is scheduled to go to a 0 at time t_6. At times t_4 and t_6 B is set to its scheduled values and S is decremented.   □

The major difficulty with Procedure 4.7 is that it is often not a simple task to unschedule an event in the scheduler. First, it is not known in which time frame the element is scheduled. Secondly, finding the scheduled event entry in the corresponding event's list often requires a sequential search. Many schemes can be employed to simplify this unscheduling task. One is to store with each element an address pointing to each entry in the scheduler associated with this element. Schemes similar to the one presented here can be employed for dealing with more complex inertial delay models, such as input inertial delay, or where $\Delta_I < \Delta_T$.

u-events

In a three valued simulator, events are usually considered to occur when a line changes from value v_1 to v_2, where $v_1\epsilon$ $\{0,1,u\}$ and $v_2\epsilon$ $\{0,1,u\} - \{v_1\}$. However, there are two additional events, called *definite* and *potential* u events, which occur and which may be required to be propagated through a circuit. A *definite u event* is an event where $v_1 = v_2 = u$, but where it is known that in the actual circuit $v_1 = \bar{v}_2$. Two simple cases which create definite u-events are the following: (1) triggering a flip-flop in the u state, i.e., $y = u$ before and after triggering though the output certainly changes state; (2) given an exclusive-or gate with one or more u inputs and one or more binary inputs. When one of the binary inputs takes its complementary value a definite u-event occurs on the output.

A *potential u-event* is an event where $v_1 = v_2 = u$ and where it is not known whether or not in the actual circuit $v_1 = v_2$ or $v_1 = \bar{v}_2$. This type of event can occur as follows. Consider a multiplexer all of whose data inputs are u's, hence $v_1 = u$, and where a logic event (binary) occurs on an address line. Now the output is still $u(=v_2)$, but in the actual circuit this line may take on a new value.

Now consider an element which triggers on both a positive and negative edge on its input T. Assume the element has been preset to the 0-state and $T = u$. Now a definite u-event on T would set this device to the 1-state, while a potential u event would set this device to the u state.

Hence it is important to process u-events since they can change the state of memory devices. Note that a definite (potential) u-event corresponds to a (potential) dynamic $\bar{u}$ and can be processed by employing special flags so that these events can be differentiated from an event such as "$0 \rightarrow u$." Though these added events lead to more accurate simulation, the occurrence of u-events causing changes in memory devices is quite infrequent. Their existence is a function of the level of modeling used. For example if edge triggered devices are modeled such that a u on an edge sensitive input always drives the device to the u state, then these u-events may not be needed.

4.5 ELEMENT EVALUATION

The process of evaluation of the output and/or next state of an element given its present input and state is called *element evaluation*. We will be primarily concerned with table driven simulators. Four methods for element evaluation to be considered in this section are subroutine, input count, truth table, and zoom table. We will illustrate our concepts on combinational elements, though most are also applicable to sequential elements. Before we discuss how an element is evaluated, we will first present a very important concept, *parallel simulation*.

4.5.1 Parallel Simulation

The data structure used for representing the input values of an element is closely related to how the element can best be evaluated. Consider an AND gate having two inputs A and B. If the value of A and B is stored in the i-th bit of words (or strings) A and B, respectively, then the AND of these two words will have the value of the output of the gate in the i-th bit of the resulting computer word. If the word (string) has W bits, then W different problems can be handled simultaneously (i.e., in parallel), each in a different bit of the word. For example, we may desire to simulate a circuit for a given input sequence and K different values for the initial state, or for K different input sequences, or for K different faults. In any case, W independent problems can be simultaneously simulated as long as all element evaluation operators employed process each bit independently of all others. Hence arithmetic operators cannot be used. A simulator operating in this manner is called a *parallel simulator*. Almost all compiler driven simulators are parallel simulators. In a compiler driven simulator, W cases can be simulated in parallel in about the same time that one case can be processed, where W is the number of bits in a word. Some time is lost in packing and unpacking the data words, and not using special time-saving techniques such as stimulus bypass. We refer to the processing of W problems in parallel as a *pass*. If there are a total of K problems to be handled, e.g., K faults, then via parallel simulation we would require $\lceil K/W \rceil$ passes, where $\lceil x \rceil$ is the smallest integer greater than or equal to x.

Parallel simulation can also be employed in a table-driven event-directed simulator. In doing so, when $v(i)$ is compared with $v'(i)$, two vectors are compared. If they differ in any bit, then an event exists. Hence in parallel simulation it might be expected that the total activity of the circuit would substantially increase as a function of W. It is interesting to note that when simulating faults, this is not the case. That is, W faults can be selected in such a manner that the activity in the simulator is not substantially increased, i.e., it is much less than $A \cdot W$, where A is the normal activity in the circuit. Usually the set of W faults are selected from the same physical portion of the circuit.

4.5.2   Element Evaluation Techniques — Two-valued Logic

Subroutine Evaluation

For this method a unique subroutine is developed for each element type. The parameter list includes the input and output signal names. From this information the subroutine can calculate the new output values. Usually the subroutine consists of the Boolean instructions of the host computer, or is written in terms of the Boolean operator in some high level language. This code can be identical to that in a compiler driven simulator, except subroutines are used rather than in-line code. The advantage of this procedure is that parallel simulation can be easily implemented. Some time is lost, however, in the overhead of dealing with subroutine calls and because the inputs to the element are processed serially. Hence the amount of time required to process an element usually increases linearly with the number of inputs to the element. This approach requires the use of the fanin list for each element.

The next three methods are intended for non-parallel type simulators, and will outperform the subroutine approach when only one circuit condition is being simulated.

Input Count Evaluation

Note that for the most common gate types, AND, OR, NAND, and NOR, a count of the number of inputs at 0 or 1 is enough information to determine the output. Hence, for an OR gate, let COUNT equal the number of inputs at value 1, the dominant input value. For an input activity causing a 0 to 1 transition, COUNT would be incremented. For a 1 to 0 transition, COUNT would be decremented. After incrementing COUNT, if COUNT = 1, then the output is *set* to 1. After decrementing COUNT, if COUNT = 0 then the output is *set* to 0. In all other cases no output activity occurs. This procedure is very fast.

Truth Tables

The truth table method employs the input state vector, such as *ILV*, as an address to a table. The value in the table is the output value of the gate. This value must then be compared with the current value to determine if an event has occurred. This procedure can be used for both gates and flip-flops, as well as more complex elements such as decoders and multiplexers.

Zoom Tables

The zoom table approach [27] is a generalization of the truth table approach. It uses the Σ word of the element descriptor data structure shown in Section 4.3. This technique is based upon the fact that all data should be considered as pointers (addresses), and information located via these addresses. The data required to determine whether or not a new event should be scheduled, and if so, when, is inherent in Σ, i.e., the type of gate T, its delay D, whether or not it is scheduled S, its present logic value OLV, and its input logic values ILV. If we use the 5-tuple (T, D, S, OLV, ILV) as an address to a zoom table, we can directly determine what scheduling action if any to take by the corresponding entry (address to a routine) encountered in this table. Some typical actions are as follows:

(a) schedule a 0 to 1 transition
(b) schedule a 1 to 0 transition
(c) no action
(d) unschedule a previously scheduled transition (inertial delay) etc.

Zoom tables can be quite large, but are probably the fastest method available for processing the effect of an input event on an element.

4.5.3 Element Evaluation — Multi-valued Logic

For three valued simulation, one bit is not adequate to represent a signal value. For parallel simulation, a convenient code to use for three valued simulation is shown in Figure 4.34. Here two W-bit words, A and A', are used to store W signal values. Using this code, the logical AND and OR operators can be applied directly to the words A and A' and the resulting code is preserved. To simulate inversion, it is necessary to complement

logic value	bit i of word A	bit i of word A'
0	0	0
1	1	1
u	0	1
illegal	1	0

Figure 4.34 Binary code for 3-valued logic

words A and A' and then interchange them. A sample computation is
shown in Figure 4.35. The fourth word in the $A(A')$ column is the logical
AND of the first two words in that column, and the fifth word is the logical
AND of the third and fourth words. The two words are then complemented and interchanged. The resultant words represent the values of
$\overline{X \cdot Y \cdot Z}$ for the three simulations. The increased cost in handling three
valued simulation is about a factor of two in both time and storage.

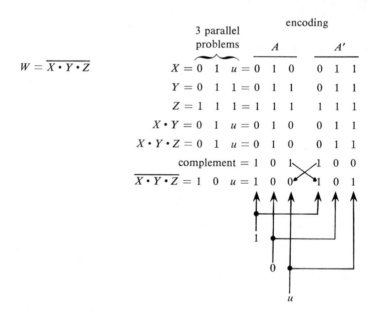

Figure 4.35 Parallel processing of three problems using 3-valued logic

All four techniques previously described for element evaluation can be
generalized to handle multi-valued logic, but at a varying cost in storage

and speed. We will first consider only the case of three valued logic. For the subroutine method, the technique just presented is quite suitable as long as logical operators are employed. For the input count method, it is necessary to keep track of both the number of inputs in the dominant input state and in the u state. The cost here in time is about three times that required for two valued simulation. For the truth table and zoom table methods, there need not be any significant loss in speed, but the storage requirements increase by a factor of $3^n/2^n$ for an n-input element. For these methods a compromise between speed and storage can be achieved. For example, a bit in the Σ word of the data descriptor can be used to indicate whether or not any inputs are u. If not, then the zoom table can be entered, otherwise a special routine can be evoked. For an AND gate the special routine would scan ILV for a 0 entry. If one existed then the new output is 0, otherwise the output is u.

For five valued logic (0, 1, 0/1, 1/0, u) three bits are required for each signal value, and a table look-up approach is usually best. For 1-st order indeterminant initialization, assume the allowable signal values are 0, 1, u_i and $\bar{u}_i$. Then, for N signal lines in a circuit, $\gamma = \log_2\lceil 2 \cdot N \rceil$ bits are required to represent the u's. Normally $\bar{u}_i$ is denoted as $-u_i$. A common storage structure for this data is shown in Figure 4.36.

Machine format $\log_2 \lceil N \rceil$ bits			logic value
1	0	————————	0
1	1	————————	1
0	0	i	u_i
0	1	i	$-u_i$

Figure 4.36

Efficient handling of element evaluation is a critical aspect in reducing simulation time. The technique to be employed is closely related to both the data structure used to store the line values, the coding used for these line values, and the facility of fanin and fanout list manipulation. There is a significant cost in CPU time and storage as the number of logic values increases. These penalties can only be compensated for by the increased accuracy and power inherent in multi-valued simulators.

4.6 FAULT SIMULATION

4.6.1 Introduction

Besides simulating the fault free circuit it is often desirable to simulate a circuit under various fault conditions. The main applications of fault simulation are:

(1) evaluation of a test sequence in terms of its fault detection and location capability

(2) the analysis of the operation of a circuit under circuit failure conditions.

In this section we will consider the design of simulators which can simulate circuits containing component failures, referred to as fault simulators.

Accuracy

Often, faults induce circuit behavior that was not considered by the circuit designer. For example, faults can create races and hazards which did not exist in the fault free circuit. A fault can inhibit the initialization of a circuit. It can create an asynchronous circuit from a synchronous one, or a sequential circuit from a combinational circuit! Hence, to process faults accurately it is often necessary to employ good timing analysis as well as techniques for processing race and hazard conditions.

Fault Modes

Besides the failures which can be modeled as stuck-at-faults, a designer may desire to simulate other faults such as bridging faults and timing (delay) faults. Relevant fault modes are usually a function of technology. For example, open conductors in CMOS circuits often act as antennas and must be modeled as intermittent faults. It may also be necessary to handle both single and multiple faults.

Fault Collapsing

Faults can be partitioned into classes based upon the concepts of dominance and equivalence. Once the faults are partitioned into equivalence classes, only a single representative of each class need be processed. The process of fault collapsing can significantly reduce the amount of required computation. The general concepts of fault collapsing were presented in sections 2.5 and 3.4.

Extraction of Information to be Used for Fault Detection and Isolation

Let C be an arbitrary circuit, and $f = 1, 2, \ldots, N_F$ be an enumeration of the faults of interest in C. Let $f = 0$ refer to the fault free condition. By

C^f we denote the circuit C under fault condition $f\epsilon \{0,1,2, \ldots,N_F\}$, where C^0 is the fault free circuit. For an input sequence $\mathbf{X} = \mathbf{x}(1)\mathbf{x}(2) \ldots \mathbf{x}(L)$, let $z_1^f(i),z_2^f(i), \ldots,z_p^f(i)$ be the steady state output values on the output lines, $z_1, \ldots,z_p$, created in response to $\mathbf{x}(i)$ for $i = 1,2, \ldots,L$, under fault condition f. We assume that $z_j^f(i) \epsilon \{0,1,u\}$. The input sequence $\mathbf{X}$ *detects* fault f if and only if for some i and j, $z_j^0(i) \neq z_j^f(i)$ for $z_j^0(i),z_j^f(i) \epsilon \{0,1\}$ and $\mathbf{X}$ *potentially detects* f if and only if $z_j^0(i) \neq z_j^f(i)$ where $z_j^0(i) \epsilon \{0,1\}$ and $z_j^f(i) = u$.

If the circuit contains N elements, N_F faults, and p outputs, then the $\mathbf{Z} = [z]$ matrix consists of L p-bit vectors for each fault. Fortunately, very little of this data is necessary for fault detection and isolation, and the data can be drastically reduced by keeping only the essential information. For example, many systems simulate faults up to the first K detects, where K is a user's input parameter. Simulation up to the first K detects means that the fault f is no longer processed once K (j,i) pairs which detect f are found. Similarly response bits $z_j(i)$ which do not distinguish any previously indistinguishable faults can be ignored. Using these two techniques, the amount of output response data that must be stored can be drastically reduced.

Given the response from a UUT, it is easy to scan this fault dictionary in order to isolate the fault. All one need do is determine those response bits which are in error, enter the fault dictionary and determine for each erroneous bit, the corresponding faults detected. Intersecting these sets gives the desired result. Due to inaccuracies in the simulation process, modeling, or selection of fault modes, this intersection may be empty. In this case, techniques for carrying out "closest match" analysis can be employed. "Probabilistic" matching analysis is also required when potential detects are employed.

Often the fault dictionary is processed so that each fault has a *fault signature*. This signature consists of the characteristic function of the erroneous response produced by the fault, and is calculated as follows. Let $z_{i_1}(j_1),z_{i_2}(j_2), \ldots,z_{i_q}(j_q)$ be those response bits which have been found to be useful for fault detection and isolation. Relabel these bits as $z_1,z_2, \ldots,z_q$. Then the signature associated with fault f is $\mathbf{S}^f = S_1^f S_2^f \ldots S_q^f$, where $S_r^f = 0$ if $z_r^0 = z_r^f$, otherwise $S_r^f = 1$, for $r = 1,2, \ldots,q$. The signatures $\mathbf{S}^f$ can now be sorted numerically and stored along with their corresponding faults. More than one fault may have the same fault signature. Given the fault signature as calculated from the response of a UUT, the fault can be easily determined via table look-up. By using *hash coding,** a long signature can be hashed into a short address.

Efficiency and Capability of Handling Large Number of Faults

The oldest method of processing faults is referred to as *fail-all* fault simulation. Here, for each fault f, the simulation circuit model is modified so that it models C^f. The circuit C^f is then simulated, i.e., each fault is simulated one at a time. The advantage of this method is that if a powerful multi-valued simulator with complex timing capabilities is available, this tool can be used to process faulty circuits. The disadvantage of this form of fault simulation is that it is quite time consuming.

Because simulation is a slow process and a large circuit can have a great number of nonequivalent faults, it is important to use very efficient techniques to process these faults in order to reduce simulation time. There are three major techniques for efficiently carrying out fault simulation. They are *parallel simulation, deductive or fault list propagation,* and *concurrent simulation.* These three techniques will be described in the following sections.

4.6.2   Parallel Fault Simulation

In Section 4.5.1 we discussed the concept of parallel simulation and showed how W problems can be processed simultaneously. For parallel fault simulation these W problems refer to W different faults. The most common way to process these faults is via *fault injection.* That is, while simulating an element the logical effect of the faults are injected into the computation. For example, consider the two input AND gate $A = B \cdot C$, and the parallel simulation of the four faults associated with gate A, as specified in Figure 4.37.

	fault	bit position
output fault	A s-a-0	bit 1
output fault	A s-a-1	bit 2
input fault	B s-a-1	bit 3
input fault	C s-a-1	bit 4

Figure 4.37

---

*A function F which maps a set of elements S_1 into a new set of elements S_2 is called a hash function or code. For example, the set of all n bit binary strings can be mapped into the set of all n-a bit strings by simply deleting the last a bits of each string in S_1. The element $F(x) \in S_2$ is usually taken to be an address.

We assume that the value of a signal X is stored in word X, and that a table-driven event-directed simulator is being employed. First gate A is flagged to denote that faults have been assigned to it. Masks are also associated with each of the terminals (A,B,C) of gate A and are used to inject faults. In the process of simulation, when it becomes necessary to simulate gate A, the flag is observed and special processing is carried out. This processing uses a mask M_1 to inject a logical 1 into bit 3 of word B forming B', and a mask M_2 to inject a 1 into bit 4 of word C forming C'. Then $A = B' \cdot C'$ is computed, and a 0(1) is then injected into bit 1(2) of word A. Note that in the remaining bit positions of the data words for each signal other fault conditions in the circuit can be processed.

The masks used for fault injection are generated during the preprocessing of the circuit for fault simulation. Except for the overhead required to generate the masks and carry out fault injection, W faults can be processed almost as rapidly as one fault. That is, no time is lost in element evaluation due to the fact that W faults are being processed simultaneously. Of course we assume that element evaluation is carried out using logical word operators and is bit organized. By selecting the W faults from a common portion of the hardware, the activity in the simulator will often not be substantially greater than that for a single fault.

It is relatively easy to simulate multiple faults using this scheme. For example, two stuck faults can be handled by simply processing these two faults in the same bit position. Complex (non stuck type) faults can also be handled. For example, if a NAND gate becomes an AND gate, it is possible to write a special routine to inject the desired value, that is, to take the current output in bit i and complement it.

Processing W faults simultaneously is called a pass. If there are N_F faults to be processed, $\lceil N_F/W \rceil$ passes are required. It is possible to reduce the number of passes by simulating several *independent* faults (multiple or single) simultaneously. Let f be a fault defined on signal line i. Let S_f be the set of signal lines in a circuit which can be effected by the value of line i. Then faults f and g are said to be *independent* if and only if $S_f \cap S_g = \phi$, i.e., faults f and g cannot affect any common portion of the circuit. In a parallel fault simulator independent faults can be simulated in the same bit position. The least upper bound on the number of independent faults which can be processed simultaneously in the same bit position is the number of output lines p in the circuit. Hence the minimum number of passes is $\lceil N_F/(W \cdot p) \rceil$. The main disadvantage with this procedure is that of identifying the independent faults. If this cannot be done efficiently, then the time saved in simulation is lost.

In compiler driven simulators, faults are usually processed by logic level. If it is desired to simulate W faults affecting the output of elements having logic level L, then the simulation proceeds by first simulating all elements at logic levels 1 through L. At this time the faults are injected, and subsequently the elements at logic level $L + 1, L + 2, \ldots$ are simulated. This procedure is quite efficient, especially for 2-valued logic and a zero delay model.

The efficiency of parallel simulation depends on the width W of a computer word as well as the instruction set and architecture of the host machine. Assuming a fixed memory cycle time and instruction execution time, by doubling W twice as many faults can be processed in the same time. If the host machine has string operators, then even further efficiencies can be achieved. For example some machines have memory to memory instructions of the form (OP,ADR,LG) where OP is an operator (op-code), ADR is the address of the first word (or byte) in a string of words (bytes), and LG is the length of this string. Then the instruction sequence

$$NOP \quad A \quad 256$$
$$AND \quad B \quad 256$$
$$SLW \quad C \quad 256$$

would process 256 W bit words (bytes) in forming the quantity $C = A \cdot B$. Typically long string operations outperform accumulator type operations, even when register to register instructions are available.

4.6.3 Deductive Simulation

Deductive simulation is based upon the concept that if the inputs to a logic element and the affect of faults on the circuit for these input values are known the output of the element under all fault conditions can be deduced. This is accomplished by using the concept of *fault list propagation*.

Recall that using the concept of parallel simulation, N_F faults require $\lceil N_F/W \rceil$ passes to process. If $W = N_F$, then only a single pass is required. Figure 4.38(a) illustrates the case where $W \geq N_F + 1$. Here bit 0 is associated with the fault free circuit, and bit j with fault number j. For signal X and time t, $X^0 = 1, X^1 = 0, X^2 = 1$, where X^j is the value of line X in the circuit under fault number j. These values are elements of the string X stored in the host computer memory, where X^j is stored in bit position j.

In general, only a small fraction of the faults will cause an error on a particular signal line X. Figure 4.38(b) illustrates the *characteristic vector* string corresponding to string X, in which bit j is 1 if and only if $X^j \neq X^0$.

Since string C usually has very few 1's, it is more efficient to store C as a list containing only the indices $j > 0$ corresponding to faults for which $X^j \neq X^0$. This list is called a *fault list*.

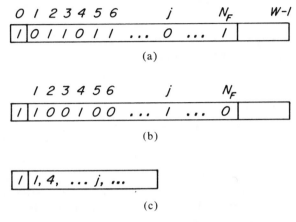

(a)

(b)

(c)

Figure 4.38 Evolution of a fault list (a) String X (at time t) used in parallel simulation (b) Characteristic string C associated with X (c) Fault list L associated with X

4.6.3.1 Two-valued Deductive Simulation

In this section we assume that all line values are binary. Using the concept of deductive simulation we can, in principle, process all faults via a one pass simulation. This is accomplished by simulating the fault free circuit, and by associating with each line α in the circuit a set or list L_α which contains the name (index) of every fault which produces an error on line α. These fault lists are then propagated through the circuit. The simulator is typically table-driven event-directed. However, there are now two types of events, *logic events* which occur when a signal line takes on a new logic value, and, *list events* which occur when a fault list L_α changes, i.e., either gains or loses one or more entries.

To illustrate this concept, consider an AND gate having inputs $a = 0$, $b = 1$, and $c = 1$. Then the output d has value 0. The faults which cause an error at line d, are the fault d s-a-1, and any fault in L_a which is not in L_b or L_c, i.e., any element in the set $L_a \cap \overline{L}_b \cap \overline{L}_c$, where $\overline{L}_\alpha$ is the complement of L_α and consists of all faults not in L_α. We therefore have

$$L_d = \{d \text{ s-a-1}\} \cup \{L_a \cap \overline{L}_b \cap \overline{L}_c\}.$$

Similarly if we consider the same gate but where $a = b = c = 1$, and hence $d = 1$, any fault which causes a 0 on any input line will cause an error at d, i.e., $d = 0$. Hence, we have

$$L_d = \{d \; s\text{-}a\text{-}0\} \cup L_a \cup L_b \cup L_c.$$

The following procedure can be used to construct the output fault list associated with an element realizing an arbitrary switching function ψ from the input fault lists.

Procedure 4.8 *(Propagation of fault lists):*

(1) If the value of ψ in the normal circuit is 0(1), let $E(x_1, x_2, \ldots, x_n)$ be a sum of products or product of sums Boolean expression for $\psi(\bar\psi)$ in terms of the inputs to the element $x_1, x_2, \ldots, x_n$. If the value of an input variable x_i in the normal circuit is 0, replace (all appearances of) x_i in E by L_{x_i}, and all appearances of $\bar x_i$ by $\bar L_{x_i}$; if the value of x_i in the normal circuit is 1, replace x_i by $\bar L_{x_i}$ and $\bar x_i$ by L_{x_i}. Replace $\cdot$ by $\cap$ and $+$ by $\cup$.

(2) If d is the element output add $d_1(d_0)$ to the fault list obtained in (1). $\square$

To illustrate this result, again consider the case $a = 0$, $b = c = 1$, for a 3-input AND gate. Since $d = 0$, we have

$$E(a,b,c) = d = a \cdot b \cdot c \big|_{a=L_a, \, b=\bar L_b, \, c=\bar L_c}.$$

Hence the resulting fault list is

$$(L_a \cap \bar L_b \cap \bar L_c) \cup d_1.$$

For the case $a = b = c = 1$, since $d = 1$,

$$E(a,b,c) = \bar d = \bar a + \bar b + \bar c \big|_{\bar a=L_a, \, \bar b=L_c, \, \bar c=L_c}.$$

Hence the resulting fault list is

$$(L_a \cup L_b \cup L_c) \cup d_0.$$

In Figure 4.39 we illustrate the propagation of fault lists through a circuit. Let α_1 and α_0 denote, respectively, the faults line α $s\text{-}a\text{-}1$ and line α $s\text{-}a\text{-}0$. Assume the input test vector is $a = b = f = i = h = 1$ and $d = 0$.

Then

$$L_a = \{a_0\}, \; L_b = \{b_0\}, L_c = \{L_a \cap L_b\} \cup \{c_1\} = \{c_1\}$$

$$L_d = \{d_1\}, \; L_e = L_d \cup L_c \cup \{e_1\} = \{c_1, d_1, e_1\}$$

$$L_f = \{f_0\}, \; L_g = L_e \cup \{g_1\} = \{c_1, d_1, e_1, g_1\}$$

$$L_h = \{h_0\}, \; L_i = \{i_0\}, L_j = L_e \cup \{j_1\} = \{c_1, d_1, e_1, j_1\}$$

$$L_k = L_i \cup L_h \cup \{k_1\} = \{i_0, h_0, k_1\}$$

$$L_l = L_j \cup \{l_0\} = \{c_1, d_1, e_1, j_1, l_0\}$$

$$L_m = \{L_k \cap \bar{L}_l\} \cup \{m_1\} = \{i_0, h_0, k_1, m_1\}$$

$$L_n = \{L_g \cap \bar{L}_f\} \cup \{n_1\} = \{c_1, d_1, e_1, g_1, n_1\}$$

$$L_p = L_n \cup L_m \cup \{p_1\} = \{c_1, d_1, e_1, g_1, n_1, i_0, h_0, k_1, m_1, p_1\}.$$

This result implies that any fault in L_p will be detected by the input test vector $(a,b,d,f,i,h) = (1,1,0,1,1,1)$. Now assume that the input h changes

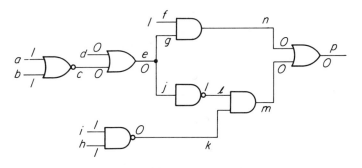

Figure 4.39   Propagation of fault lists through a circuit

to 0. The event directed approach can be used so that all lines need not be re-evaluated. Namely, we have $h:1 \to 0$; $L_h = \{h_1\}$, $k:0 \to 1$, $L_k = (L_h \cap \bar{L}_i) \cup k_0 = \{h_1, k_0\}$; $m:0 \to 1$, $L_m = (L_k \cup L_l) \cup m_0 = \{h_1, c_1, d_1, e_1, j_1, l_0, k_0, m_0\}$; $p:0 \to 1$, $L_p = (L_m \cap \bar{L}_n) \cup p_0 = \{h_1, k_0, m_0, j_1, l_0, p_0\}$. Note that faults c_1, d_1, e_1 are not detected by this new input since they are related to reconvergent fanout lines. The other fault lists remain unchanged. Next consider the change $i:1 \to 0$. We have that $L_i = \{i_1\}$. Simulating gate k produces no logic event, but now $L_k = \{i_1, h_1, k_0\}$ and now a *list-event* has occurred. Next gate m is simulated and L_m is re-evaluated, followed by gate p and L_p. The result is that the fault i_1 is added to the lists L_k, L_m and L_p.

Note that when L_α is computed, to determine if a list event has occurred the new L_α must be compared with the old L_α, denoted by $\tilde{L}_\alpha$, before the latter is destroyed, i.e., we must determine whether or not $L_\alpha = \tilde{L}_\alpha$.

Fault propagation becomes more involved when there is feedback. Care must be exercised when the effect of a fault, say α_0 or α_1, feeds back onto the line α itself. If the fault list propagating to line α contains an α_0 and if the normal (fault free) value of α is 0, then α_0 should be replaced by α_1. If the fault list contains α_1, then no change is necessary. Similarly α_1 should be replaced by α_0 if the normal value of α is 1.

Additional complexities occur in propagation of fault lists through memory elements. Consider the SR latch shown in Figure 4.40. Let the state at time t_1 be $(y_1, y_2) = (0, 1)$, and the input be $(S, R) = (1, 1)$. If at time t_2 R changes to a 0, the outputs should remain the same. Let L_S and L_R be the input fault list at time t_2 associated with lines S and R, and let $\tilde{L}_1$ and $\tilde{L}_2$ be the fault lists associated with lines y_1 and y_2 at time t_1. The new fault lists L_1 and L_2 associated with lines y_1 and y_2 due to the input logic event at t_2 can be computed as follows, where faults internal to the latch will be ignored.

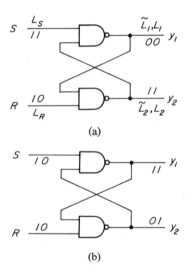

(a)

(b)

Figure 4.40 Propagation of fault lists through an SR latch (a) Normal circuit (b) Faulty circuit for some fault f in the set $\{L_S \cap L_R \cap \tilde{L}_1 \cap \tilde{L}_2\}$

Initially set $L_1 \leftarrow \tilde{L}_1$ and $L_2 \leftarrow \tilde{L}_2$. The new values for L_1 and L_2 are given by the expressions $L_1 \leftarrow L_S \cup L_2$ and $L_2 \leftarrow L_R \cap L_1$. Since a change in the fault lists for y_1 and y_2 may have occurred, this calculation must be repeated until the fault lists stabilize. Under some conditions, such as a critical race, the lists may not stabilize and special processing is required. This problem is dealt with later in this section.

A second and faster approach for dealing with the propagation of fault lists through a latch is to consider this element to be a primitive and calculate the rules for determining the steady state fault lists for y_1 and y_2 in terms of L_S, L_R, $\tilde{L}_1$, and $\tilde{L}_2$. These rules can be derived by inspecting all 16 minterms over the variables L_S, L_R, $\tilde{L}_1$, and $\tilde{L}_2$, i.e., $(L_S \cap L_R \cap \tilde{L}_1 \cap \tilde{L}_2)$, $(L_S \cap L_R \cap \tilde{L}_1 \cap \bar{\tilde{L}}_2)$, ..., $(\bar{L}_S \cap \bar{L}_R \cap \bar{\tilde{L}}_1 \cap \bar{\tilde{L}}_2)$.

For example, again consider the initial state condition $(S,R,y_1,y_2) = (1,1,0,1)$. Any fault f in the set (minterm) $L_S \cap \bar{L}_R \cap \tilde{L}_1 \cap \tilde{L}_2$ causes both outputs to be incorrect at time t_1 (due to $\tilde{L}_1$ and $\tilde{L}_2$), and input S to be incorrect at time t_2 (see Figure 4.40b). Hence at t_2 we have that $(S,R) = (0,0)$ in the faulty circuit, and this fault produces $(y_1,y_2) = (1,1)$ and hence is an element in L_1 but not L_2 (note that $y_1 \neq \bar{y}_2$, hence the outputs are not labeled y_1 and $\bar{y}_1$). In a similar manner each of the remaining 15 minterms can be processed and the rules for calculating L_1 and L_2 developed. These rules become more complex if internal faults are considered, or if an internal fault propagates around a loop and appears in L_S or L_R. Finally, the rules for L_1 and L_2 must be developed for each initial state vector (S,R,y_1,y_2).

For other types of flip-flops the rules for generating the output fault lists are independent of the value of the input and state, and correspond to the flip-flop characteristic equations, namely

$$L_Y = L_D \qquad \qquad (D \text{ flip-flop})$$

$$L_Y = L_T \oplus L_y \qquad \qquad (T \text{ flip-flop})$$

$$L_Y = (L_J \cap \bar{L}_y) \cup (\bar{L}_K \cap L_y) \qquad (JK \text{ flip-flop})$$

where $L_Y(L_y)$ is the new (old) fault list associated with the state or true output of the flip-flop. The reason for the complexity associated with the SR latch is that it is the only element for which the outputs may not be complementary due to an external fault. For all other devices the outputs are complementary and hence $L_{\bar{Y}} = \bar{L}_Y$. We shall now consider several aspects related to the efficiency of deductive simulators.

Fault Storage and Processing

Fault lists can be stored as either linked lists, sequential tables, or as characteristic vectors. These three structures are shown in Figure 4.41. For a list structure, the faults should be stored in an ordered sequence to facilitate the computation of set union and intersection. List structures require the overhead of an available space list as well as a pointer to find the next element in a list. However, insertion and deletion of elements is a simple task. Lists can be easily destroyed by assigning them to the available space list. Using a sequential memory organization leads to faster processing and eliminates the need for pointers. However, repacking of storage is required occasionally in order to make a section of core reusable.

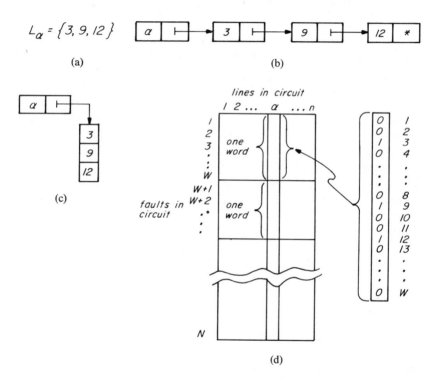

Figure 4.41   Three storage structures for lists (a) fault list (b) linked lists
(c) sequential memory (d) characteristic vector

The computation of set union and intersection for unordered and ordered sequential tables is about of the same complexity. It is easier to add a single element to an unordered set, since it can be placed at the end of the table. In an ordered table it must be inserted in its correct position, and all entries below it re-positioned in memory. It is easier to delete an arbitrary element in an ordered table than in an unordered one, since its position can be found using a binary search process.

Using the characteristic vector structure, all list operations are simple and fast. Insertion and deletion of a fault is done by either storing a 1 or 0 in the appropriate bit. Set union and intersection are carried out by simple OR and AND word operations. However, this structure typically requires more storage than the preceding two, though it is of fixed size. An exact comparison of the storage requirements requires knowledge of the average size of a fault list.

For large circuits, it is possible to run out of memory while processing the fault lists, which are dynamic and unpredictable in size. If this can occur the set of faults must be partitioned, and each subset processed separately. This process can be done dynamically, and leads to a multi-pass simulation process, which is similar in concept to parallel simulation.

Oscillation and Active Faults

It is possible that the fault free circuit will stabilize while the circuit with some fault f oscillates. For this case there will be an arbitrarily long sequence of list events. Unfortunately, even though only one fault may be causing the oscillation, repeated complex processing of long lists may be required. This is a very unsatisfactory situation. Faults which produce circuit oscillation, as well as those which lend to circuit stability only after a great amount of logical activity should be purged from fault lists whenever possible. These two problems are discussed in more detail in Sections 4.6.6 and 4.6.7.

4.6.3.2   Three-valued Deductive Simulation

When three valued logic is employed, the complexity of deductive simulation greatly increases. In this section we will briefly outline two approaches of varying degree of accuracy (pessimism). We refer to these as third order analysis (least pessimistic) and second order analysis (most pessimistic).

Third Order Analysis

Since each line α in the fault free and faulty circuits can take on the logic values 0,1 and u, two lists L_α^δ and L_α^ϵ will be associated with a line α whose normal value is v, where $\{\delta,\epsilon\} = \{0,1,u\} - \{v\}$. For example, if $v = 1$, then the lists L_α^0 and L_α^u are associated with line α. Since the set of all faults equals the set $L_\alpha^0 \cup L_\alpha^1 \cup L_\alpha^u$, we have that $L_\alpha^v = \overline{L_\alpha^\epsilon \cup L_\alpha^\delta}$.

Example 4.6:   For the gate and input conditions shown in Figure 4.42,

$$L_d^0 = (L_a^1 \cap L_b^1 \cap (\overline{L_c^0 \cup L_c^u})) \cup d_0$$
$$L_d^u = (L_a^u \cup L_a^1) \cap \overline{L_b^0} \cap \overline{L_c^0} -$$
$$\underbrace{L_a^1 \cap L_b^1 \cap \overline{L_c^0 \cup L_c^u}}_{111 \text{ input}}.$$

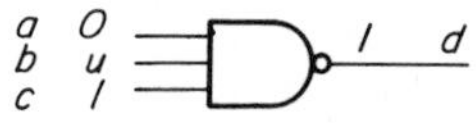

Figure 4.42

One disadvantage of this approach is that two lists exist for each line, and the complexity of the processing required to propagate the fault lists through an element is more than doubled.   □

Second Order Analysis

In order to reduce computational complexity, we can associate a single fault list L_α with each line α. If the value of line α in the fault free circuit is u, then the output fault list is indeterminant. This implies that if the value of the line is u, we will make no predictions on the value of this line in any of the faulty circuits. Hence some information is lost, and in fact incorrect initialization of some faulty circuits is possible. When calculating the output fault list of an element, all indeterminant input fault lists are ignored. If f is a fault which produces a u on a line α whose fault free value is 0 or 1, then the entry in L_α corresponding to fault f is flagged (denoted by $*f$), and is called a *star fault*.

The rules for set union and intersection for star faults are given in the table of Figure 4.43.

A	B	$A \cup B$	$A \cap B$	$A - B = A \cap \bar{B}$	$B - A$
$*f$	λ	$*f$	λ	$*f$	λ
$*f$	f	f	$*f$	λ	$*f$
$*f$	$*f$	$*f$	$*f$	$*f$	$*f$

λ indicates the absence of f or f^*.

Figure 4.43

Whenever a race or oscillation condition is identified on line α due to fault f, the corresponding fault f is entered as a star fault on the associated list (see Section 4.7). If it is decided that line α is oscillating, then those faults causing oscillation are precisely those elements in the set $(\tilde{L}_\alpha - L_\alpha)$ $\cup (L_\alpha - \tilde{L}_\alpha)$ where $\tilde{L}_\alpha$ and L_α are the old and new fault lists. By changing these elements to star faults, the simulation can be continued and the simulation oscillation should cease [9]. It is possible to make the initialization process more accurate by placing every star fault in the initial list for each line whose initial value is u.

An interesting open problem is what should be the initial contents of the fault lists? It is often not known how the initial state of the circuit was arrived at, and therefore is not apparent whether or not a fault f would have influenced the initializing of line α. It is erroneous to set all fault lists initially to the empty set, and it is too pessimistic to place all faults into the set L_α^u. However, the former approach is usually taken.

4.6.4 Concurrent Fault Simulation

Ulrich and Baker [24] have proposed another method for simulating faults in circuits, referred to as *concurrent simulation*. Like deductive simulation this approach is also a one pass process. For large circuits, partitioning is of course required, hence multiple passes may occur. We will first illustrate the concept of concurrent simulation, and then compare these two approaches. For simplicity we assume all lines have binary values.

Consider a single output n-input combination element E. At a particular simulation time t for fault f this element has input values $a_1^f, a_2^f, \ldots, a_n^f$ and output value b^f, where $f = 0$ refers to the fault free circuit. Consider the set of faults $F' \subset F$ (where F is the set of all single stuck faults) such that for each $f \epsilon F'$, either $b^f \neq b^0$, or $a_j^f \neq a_j^0$ for some input j. That is, for each $f \epsilon F'$ either an input or the output b of E is in error. We can now associate with b a super fault list (SFL) S_b, where each entry in this list is of the form

$$f; a_1^f a_2^f \ldots a_n^f; b^f$$

for $f \epsilon F'$. We illustrate this list in pictorial form in Figure 4.44. Here, the first element in S_b is 9;00;1 which implies that fault 9 causes inputs (0,0) and output 1. The elements are sorted by fault index, and can be stored in a sequential table or in a list structure as for L_b. We call S_b a super fault list since the deductive fault list L_b is a subset of this list in the sense that $f \epsilon L_b$ if and only if $b^f \neq b^0$. It is therefore evident that concurrent simulation requires more storage than deductive simulation.

fault free gate E

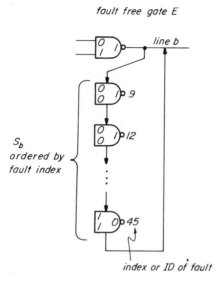

index or ID of fault

Figure 4.44   Super fault list S_b associated with a line b

In deductive simulation the fault free circuit is explicitly simulated and the faulty circuits are deductively simulated. In concurrent simulation only those elements in the faulty circuit which do not agree, in terms of input and/or output values, with the same element in the fault free circuit are explicitly simulated. In parallel simulation elements in both the fault free and faulty circuit are explicitly simulated even when they agree with each other.

Example 4.7:   We will illustrate the computation of the super fault lists S_b, using the circuit shown in Figure 4.45(a) to show how these lists differ from L_b. List $\tilde{S}_b$ and $\tilde{L}_b$ refer to the present (initial) fault lists.

For gate c there is an entry $a_1;$ 10; 1 in $\tilde{S}_c$ which implies that if a is s-a-1, the input to the gate will be $a = 1$, $b = 0$ rather than $a = 0$, $b = 0$, and the output is 1. Now assume that line a changes to a 1. The deductive simulator would re-evaluate c and see that no logic activity has occurred. However, since $L_c \neq \tilde{L}_c$ a list-event has occurred. Therefore $L_e = L_c \cup L_d \cup e_1$ is computed. Then, since $L_e \neq \tilde{L}_e, L_i = L_e \cup L_h \cup i_1$ is computed. Thus it is necessary to recompute 3 fault lists and check to see if they differed from their previous status. In general, with long lists this can be quite time consuming.

We will now consider how a concurrent simulator would handle this

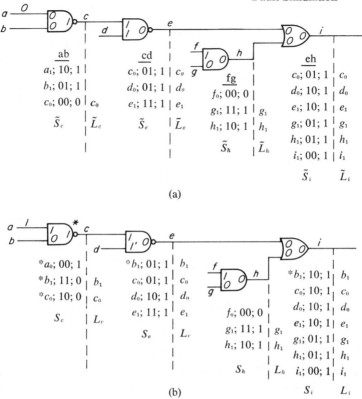

Figure 4.45 Comparison of lists for deductive and concurrent simulation

same problem. When line a changes to a 1 there is an activity and the entire list $\tilde{S}_c$ as well as gate c must be processed. For gate c, only its input changes. For the entry a_1;1 0;1 since $a = 1$, this term is deleted and the term a_0;0 0;1 is added to $\tilde{S}_c$. Similarly, b_1;0 1;1 changes to b_1;1 1;0 and c_0;0 0;0 changes to c_0;1 0;0. These computations produce the list S_c. Now *all* entries, and *only* these entries, which have either caused a change in the logic value of line c, or which create a new element to be added to a list due to an output error are processed. Such events are called *logic list events*. In this example, only entry b_1 qualifies for further processing. The list $\tilde{S}_e$ is scanned looking for a b_1 entry. (Note that all entries on a list S are ordered by fault index. In our example the order is alphabetic.) Since the first entry encountered on $\tilde{S}_e$ is c_0, b_1 is not an entry on $\tilde{S}_e$ and therefore the entry b_1;0 1;1 is added to $\tilde{S}_e$, forming S_e. Again this causes a logic list event and $\tilde{S}_i$ is processed next by adding b_1;1 0;1 to it, thus forming S_i. Those gates (entries) which have been processed are flagged in Figure 4.45(b) by an *. There are six such entries. For the fault list propagation technique three gates, (c, e, and i) would be processed and their associated fault lists recomputed. Hence the concurrent simulation process can potentially lead to a reduction in CPU time. This savings is related to the ratio of logic list events to the total length of the fault sets. □

The reason the input vector $(a_1^f, a_2^f, \ldots, a_n^f)$ is stored along with its entry in S is because each element E^f, is actually simulated one at a time, as long as there is an activity associated with it. That is, if gate c has some activity due to faults i, j and k, then three separate copies of c are simulated and these entries are placed in S. Because of this, the input values for these three versions of gate c must be known.

Since faulty circuits and good circuits are processed (scheduled) concurrently, this technique is called *concurrent simulation*. Because each entry in S is processed separately, and its inputs are known, fast simulation techniques such as table look-up can be used. Thus one significant difference between deductive and concurrent simulation is related to the fact that a concurrent simulator only processes the active circuits. The difference in processing performance between deductive and concurrent simulation due to this fact becomes more apparent when a fault f causes a circuit to oscillate. We assume the fault free circuit has stabilized. In deductive simulation it is necessary to repeatedly process each gate in the circuit loop which is oscillating since a list event is present. Each gate processed requires a complex calculation over all its input lists, even though only one fault f is causing the oscillation. In concurrent simulation, only the single fault f is processed.

When an event occurs during concurrent simulation, an entry must be placed in the scheduler at the appropriate time. This entry is actually a 4-tuple consisting of (1) the name of the element E to be simulated; (2) the name of the fault causing simulation; (3) the name (index) of the input line on which an event occurred which caused E to be scheduled; and (4) the new value of this line.

The main disadvantages of the concurrent simulation procedure are that it requires more storage than the deductive procedure, and when an event occurs, due to a fault, the super fault list must be serially scanned to see if the fault is an entry on this list. However, this scan process is less time consuming than set intersection or union. The super fault list must also be processed when a logic event in the fault free circuit occurs, since it affects the input values to the element.

Since activity in both the fault free and faulty circuits must be scheduled, the length of the scheduler list is longer than in a deductive simulator. The same elements, however, are processed in both cases. That is, a change in an input causes an element E to be processed at time frame t in a deductive simulator if and only if it is scheduled in a concurrent simulator. In the deductive method, however, it will be scheduled by a simple entry such as E (multiple entries are possible but can be eliminated if desired), while in a concurrent simulator there will probably be multiple entries. These entries should be ordered by fault index (the second field) so they can be efficiently processed.

Finally, for multi-valued logic, such as the five valued system described earlier, concurrent simulation is ideal since each element in a super fault list is handled individually, hence all the tools available for fault free simulation are again available for fault simulation. In addition, complex delay models as well as functional modeled elements can be dealt with quite easily.

4.6.5   Hyperactive Faults

In a recent study [9], a class of faults, referred to as *hyperactive faults*, was identified. These faults appear to create an inordinate amount of simulation activity. Removal of hyperactive faults often reduced simulation time, using a deductive simulator, by almost an order of magnitude. Usually these hyperactive faults constitute less than 5% of the total faults in the circuit. These faults are usually associated with clock and sequencer circuits and they usually inhibit the effectiveness of critical control signals and allow the circuit to behave erratically. Usually faults which cause races and oscillations are a subset of the hyperactive faults. If these faults can be readily identified by the simulator and their effects on circuit activity quickly suppressed, a significant decrease in simulation time can be realized. Unfortunately, effective procedures for identifying hyperactive faults *a priori* do not exist.

4.6.6   Comparison of Fault Simulation Techniques

The total CPU time of a parallel simulator can usually be reduced by increasing the number of faults processed per pass. Also, by reducing the number of faults processed per pass, a parallel simulator can always be developed which requires less storage than a deductive simulator. The storage and CPU time requirements for a parallel simulator increase linearly with the number of faults processed per pass. For a deductive simulator these parameters increase linearly with the average size L of the fault lists being processed. Unfortunately there is no simple way of predicting the value of L for a given circuit.

For 2-valued logic simulation Chappell et al. [8] state that parallel simulation is faster then deductive only in simulating small (e.g., <500 gates) highly sequential circuits. Though their analysis did not include 3-valued simulation, for this case it appears that deductive simulation suffers to a higher degree than does parallel simulation.

4.7   SIMULATION OSCILLATION

Occasionally, the fault free or faulty circuit may oscillate in response to some input sequence. When this occurs, the simulator, if accurately modeling the circuit, will emulate this behavior by "looping," which we refer to as *simulator oscillation*. The mechanism required to detect and correct simulator oscillation is called *oscillation control*. The primary functions of oscillation control are: (1) to identify simulator oscillation (or what is believed to be oscillation); (2) take appropriate corrective action to eliminate the oscillation; and (3) to proceed with the normal simulation process.

A simple example of oscillation is illustrated in Figure 4.46(a) when, at time t, the inputs R and S change from (0,0) to (1,1). For this situation, most simulators would begin looping, producing the sequence 101010 . . .

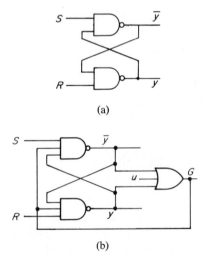

(a)

(b)

Figure 4.46   (a) Latch under oscillation condition (b) Model change
used to halt oscillation

for both y and $\bar{y}$. Oscillation control typically occurs at two levels, referred to as local and global control.

4.7.1   Local Oscillation Control

Often, when it is known that a specific subcircuit, such as a latch, is prone to oscillation, a special check can be added to the simulator to identify when oscillation is occurring. In our example, the race on the inputs causes the oscillation, and it is identified by the condition $R = S = y = \bar{y}$ = 1 or equivalently, $y = \bar{y} = 0$. Also, the states $y = u$, $\bar{y} = 0$ and $y = 0$, $\bar{y} = u$ can cause oscillation. The appropriate corrective action for these cases is to set $y = \bar{y} = u$.

Local oscillation detection can be carried out in several ways, depending on the type of simulator being employed. For a deductive simulator, where one or more faults may be causing oscillation, the fault lists must be processed in order to identify $y = \bar{y} = 0$ condition. If line α is oscillating, the faults causing oscillation are those in the set $(L_\alpha - \tilde{L}_\alpha) \cup (\tilde{L}_\alpha - L_\alpha)$. These faults become * faults.

Oscillation can also be detected and corrected automatically via modeling [27]. In Figure 4.46(b) an extra oscillation control gate G has been added to the latch circuit. Normally $G = 1$, since typically $y = 1$ and $\bar{y} = 0$, or $y = 0$ and $\bar{y} = 1$, or $y = \bar{y} = 1$. When $y = \bar{y} = 0$, $G = u$. If G is made a pseudo ouput, then this u can be used to signal an oscillation condition. If, in addition, G is allowed to drive the latch gates, then $G = u$ with $R = S$ = 1 will drive the latch to $y = \bar{y} = u$ and simulator oscillation will automatically cease.

Local oscillation control is not necessarily restricted to latch circuits. However, if the user does not specify to the simulator which subcircuits may oscillate, a global oscillation control procedure may be required.

4.7.2   Global Oscillation Control

In general, it is difficult to determine if a simulator is oscillating. True oscillation implies that, for the given input, the status of the data (line values and scheduled future changes) cycles or repeats itself. Since this data is typically not retained from time frame to time frame, such a comparison is not computationally feasible. Hence, most simulators try to "inhibit potential and real" oscillation which creates high circuit activity by limiting the number of times a signal line can change state, or the number of simulation time frames for a static input condition. Once one of these conditions is violated, the simplest form of oscillation correction is to continue the simulation process, but now, whenever a line is to change state, set its new value to a u. Eventually the circuit will stabilize and every signal line that was involved in the oscillating loop will have the value u. The limit checks can be made in the simulator by associating counters with critical points in the circuit. A counter is incremented whenever the line to which it is assigned has an activity, and is reset to zero whenever a new input vector is applied.

4.8   MODELING

The first step in the processing of a circuit for test generation or simulation is the development of the circuit model which is input to the simulator. This model is then translated by the input preprocessor into an internal input description or internal model. In this section we will discuss some of the problems involved in developing the input model, and the trade-offs between different internal circuit models.

Input Model Development

Typically, the development of the input model is a straightforward encoding of various logical elements or IC's and how they are interconnected. Unfortunately, for many classes of circuits, several complications can exist, a few of which are listed below.

1. Some elements in a circuit are not strictly digital, such as one-shots, multivibrators, delay lines, RC networks, etc.

2. Some digital elements cannot be effectively dealt with by the processing program, such as large counters, ROM's and RAM's, etc.

3. Some circuit topologies cannot be accurately handled. For example, a simulator built for synchronous circuits cannot simulate asynchronous circuits.

4. Some fault modes cannot be processed, e.g., a stuck type fault in some elements may cause indeterminant signal values.

These problems can sometimes be circumvented by clever modeling techniques. The basic concept is to develop a model of the subcircuit C such that this model behaves similarly to C. The model should also cover the fault modes of C and must be directly translatable into the primitives of the system.

One situation which often occurs is the necessity of modeling an analog device by digital devices. As an example, a delay line can be modeled by a chain of single input OR gates, or by a shift register. The choice is dependent on the function of the delay line in the circuit. Often analog portions of a circuit must be partitioned from the digital portion and handled separately.

Complex digital elements can often be modeled by simpler elements, and the results patched to compensate for the modeling change. Thus a one-shot having a 50 ms pulse might be modeled by one which has a 20 unit pulse, where a unit is 5 μs. Here only 100 μs of real time is being simulated, hence the need for the rescaling of the results. Often large counters and shift registers can be modeled by smaller counters and registers, and again the results patched accordingly.

Often modeling techniques are used to compensate for deficiencies in the simulation system. As an example, assume that a simulator is unable to initialize a circuit when it is known that the input sequence does indeed initialize the circuit. This situation can often be rectified by adding logic to the model which does not exist in the actual simulator. For example, possibly a pre-reset line can be added to a *JK* flip-flop to insure that it is initialized by the simulator.

Once a model has been developed, it must be analyzed to see if it is a realistic representation of the actual circuit before costly test generation and simulation studies are carried out. This can be done by determining (manually) functional input patterns for which the response of the circuit is known. By comparing this information with the response from the simulator, some degree of confidence in the model is gained. These same inputs should be processed through the ATE to see if the correct response is obtained. This last step is required in order to insure that the simulation model includes all aspects of the ATE which may influence test pattern application and response measurement.

Internal Model Representation

In logic simulation an element, such as an MSI, can either be modeled functionally or at the gate level. At the functional level, the principle elements may consist of functional blocks such as counters, shift registers, flip-flops, decoders and multiplexers. At the gate level, the primitives would be elements such as NAND, NOR, AND, OR, and INVERTER gates.

As an example of a functional level model, consider the decoder circuit shown in Figure 4.47. Here, a simple functional level element evaluation

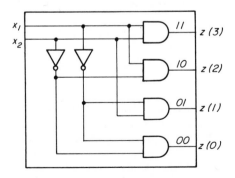

Figure 4.47   Decoder circuit

and scheduling scheme might consist of the following two steps, carried out when the input changes from I to I', where I and I' are the integer values of the old and new input vector (x_1, x_2).

Step 1: Schedule the event $z(I)$: $1 \to 0$

Step 2: Schedule the event $z(I')$: $0 \to 1$.

Note that here we have dealt with the circuit (chip) strictly as a functional element and have not considered its internal organization. In general, very fast element evaluation routines can be developed for handling many functional elements at the functional level. Unfortunately, many of these efficiencies can be realized only if two valued logic is being employed. Parallel simulation techniques often cannot be used because they require the use of logical operators. Concurrent simulation techniques are applicable to functional level processing.

The level of internal modeling employed is dictated by several factors such as timing requirements and fault modes. In a functional level model, internal fault modes cannot be processed. Also, detailed timing analysis cannot be carried out because internal delay values are not processed. Functional level simulation is necessary in many situations, such as when the detailed logic design of an element is not available. An example of this occurs in present day microprocessor chips, where typically it is impossible to obtain their gate level description. In the future we will probably see more simulation carried out at the functional level than at present. Functional simulators will be useful tools to help create digital systems which are correct, reliable and easily testable.

REFERENCES

[1] Armstrong, D. B., "A Deductive Method for Simulating Faults in Logic Circuits," *IEEE Transactions on Computers,* Vol. C-21, pp. 464–471, May 1972.
[2] Breuer, M. A., "Techniques for the Simulation of Computer Logic," *Communications ACM,* pp. 443–446, July 1964.
[3] Breuer, M. A., "Functional Partitioning and Simulation of Digital Circuits," *IEEE Transactions on Computers,* Vol. C-19, pp. 1038–1046, November 1970.
[4] Breuer, M. A., "A Note on Three Valued Logic Simulation," *IEEE Transactions on Computers*, Vol. C-21, pp. 399–402, April 1972.
[5] Breuer, M. A., and L. Harrison, "Procedures for Eliminating Static and Dynamic Hazards in Test Generation," *IEEE Transactions on Computers,* Vol. C-23, pp. 1069–1078, October 1974.

[6] Chang, H. Y., Manning, E. G., and G. Metze, *Fault Diagnosis of Digital Systems,* John Wiley & Sons, Inc., New York, 1970.

[7] Chappel, S. G., and S. S. Yau, "Simulation of Large Asynchronous Logic Circuits Using an Ambiguous Gate Model," *Proc. Fall Joint Computer Conference,* pp. 651–661, 1971.

[8] Chappell, S. G., Chang, H. Y., Elmendorf, C. H., and L. D. Schmidt, "Comparison of Parallel and Deductive Simulation Techniques," *IEEE Transactions on Computers,* Vol. C-23, pp. 1132–1139, November 1974.

[9] Chappell, S. G., Elmendorf, C. H., and L. D. Schmidt, "LAMP: Logic Circuit Simulation," *The Bell System Technical Journal,* Vol. 53, pp. 1451–1476, October 1974.

[10] Eichelberger, E. B., "Hazard Detection in Combinational and Sequential Switching Circuits," *IBM J. Res. Develop.,* Vol. 9, pp. 90–99, March 1965.

[11] Fantauzzi, G., "An Algebraic Model for the Analysis of Logical Circuits," *IEEE Transactions on Computers,* Vol. C-23, pp. 576–581, June 1974.

[12] Friedes, A., "The Propagation of Fault Lists Through Combinational or Sequential Circuits," *Proc. Workshop on Fault Detection and Diagnosis in Digital Circuits and Systems,* Lehigh University, pp. 12–41, December 7–9, 1970.

[13] Hardie, F. H., and R. J. Suhocki, "Design and Use of Fault Simulation for Saturn Computer Design," *IEEE Transactions on Electronic Computers,* Vol. EC-16, pp. 412–429, 1967.

[14] Jephson, J. S., McQuarrie, R. P., and R. E. Vogelsberg, "A Three-Value Computer Design Verification System," *IBM System J.,* Vol. 8, pp. 178–188, 1969.

[15] Koford, J. and R. Walker, *FAIRSIM II User's Manual,* Fairchild Semiconductor Corp., 1969.

[16] *D-LASAR User's Guide,* University Computing Company, Report No. 3544, November 1, 1973.

[17] Lewis, D. W., "Hazard Detection by a Quinary Simulation of Logic Devices with Bounded Propagation Delays," M. S. Thesis, Syracuse University, January 1972.

[18] Menon, P. R., "A Simulation Program for Logic Networks," Bell Telephone Labs. Internal Technical Memorandum, No. MM65-1271-3, 1965.

[19] Seshu, S. and D. N. Freeman, "The Diagnosis of Asynchronous Sequential Switching Systems," *IEEE Transactions on Electronic Computers,* Vol. EC-11, pp. 459–465, August 1962.

[20] Szygenda, S. A., and E. W. Thompson, "Fault Insertion Techniques and Models for Digital Logic Simulation," *Proc. Fall Joint Computer Conference,* pp. 875–884, 1972.

[21] Szygenda, S. A., Rouse, D. M., and E. W. Thompson, "A Model and Implementation of a Universal Time Delay Simulator for Large Digital Nets," *Proc. Spring Joint Computer Conference,* pp. 207–216, 1970.

[22] Szygenda, S. A., "TEGAS 2—Anatomy of a General Purpose Test Generation and Simulation System for Digital Logic," *Proc. 9-th ACM-IEEE Design Automation Workshop*, Dallas, Texas, pp. 116–127, June 1972.

[23] Szygenda, S. A., Hemming, C., and J. M. Hemphill, "Time Flow Mechanisms for Use in Digital Logic Simulation," *Proc. of the 1971 Winter Simulation Conference*, December 1971.

[24] Ulrich, E. G., and T. Baker, "Concurrent Simulation of Nearly Identical Digital Networks," *Computer*, Vol. 7, pp. 39–44, April 1974.

[25] Ulrich, E. G., "Time-sequenced Logical Simulation Based on Circuit Delay and Selective Tracing of Active Network Paths," *Proc. ACM 20-th Nat'l. Conf.*, pp. 437–448, 1965.

[26] Ulrich, E. G., "Exclusive Simulation of Activity in Digital Networks," *Communications of the ACM*, Vol. 13, pp. 102–110, February 1969.

[27] Ulrich, E. G., Baker, T., and L. R. Williams, "Fault-test Analysis Techniques Based on Logic Simulation," *Proc. 9th Design Automation Workshop*, 1972.

PROBLEMS

4.1 For each of the five cases shown below, analyze the operation of the latch shown in Figure 4.15 for the input sequence shown in Figure 4.48, assuming initially that $\bar{y} = 0$ and $y = 1$.

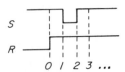

Figure 4.48

a) $\Delta_T = 2$

b) $\Delta_I = 2$

c) $\Delta_I = 1$

d) $\Delta_R = 3, \Delta_F = 1$

e) $\Delta_R = 1, \Delta_F = 3$

4.2 Consider the circuit shown in Figure 4.49, and the input sequence shown. Calculate the output sequence at J and K using Eichelberger's 3 valued logic simulation and Procedure 4.4 for 8 valued logic. Verify that the 8 valued logic system correctly identifies a dynamic hazard at K, while the 3 valued logic system produces the same result for lines J and K.

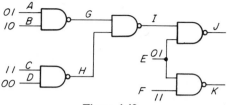

Figure 4.49

4.3 Prove Corollary 4.1

4.4 The switching circuit shown in Figure 4.50 contains a hazard for the input sequence a c, where a = (1,0,1) and c = (0,0,1).

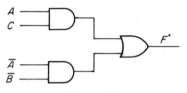

Figure 4.50

If the redundant AND term $\bar{B}C$ is added to this circuit, the hazard no longer appears. Verify these statements using 3 valued logic simulation. (Note that the stuck-at-fault which clamps the output of this new AND gate to zero is statically undetectable but can cause a hazard to appear.)

4.5 Simulate the latch shown in Figure 4.15 using the input sequence shown in Figure 4.51 assuming 5 valued logic, $\Delta_m = 1$, $\Delta_M = 2$, $R = 1$ and initially $\bar{y} = 0$ and $y = 1$.

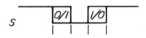

Figure 4.51

4.6 In Figure 4.52 treat the flip-flops as functional elements and assume the input sequence X = 010.

a) Show that 3 valued logic $(0, 1, u)$ fails to initialize this circuit.

b) Show that second order indeterminant initialization does initialize this circuit.

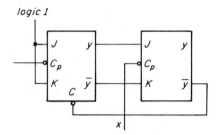

Figure 4.52

4.7 Show that an *SR* master-slave flip-flop consisting of 9 NAND gates can be initialized using only three valued simulation.

4.8 The mod 16 state counter in the circuit shown in Figure 4.53 operates as follows. In response to a clock pulse the state of the counter is incremented by one. When the state reaches 15 the output *TC* becomes a 1. If clocked again the state becomes 0. *MR* is a master reset and a 0 input drives the state of the counter to 0. Analyze the response to this circuit to 16 clock pulses. Will a 3 valued logic system initialize this circuit?

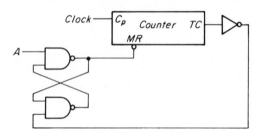

Figure 4.53

4.9 For the computer available to you at your local installation, determine the most efficient compiled code for the following elements.

a) 5 input NAND gate

b) *SR* latch

c) *SR* master-slave flip-flop with preset and clear. Assume a functional model.

What is the most efficient number of faults that can be simulated in parallel on this machine?

4.10 Construct a descriptor type data base for the latch shown in Figure 4.15.

4.11 Extend the data base shown in Figure 4.27 to handle multi-output elements with memory.

4.12 Construct a zoom table for a 2 input NAND element, assuming 2 valued logic and unit transport delay. Repeat for 3 valued logic.

4.13 Consider the circuit shown in Figure 4.54, where only single stuck-at-faults are of interest.

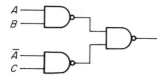

Figure 4.54

Assume a test sequence consisting of the binary equivalent of the integers 0,1,2 ...,7, in this order.

a) Construct a fault detection table where after the first 2 detects the fault is no longer processed.

b) Determine which output bits can be ignored in isolating a fault.

4.14 Carry out a hand simulation of the latch shown in Figure 4.15, assuming $\bar{y} = 0$, $y = 1$, and input sequences $\mathbf{S} = 10$ and $\mathbf{R} = 11$. Use a simple event directed unit delay simulation process with 0,1 logic states. Assume a parallel simulator with the following faults.

fault	bit position
fault free	bit 1
S s-a-1	bit 2
S s-a-0	bit 3
$\bar{y}$ s-a-1	bit 4
$\bar{y}$ s-a-0	bit 5

Show the value of y and $\bar{y}$ for each time frame.

4.15 Flow chart the following procedures for processing a sequential table structure used to store fault lists:

a) set intersection assuming ordered lists;

b) set intersection assuming unordered lists;

Compare the complexity of these two procedures.

4.16 For the latch shown in Figure 4.15, assume $\bar{y} = 0$, $y = 1$, and $S = R = 1$. Assume the initial fault lists associated with lines y, $\bar{y}$, R and S are L_y, $L_{\bar{y}}$, L_R, and L_S. Let S change to a 0. Determine the new output fault lists in terms of the given fault lists produced by this input event. Also, include all s-a-faults associated with this circuit.

4.17 Flow chart the design of a complete logic simulator. Assume the following constraints:

a) a descriptor type data structure for the circuit.

b) arbitrary inertial delay for each element ($\Delta_I = \Delta_T$).

c) three valued logic simulation.

d) concurrent fault simulation.

Specify all other design constraints you require.

4.18 It is desired to correctly process a *JK* master-slave flip-flop using 3 valued simulation. It was shown that employing a gate equivalent model leads to errors in initialization. Determine a state table model for this device. Assume that the master, slave, *J*, *K*, and clock lines can be either 0, 1 or u. There are therefore $3^3 = 27$ possible input vectors and $3^2 = 9$ possible internal state configurations.

4.19 Associate with each line α a list L_α^1, called the *one-list*, where fault $f \epsilon L_\alpha^1$ if and only if line α in the circuit under fault f has the value 1. Note that $L_\alpha^1 = L_\alpha$ if line α in the normal circuit has the value 0, and $L_\alpha^1 = \bar{L}_\alpha$ if the line has the value 0. Show that for an AND (OR) gate with inputs a and b and output c, that $L_c^1 = L_a^1 \cap L_b^1 \cup c$ s-a-1 ($L_c^1 = L_a^1 \cup L_b^1 \cup c$ s-a-1). Hence the output one list can be constructed independent of the logic values of the input lines. What are the major advantages and disadvantages of carrying out fault analysis using L_α^1 rather than L_α?

4.20 Prove the validity of the following procedure, which is an alternative to Procedure 4.8, for determining the output fault list of an element (function) ψ in terms of its input faults lists.

Procedure: The output fault list L for ψ is given by the equation $L = E(a_j) \oplus \tilde{E}(a_j \oplus L_j)$ where $E(a_j)$ is the value of the function ψ (or expression E for ψ) evaluated for a particular binary n-tuple a $= (a_1, a_2, \ldots, a_n)$, and $\tilde{E}$ is the same expression as E except where the arguments are fault lists, where $0 \oplus L = L$ and $1 \oplus L = \bar{L}$, and where "$\cdot$" is replaced by "$\cap$" and "$+$" is replaced by "$\cup$".   □

4.21 Consider the *JK* master-slave flip-flop shown in Figure 1.14, ignoring the preset and reset inputs. Let $J = 1$ and $K = 0$ and let the input clock sequence be 010. Assume the initial state of each line is unknown.

a) Verify functionally that this input condition initializes the flip-flop.

b) Verify that by using 3-valued simulation $(0,1,u)$ that the flip-flop is not initialized.

c) Verify that by using first order indeterminant initialization (i.e., the output of each gate can be $0,1,u_i,$ or $\bar{u}_i$) that the flip-flop is not initialized.

d) Verify that by using second order indeterminant initialization (i.e., the output of each gate can be $0,1,u_i,\bar{u}_i$ or an arbitrary function of two variables, say u_j and u_k) that the flip-flop can be initialized.

e) Assume the latches in the flip-flop are identified, and we use the rule that $(u_i,\bar{u}_i)$ input to a latch produces the output $(\bar{u}_i,u_i)$. Show that the combination of this rule and first order indeterminant initialization is sufficient to initialize the flip-flop.

4.22 Consider the portion of a circuit shown in Figure 4.55, where $a = 0$.

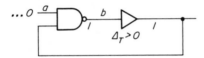

Figure 4.55   Simple circuit which oscillates for fault *a s-a-*1

Assume the initial conditions

$$L_a = L_A \cup \{a_1\}, L_b = \phi, L_c = \phi,$$

where L_A is an arbitrary fault list and $b_0 \notin L_A$. Note that the fault a_1 causes the circuit to oscillate.

a) Determine the oscillatory values for the fault set L_b.

b) Simulate this same case using concurrent simulation.

c) Compare the complexity of these two simulation procedures for this case.

4.23 The following procedure computes the union L of two unordered fault lists (sets) L_1 and L_2, where $|L_1| \le |L_2|$. Let the elements of L_1 and L_2 be integers between 1 and K, and assume a working space vector $\mathbf{w} = (w(1), \ldots,w(K))$, where $w(i) = 0$ or 1. Initially $w(i) = 0$ for all i.

Procedure:

1) For each $e \in L_1$, place e into L and set $w(e)$ to 1.

2) For each $e \in L_2$ such that $w(e) \neq 1$, place e into L.

3) For each $e \in L_1$, set $w(e) = 0$.   □

The execution of this procedure requires the processing of $2|L_1| + |L_2|$ elements. Devise an efficient procedure for carrying out the union of two ordered fault lists. Compare the complexity of this procedure with the one just presented. Consider the special cases when $L_1 \cap L_2 = \phi$ and when $L_1 \subset L_2$.

Chapter 5

RELIABLE DESIGN–THEORY AND TECHNIQUES

In the previous chapters we have considered the problems associated with detection of faults by observation of responses to excitations called tests. In this chapter we will consider three classes of design procedures which simplify system maintenance and/or fault diagnosis: (1) design of *self checking digital systems* in which faults can be automatically detected by a subcircuit called a *checker*, (2) design of *fault tolerant circuits*, in which faults do not cause system malfunctions, and (3) design of *easily testable systems*, in which the problems associated with test generation are considerably alleviated. We shall also consider several models for evaluating the diagnosability of digital systems.

5.1 SELF CHECKING CIRCUITS

In some cases it may be possible to determine from the outputs of a circuit C whether a certain fault α exists within the circuit. In this case it is unnecessary to explicitly test for α and the circuit is said to be self checking for α. Another circuit, called a checker, can be designed to generate an error signal whenever the outputs of C indicate the presence of a fault within C. It is desirable to design circuits, including checkers, to be self checking to as great an extent as possible (i.e., for as many faults as possible).

For an arbitrary combinational circuit with p inputs and q output all 2^p input combinations can occur as can all 2^q possible outputs. If all 2^q outputs can occur, it is impossible to determine whether a fault is present, assuming no knowledge of the inputs, by just observing the outputs of the circuit. However, if only $k < 2^q$ output configurations can occur during normal operation, the occurrence of any of the $2^q - k$ unallowable configurations indicates a malfunction independent of the corresponding input configuration. Thus, faults which result in such an unallowable output can be detected by a hardware checker, as illustrated in the following example.

Example 5.1:   Consider a circuit which realizes the combinational functions $f_1(x_1,x_2)$ and $f_2(x_1,x_2)$ described by the truth table of Figure 5.1(a).

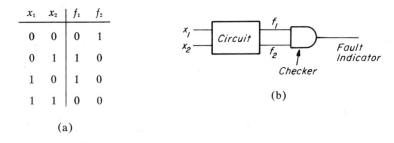

x_1	x_2	f_1	f_2
0	0	0	1
0	1	1	0
1	0	1	0
1	1	0	0

(a)

(b)

Figure 5.1   Automatic Fault Checking for Example 5.1

Note that the output configuration $f_1 = f_2 = 1$ never occurs. Any fault which leads to this configuration can be automatically detected by the checker shown in Figure 5.1(b) which generates a 1-output, indicating an error, if and only if $f_1 = f_2 = 1$. Note that this checker will fail to detect faults which cause an incorrect but "possible" output configuration.   □

In a circuit which has output configurations which do not occur during fault-free (i.e., normal) operation the outputs which do occur are called *(valid) code words* and the unallowable configurations are called *invalid* or *non-code words*. We will speak of both input codes and output codes in this manner. Considerable work has been done on specifying codes which are useful for error detection and correction.

5.1.1   Application of Error Detecting and Correcting Codes

Codes are usually classified in terms of their ability to detect or correct classes of faults which affect some fixed number of bits. Thus a code is *e-error detecting* if any fault which causes at most *e* output bits to be erroneous can be detected. This implies that any such error does not transform a code word into another code word. A code is *e-error correcting* if, for any fault which causes at most *e* erroneous output bits, the set of all correct output bits can be automatically determined. This implies that any two such errors e_1, e_2, affecting code words w_1, w_2 respectively do not result in the same word.

The *Hamming distance d* of a code is the minimum number of bits in which any two code words differ. The error detecting and correcting capability of a code can be expressed in terms of d as shown in the table of Figure 5.2. (The proof of these results can be found in almost any book on coding theory and is left as an exercise.)

d	capability
1	none
2	1-error detection, 0-error correction
3	2-error detection, 1-error correction
$\vdots$	
$e + 1$	e-error detection, $\left\lceil \dfrac{e}{2} \right\rceil^*$-error correction
$\vdots$	
$2e + 1$	$2e$-error detection, e-error correction

Figure 5.2   Capability of a Code with Distance d

In general, additional outputs, called *check bits*, must be generated by a circuit in order for its output words to constitute a code with useful error capabilities. The *parity check code* is the simplest such code. For this code $d = 2$, and the number of check bits is one (independent of the number of outputs in the original circuit). There are two types of parity checks, even and odd. For an even (odd) code, the check bit is defined so that the total number of 1-output bits is even (odd) at all times. Any error affecting a single bit causes the output to have an odd (even) number of 1-bits and hence is automatically detected. Note that in an arbitrary circuit a single fault may cause an error in several output bits due to the presence of fanout. Hence care must be taken in designing a circuit if a limited number of erroneous bits is presumed.

Example 5.2:   For the functions f_1, f_2 of Example 5.1, the check bit y_e for an even parity code is defined so that for any input, the total number of 1-outputs among f_1, f_2 and y_e is even (Figure 5.3). Thus, if $x_1 = 0$, $x_2 = 1$,

---

$*\left\lceil \dfrac{e}{2} \right\rceil$ denotes the smallest integer not less than $\dfrac{e}{2}$.

since $f_1 = 1$ and $f_2 = 0$, then y_e must be 1. For an odd parity check, the check bit y_o would be as shown in Figure 5.3. Note that y_o is always equal to $\overline{y_e}$.   □

x_1	x_2	f_1	f_2	y_e	y_o
0	0	0	1	1	0
0	1	1	0	1	0
1	0	1	0	1	0
1	1	0	0	0	1

Figure 5.3

The check bits required in a code can be thought of as constituting redundancy since they are only required for error detection. The other bits are called *information bits*.* A generalized class of parity check codes can be defined which have greater error detecting and/or correcting capability. A single error correcting code for q information bits requires c check bits where $2^c \geq q + c + 1$. The value of c for various values of q is shown in Figure 5.4.

q	c
1	2
4	3
11	4
26	5
57	6
120	7

Figure 5.4   Values of q and c for Single Error Correcting Parity Check Codes

The c check bits and q information bits constitute a $(c + q)$-bit word $b_{c+q} \ldots b_2 b_1$. In the conventional Hamming code the check bits occur in positions $b_{2^0}, b_{2^1}, b_{2^2}, \ldots, b_{2^{c-1}}$. The values of these check bits are defined by c parity check equations. Let p_j be the set of integers whose binary

---

*Redundancy has been defined as that which is not necessary for correct system operation. The number of check bits used as compared with the number of information bits is a measure of the amount of redundancy.

representation has a 1 in position b_j, i.e., $p_j = \{I \mid b_j(I) = 1\}$, where $b_j(n)$ denotes the value of the jth bit (from the right) of a binary number N. Then the value of the check bits are defined by the c parity equations of the form

$$\sum_{k \in p_i} b_k = 0 \qquad i = 1, \ldots, c$$

where the sum is modulo 2.

An error in bit b_j will result in incorrect parity for exactly those equations for which $j \in p_i$. Thus the erroneous bit can be computed from these c parity check equations.

Example 5.3: Let $q = 4$. Then $2^c \geq q + c + 1 = 5 + c$, and hence $c = 3$. The single error correcting code defines a seven bit word with bits b_1, b_2, b_4 being the check bits. The value of the check bits can be determined from the following three parity check equations.

$$b_1 \oplus b_3 \oplus b_5 \oplus b_7 = 0 \qquad \text{defined by } p_1$$
$$b_2 \oplus b_3 \oplus b_6 \oplus b_7 = 0 \qquad \text{defined by } p_2$$
$$b_4 \oplus b_5 \oplus b_6 \oplus b_7 = 0 \qquad \text{defined by } p_3.$$

Thus if the information bits have the values $b_3 = 1$, $b_5 = 0$, $b_6 = 0$, $b_7 = 1$, then the check bits have the values

$$b_1 = b_3 \oplus b_5 \oplus b_7 = 1 \oplus 0 \oplus 1 = 0$$
$$b_2 = b_3 \oplus b_6 \oplus b_7 = 1 \oplus 0 \oplus 1 = 0$$
$$b_4 = b_5 \oplus b_6 \oplus b_7 = 0 \oplus 0 \oplus 1 = 1$$

and the encoded word is 1 0 0 1 1 0 0. If an error occurs in bit position b_5, the word becomes 1 0 1 1 1 0 0. Let us now recompute the three parity check equations for this erroneous word.

$$b_1 \oplus b_3 \oplus b_5 \oplus b_7 = 0 \oplus 1 \oplus 1 \oplus 1 = 1$$
$$b_2 \oplus b_3 \oplus b_6 \oplus b_7 = 0 \oplus 1 \oplus 0 \oplus 1 = 0$$
$$b_4 \oplus b_5 \oplus b_6 \oplus b_7 = 1 \oplus 1 \oplus 0 \oplus 1 = 1$$

Thus the first and third equations are erroneous indicating an error in bit b_j where $j \in p_1$, $j \notin p_2$, $j \in p_3$. Thus j corresponds to the binary number 1 0 1 and the erroneous bit is b_5. Thus the single bit error can be corrected.   □

The use of codes enables hardware to be designed which can automatically detect or correct errors in the circuit (but not in the checker itself) as shown in Figure 5.5(a) and 5.5(b) respectively. Many codes have been derived which can be used in the design of self checking circuits. The type of code to be used may vary depending on the type of circuit. For data

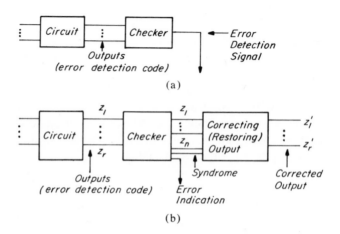

(a)

(b)

Figure 5.5   (a) Error Detecting Circuit (b) Error Correcting Circuit

transmission buses, a parity check code may be adequate. However, to check for errors in an arithmetic unit another type of code is required. This is because the value of the parity check bits for the operation $A + B$ cannot be determined from the check bits of A and the check bits of B. For the two additions illustrated in Figure 5.6, in both cases the operand check bits (even parity) are 1 and 0 respectively but the check bit of the sum $A + B_1$ is 0 and the check bit of the sum $A + B_2$ is 1. Thus the parity check bit must effectively be recomputed after each addition.

$$A = 0\ 0\ 0\ 1 \qquad\qquad A = 0\ 0\ 0\ 1$$
$$\underline{B_1 = 0\ 1\ 0\ 1} \qquad\qquad \underline{B_2 = 0\ 0\ 1\ 1}$$
$$A + B_1 = 0\ 1\ 1\ 0 \qquad\qquad A + B_2 = 0\ 1\ 0\ 0$$

Check bit of $A = C(A) = 1, C(B_1) = C(B_2) = 0, C(A + B_1) = 0, C(A + B_2) = 1$

Figure 5.6   Addition Does Not Preserve Parity

Another class of codes, called *residue codes*, has the desirable property that for the arithmetic operations of addition, subtraction and multiplication, the check bits of the result can be determined from the check bits of the operands. This property is called *independent checking*. Several different types of residue codes have been formulated. We will only consider one such class. In this code the rightmost p bits are the check bits. The check bits define a binary number C, and the information bits define another number N. The check bits are defined in such a manner that $C = (N)$ modulo m^* where m is a parameter (*the residue*) of the code, and the number of check bits is $p = \lceil \log_2 m \rceil$.

Example 5.4: Consider the derivation of the check bits for a residue code with three information bits I_2, I_1, I_0 and $m = 3$. Since $\lceil \log_2 m \rceil = 2$, check bits C_1 and C_0 are required. Their values are defined so that for the binary number $C = C_1 C_0$, $C = (N)$ mod 3 where N is the binary number $I_2 I_1 I_0$, as shown in Figure 5.7, for all possible values of I_2, I_1, I_0. □

I_2	I_1	I_0	N	C	C_1	C_0
0	0	0	0	0	0	0
0	0	1	1	1	0	1
0	1	0	2	2	1	0
0	1	1	3	0	0	0
1	0	0	4	1	0	1
1	0	1	5	2	1	0
1	1	0	6	0	0	0
1	1	1	7	1	0	1

Figure 5.7 A 3-Bit Residue Code with $m = 3$

We will now prove that for this type of residue code, the check bits of the sum (product) of a set of operands is equal to the sum (product) of the check bits of the operands.

---

*Given integers N,m, where $0 < m$, there is a unique representation of N of the form $N = b_1 \cdot m + b_2$ where b_1, b_2 are integers and $0 \le b_2 < m$. Then (N) modulo m equals b_2.

Theorem 5.1:   Let $\{a_i\}$ be a set of operands with check bits $C^i = (a_i)$ mod m. The residue of the sum is $(\Sigma\ a_i)$ mod m and the residue of the product is $(\Pi\ a_i)$ mod m. Then

(a) $(\Sigma\ a_i)$ mod $m = (\Sigma\ (a_i)$ mod $m)$ mod m. (Check bits of sum equal sum of check bits modulo m.)

(b) $(\Pi\ a_i)$ mod $m = (\Pi\ (a_i)$ mod $m)$ mod m. (Check bits of product equal product of check bits modulo m.)

Proof: Let $a_i = k_{i1}m + k_{i2}$ where $0 \leq k_{i2} < m$.

(a) Then $(\Sigma\ a_i)$ mod $m = (\Sigma\ (k_{i1}m + k_{i2}))$ mod $m = (\Sigma\ k_{i2})$ mod $m = (\Sigma\ (a_i)$ mod $m)$ mod m.

(b) Then $(\Pi\ a_i)$ mod $m = (\Pi\ (k_{i1}m + k_{i2}))$ mod $m = (\Pi\ k_{i2})$ mod $m = (\Pi\ (a_i)$ mod $m)$ mod m.   □

Example 5.5:   (a) Consider the addition shown below, using residue codes with $m = 3$.

information bits				check bits	
0	0	1	0	1	0
0	1	0	0	0	1
0	1	1	0	1	1

The information bits of the sum represent the number 6, and (6) mod 3 $=0$. The sum of the check bits mod 3 is also 0. Thus, the sum of the check bits modulo m is equal to the check bits of the sum.

(b) Consider the multiplication shown below using residue codes with $m = 3$. The product of the check bits modulo m is equal to 2. The information bits of the product represent the number 8 and (8) mod 3 = 2. Thus the product of the check bits modulo m is equal to the check bits of the product.

information bits				check bits	
0	0	1	0	1	0
0	1	0	1	0	1
1	0	0	0	1	0

□

The use of residue codes to check addition is illustrated by the system of Figure 5.8 which computes the check bits $C(A + B)$ of the sum $A + B$

and compares it to the modulo m sum of the check bits $(C(A) + C(B))$ mod m.

Let us now consider the error detecting capabilities of this class of residue codes. If an entire word has s bits (i.e., $q + p = s$), then an error pattern E can be defined as an s-bit binary vector $(e_{s-1}, e_{s-2}, \ldots, e_0)$ where $e_i = 1$ if bit i is in error and $e_i = 0$ if bit i is correct. For a number N with check bits C, where $C = (N)$ mod m, such an error changes N to N' and C to C'. If $C' = (N')$ mod m, the error will not be detected. Let us first consider error patterns affecting a single bit.

Theorem 5.2:   In a residue code with m odd, all single bit errors are detected.

Proof: We must consider two cases.

Case 1: The single erroneous bit is an information bit. Then $N' = N \pm 2^i$ if bit i of the information segment is in error. Since there is just a single error $C = C'$. Thus $C' = (N')$ mod m if and only if (N') mod $m = (N)$ mod m. This implies that $(N \pm 2^i)$ mod $m = (N)$ mod m. But $(N \pm 2^i)$ mod $m = ((N)$ mod $m \pm (2^i)$ mod $m)$ mod m. For m odd, (2^i) mod $m \neq 0$ and hence the error is detected.

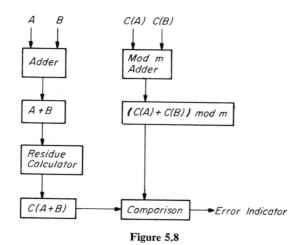

Figure 5.8

Case 2: The single erroneous bit is a check bit. Then $N = N'$ and $C' = (C \pm 2^i)$ mod m where bit i of the check segment is in error. The error is detected unless $C' = C$. This implies that $C = (C \pm 2^i)$ mod m which is impossible for m odd and hence all single errors are detected.   □

If m is odd, some single bit errors may be indistinguishable. For m even, some single errors may not even be detected.

Example 5.6:   (a) Let $m = 3$. Consider the code word 1 1 0 0 0 (rightmost two bits are check bits) with error pattern 0 1 0 0 0. The erroneous word is 1 0 0 0 0 which is not a code word and hence the error is detected. The same erroneous word may result from the code word 0 0 0 0 0 and the error pattern 1 0 0 0 0. Thus this code is not error correcting for single bit errors.

(b) Let $m = 2$. Consider the code word 1 1 0 0 (rightmost bit is only check bit) with error pattern 0 1 0 0 resulting in the word 1 0 0 0. Since this is a valid code word, the error will not be detected.   □

Thus the parameter m must be odd for the code to be single error detecting. As m increases, the number of check bits required increases. The error detecting capability remains unchanged for single bit errors. However, the error correcting capabilities and multiple bit error detecting capabilities vary with the specific value of m [32] in a complex manner. These capabilities will not be considered herein.

Multiple Bit Errors

The error detecting capabilities of codes with respect to multiple bit errors are also of interest. For a parity check code, all errors which affect odd number of bits will be detected. It should be noted, however, that the most probable multiple bit errors in many technologies are not random, but have some special properties associated with them such as *unidirectional errors* (all erroneous bits have the same value), and *adjacent bit* errors (all bits affected by an error form a connected string of bits). Some common codes are useful with respect to such error patterns.

The k/n (k out of n) code consists of n-bit words in which each code word has exactly k 1-bits. These codes detect all unidirectional multiple faults (Exercise).

In the *modified residue check code,* $m - 1$ check bits are defined so that the total number of 1-bits in a code word is a multiple of a parameter m. This code, which is a generalization of the parity check code, detects all unidirectional errors affecting less than m bits.

Given a set of kn bits arranged as k n-bit words, adding a parity check bit to each word results in k ($n + 1$)-bit words in which any single bit error can be detected as well as any multiple bit error so long as no word has more than one erroneous bit. Alternatively, we can define one n-bit check word C, where for all i, $1 \leq i \leq n$, the ith bit of C is a parity check over the ith-bit of all k words. This results in ($k + 1$) n-bit words in which all single faults are detected, all multiple faults within one word are detected, as are multiple faults involving different bits of different words. This technique can also be used with error correcting codes to obtain multiple bit error correction.

5.1.2 Checking Circuits

The use of hardware (i.e., checking circuits in conjunction with coded outputs) to detect faults has the following advantages over testing by the use of diagnostic software programs.

(1) Intermittent faults are detected.

(2) Errors are immediately detected upon occurrence. This prevents corruption of data.

(3) The distribution of checkers throughout a digital system provides a good measure of the location of a fault by the location at which it is detected.

(4) Software diagnostic program is eliminated, or at least simplified.

The use of hardware checking can be combined with a general reliability strategy called *rollback*, in which the status of a system is stored periodically, and upon detection of an error the system is reconfigured to its most recent previous valid condition and the last sequence of operations is attempted again. Repeated failures cause an interrupt. (This strategy is effective for intermittent failures of short duration.)

There are also several disadvantages associated with hardware testing, including the following:

(1) More hardware is required, including a hardware checker.

(2) Additional hardware must be checked or tested *(checking the checker problem)*. In general, some faults cannot be automatically detected. Faults in this *hardcore* must still be tested by a diagnostic program.

Thus the use of a hardware testing philosophy raises the problem of how to handle faults in the checking unit. This has led to the study of *totally self-checking circuits (and checkers)*. A circuit is *fault secure* for a set of faults F, if for any fault in F, and any allowable (code) input, the output is a non-code word or the correct code word, never an incorrect code word. A circuit is *self-testing* for a set of faults F if for any fault α in F, there exists an allowable (code) input which detects α. A *totally self-checking circuit* is both fault secure and self testing for all faults (in the set of faults of interest). Fault secureness insures that the circuit is operating properly if the output is a code word. Self testing insures that it is possible for any fault to be detected during normal operation. Hence a totally self-checking circuit need not have a special diagnostic program but can be completely tested using hardware diagnosis.* One intrinsic difficulty associated with such diagnosis is the possibility of faults within the checker. For the system to be totally self-checking, both the circuit and the checker must also be self-testing and fault secure. Those faults which cannot be detected in this manner must be tested by a diagnostic program and are sometimes referred to as *hardcore*. It is desirable to design the checking circuit so that hardcore is localized and/or minimized.

Very little is known about the general design of self checking circuits. It is easily proven that the inputs of such a circuit must be coded in a distance d code where d is at least two in order for the circuit to be fault secure with respect to stuck type input faults. The outputs must be similarly coded to be fault secure with respect to stuck type output faults. If it is assumed that there are no input faults and the inputs are uncoded, then self testing is automatically obtained and the circuit must only be designed to be fault secure. If the outputs of the circuit are defined to be of even parity, they define a distance two code. However, it is possible for a single fault to affect

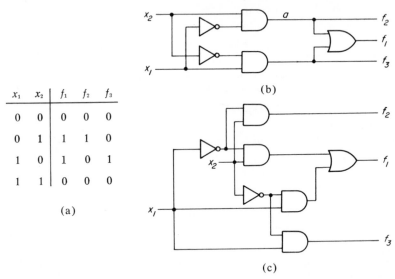

x_1	x_2	f_1	f_2	f_3
0	0	0	0	0
0	1	1	1	0
1	0	1	0	1
1	1	0	0	0

(a)

(b)

(c)

Figure 5.9

---

*If a circuit is totally self testing for a set of faults F, then it is possible for any fault in F to be detected during normal operation by hardware checking. Of significance is the probability that that fault will be detected within t units of time from its occurrence. The expected value of t has been referred to as the *error latency* of the circuit [33]. If F is the set of single stuck type faults, hardware detection is only useful if the error latency of the circuit is much less than the expected time for a second fault to occur so that a multiple fault does not exist.

two outputs as illustrated by the fault a s-a-0 with input $x_1 = 0$, $x_2 = 1$ in the circuit of Figure 5.9(b). In this case the circuit is not fault secure. Ko [22] has developed several design procedures which can be used to prevent such errors in circuits whose outputs satisfy parity conditions. One of these procedures alters the fanout of a node by generation of duplicated signals to ensure odd parity errors (Figure 5.9(c)). Thus if no input faults are considered, it is possible to design fault secure realizations of arbitrary combinational functions.

Considerably more work has been done on the design of self checking checkers. A checker (for a specific code) is usually defined as a single output circuit whose output takes the value 0 for any input corresponding to a code word and takes the value 1 for any input corresponding to a non-code input. This output is used as an error indication. Since the output is 0 for all code inputs, a checker cannot be designed so as to be self testing for a s-a-0 fault on the output of the checker since this fault can only be detected by a non-code input. Signals which have only one possible value during normal operation are called *passive*. One approach to the design of self checking checkers is to replace all passive signals by a pair of signals each of which, during normal operation, may take on both logical values, 0 and 1. Thus a checker may be designed, as shown in Figure 5.10, where the two outputs z_1, z_2 of C_1 take the values $(0,1)$ and $(1,0)$ for code inputs and the values $(0,0)$ and $(1,1)$ for non-code inputs. If we assume that a single signal is necessary for error indication, additional logic is required to generate the output z from z_1 and z_2. In this case C_2 generates the exclusive-OR of z_1 and z_2. For some codes it is possible to realize a checker in this manner so that C_1 is totally self checking. However, C_2 is always non-self

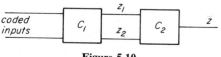

Figure 5.10

testing. Thus the hardcore (i.e., the logic which is not self testable) has actually been localized and minimized rather than eliminated.

The concept of realizing a binary valued function f with two outputs can be formalized as follows. Consider a binary function f with values 0,1, which are mapped into two binary signals z_1, z_2 in which $(z_1, z_2) = (0,1)$ or $(1,0)$ corresponds to $f = 0$ and $(z_1, z_2) = (0,0)$ or $(1,1)$ corresponds to $f = 1$. The set of functions (z_1, z_2) is called a *morphic function* corresponding to f. It is possible to design some morphic functions so as to be totally self checking.

Consider the parity check function $x_1 \oplus x_2 \oplus x_3$. The normal single output function is represented by the Karnaugh map shown in Figure 5.11. The corresponding morphic function (z_1, z_2) is represented by the Karnaugh maps of Figure 5.12 where each a_i can be 0 or 1.

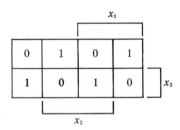

Figure 5.11   Karnaugh Map of 3-Input Parity Check Function

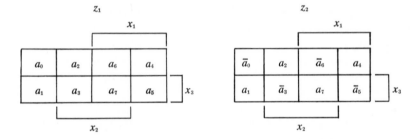

Figure 5.12   Karnaugh Maps Representing Morphic Function
Corresponding to 3-Input Parity Check Function

In general, corresponding to any n-input function there are 2^{2^n} morphic function pairs. The question remains, can these values of a_i be selected in such a manner that both z_1 and z_2 are totally self checking. For the above example, the choice $a_0, a_1, a_2, a_3 = 0$, $a_4, a_5, a_6, a_7 = 1$ leads to the circuit shown in Figure 5.13(a), which can be verified to be totally self-checking

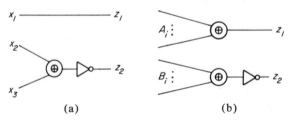

Figure 5.13   (a) Self-checking 3-bit Parity Checker
(b) General Self Checking Parity Checker

where the code inputs correspond to all inputs with an even number of 1's. This type of realization can be generalized for an n-input parity check circuit. In the totally self checking circuit, the set of n variables is partitioned into two disjoint sets, A_i, B_i each with at least one variable, and parity check functions of these two variable sets are realized. The resultant circuit, shown in Figure 5.13(b), is totally self-checking. (An inverter on one of the outputs is required to produce outputs of $(0,1)$ or $(1,0)$ for even parity inputs.) This morphic function realization can be shown to be a minor modification of a normal checker realization shown in Figure 5.14. Thus the hardcore of the normal circuit has now been placed with the decision logic (which interprets the error identification signals $(0,0)$ and $(1,1)$ and produces one error signal). Hardcore has been *localized* rather than eliminated.

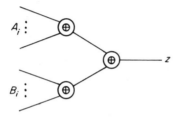

Figure 5.14 Parity Check Circuit

Anderson [2,3] has shown how a totally self-checking checker circuit can be designed for a $k/2k$ code. The totally self-checking $k/2k$ code checker is designed as follows: The checker has two outputs f and g. The $2k$ inputs are partitioned into two disjoint subsets $\mathbf{x}_A = (x_1, x_2, \ldots, x_k)$ and $\mathbf{x}_B = (x_{k+1}, x_{k+2}, \ldots, x_{2k})$. The function f will be specified to have the value 1 if and only if i or more of the variables in $\mathbf{x}_A$ have the value 1 and $k - i$ or more of the variables in $\mathbf{x}_B$ have the value 1, for i odd. Similarly, g has the value 1 if and only if i or more of the variables in $\mathbf{x}_A$ have the value 1 and $k - i$ or more of the variables in $\mathbf{x}_B$ have the value 1, for i even. If $T_i(\mathbf{x})$ represents the function which has the value 1 if and only if i or more of the variables in $\mathbf{x}$ have the value 1, then

$$f = \sum_{i=0}^{k} T_i(\mathbf{x}_A) \cdot T_{k-i}(\mathbf{x}_B) \qquad i \text{ odd}$$

and

$$g = \sum_{i=0}^{k} T_i(\mathbf{x}_A) \cdot T_{k-i}(\mathbf{x}_B) \qquad i \text{ even}$$

For code inputs (i.e., exactly k of the $2k$ variables have the value 1) $f = 1$ and $g = 0$ or $f = 0$ and $g = 1$, while for non-code inputs $f = 0$ and $g = 0$ if fewer than k variables are 1, and $f = 1$ and $g = 1$ if more than k variables have the value 1. For $k = 3$,

$$f = T_1(x_1,x_2,x_3) \cdot T_2(x_4,x_5,x_6) + T_3(x_1,x_2,x_3) \cdot T_0(x_4,x_5,x_6)$$
$$= (x_1 + x_2 + x_3)(x_4x_5 + x_4x_6 + x_5x_6) + x_1x_2x_3$$

and

$$g = T_0(x_1,x_2,x_3) \cdot T_3(x_4,x_5,x_6) + T_2(x_1,x_2,x_3) \cdot T_1(x_4,x_5,x_6)$$
$$= x_4x_5x_6 + (x_1x_2 + x_1x_3 + x_2x_3)(x_4 + x_5 + x_6).$$

The general form of the circuit is as shown in Figure 5.15. $T_{A_{odd}}$ has outputs $T_i(x_A)$, for all odd i, $0 \le i \le k$. $T_{A_{even}}$, $T_{B_{odd}}$, and $T_{B_{even}}$ are similarly defined. It can be shown that this circuit is both self-testing and fault secure for all single stuck type faults and hence is totally self checking. Other realizations of this function have a significant amount of hardcore.

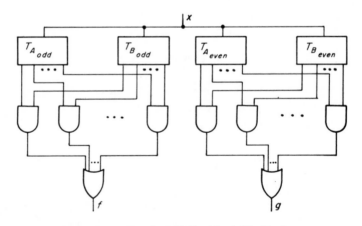

Figure 5.15 Totally Self-Checking k/2k Checker

The self checking $k/2k$ checker can also be used to realize a general k/n checker where $n \ne 2k$. The general form of the realization is shown in Figure 5.16. The AND array consists of a single level of $\binom{n}{k}$ k-input AND gates which generate all possible products of k of the n variables. Thus, for a code word input, the output of this array will have exactly one

1-signal while for non-code inputs the number of 1-signal outputs should not be equal to one. The OR array consists of a single level of OR gates which converts the $1 \big/ \binom{n}{k}$ code on the z signals to a $p/2p$ code, where p must satisfy the constraint

$$2^p \leq \binom{n}{k} \leq \binom{2p}{p}.$$

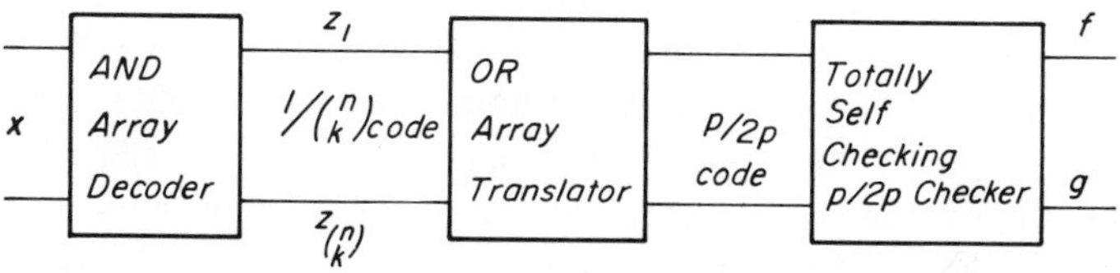

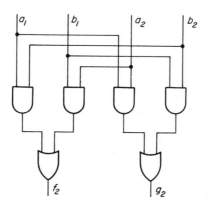

Figure 5.16

Anderson [2] has also developed procedures for the design of totally self checking equality checkers which determine if two k-bit words $(a_1, a_2, \ldots, a_k)$ and $(a'_1, a'_2, \ldots, a'_k)$ are equal (i.e., $a_i = a'_i$ for all i). For $k = 2$ the circuit is as shown in Figure 5.17, where $b_i = \bar{a}'_i$. This can be generalized to a totally self checking k-bit equality checker (Problem 5.10). Such an equality checker can be used as the basis for a checker for various

Figure 5.17

operations and codes as illustrated by the system of Figure 5.8, in which a comparison circuit is used to check addition on residue coded words.

However, no general procedures for the design of self checking checkers have been developed.

As we have seen, if we assume that a single signal is necessary for error indication, design of totally self checking circuits *minimizes* hardcore rather than actually *eliminating* it. Referring to Figure 5.10, if C_1 is to be totally self checking and C_2 is to represent hardcore, the question arises whether the logic in C_1 can be simplified substantially if C_2 is made somewhat more complex. Gogineni [14] has shown that in the case of a general k/n checker, where $n \neq 2k$, substantial savings in logic can be achieved if C_1 is defined to be a 3 output circuit and C_2 is defined to be a 3 bit parity check circuit. It thus appears likely that a general theory of self checking circuits would not be limited to two-output morphic functions and would explicitly recognize the tradeoff between hardcore and degree of self checking. In this connection Gogineni has considered a class of circuits which are totally fault secure but only partially self testing, and Wakerly [38] has considered a class of circuits which are totally self testing but are only fault secure for a subset of all possible inputs. However, no general design procedures for such circuits have yet been developed.

5.1.3   Self Checking Sequential Circuits

The use of codes and the concepts of self checking design are also applicable to the design of self checking sequential circuits. Consider the sequential circuit model of Figure 5.18, in which the outputs and state

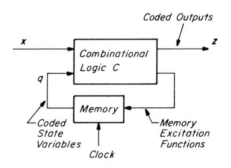

Figure 5.18

variables are coded. Self checking can be obtained by designing the combinational logic in such a way that:

(1) For any fault internal to C^*, and for any input x_i, either the output

---

*If input faults are also to be considered, the inputs x must be coded.

and the next state are both correct or the output and/or the next state is a non-code word.

(2) For any state q_e corresponding to a non-code word resulting from a fault α in C, and for any input x_i, the next state generated by C with fault α is a non-code word and the output is also a non-code word.

The net result from these conditions is that C serves as a checker on the coded state variables. Design procedures for the combinational logic for the memory excitation functions using k/n codes were initially developed by Tohma et al [36].* More economical logic designs were subsequently developed by others [10, 30].

A conceptually similar design procedure (Figure 5.19) was considered by Armstrong et al [4]. The outputs of the sequential circuit C_1 are encoded in a k/n code, which is input to a k/n checker. The checker generates a signal R_s which is required for the next clock (or for asynchronous circuits, the next input) to be generated. Thus for many faults the system will stop as soon as a faulty output is generated.

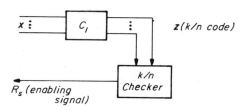

Figure 5.19

5.2 FAULT TOLERANT DESIGN

In some applications repair is impossible and hence either failure** must be eliminated or the probability of failure over a given time span must be made negligible. It is impossible to have components which are sufficiently reliable to accomplish this objective. Hence redundancy techniques, in the form of *fault masking* must be employed. The relation between fault masking (error correction) and self checking can be seen by referring to the systems of Figure 5.5(a) and (b). If the circuit output code is an error

---

*Tohma et al actually considered the design of fail-safe circuits (to be considered in Section 5.2.3) in which the generated output should not be an erroneous 0 for 0-fail safe (or an erroneous 1 for 1-fail safe). Similar procedures apply to the design of self checking circuits.

**By system failure we mean an error in an output of the system. Internal faults which do not result in output errors are permitted.

detecting code, the system can be made self-checking, while if the output code is an error correcting code, the system can be made fault masking.

The principal objectives of fault tolerant design are to increase the probability of system survival to some time T or to prolong the average (or expected) life of the system. The latter measure is referred to as the *mean time before failure (MTBF)*. For a system L, if $R(t)$ is a probability function which defines the probability that the system will not have failed up until time t, then the MTBF is defined by the following equation

$$MTBF = \int_{o}^{\infty} - t \, dR.$$

If the MTBF is assumed to be a constant, $1/\lambda$, where λ is the *failure rate* then we can solve for $R(t)$. The result is

$$R(t) = e^{-\lambda t}.$$

5.2.1   Triplicated Modular Redundancy

For a circuit having a single output, a single error correcting code requires two check bits. The code words are 0 0 0 and 1 1 1. This code corresponds to the conceptually simple redundancy scheme called *Triplicated Modular Redundancy (TMR)* in which the circuit is triplicated and the correction logic is an element with 3 inputs x,y,z which realizes the *majority function* $M(x,y,z) = xy + yz + xz$. This scheme is depicted in Figure 5.20. Barring input errors and faults in M, all single faults will lead to at most one input to M being in error, and hence the output z will be correct. For this case the redundancy ratio, which is defined as the amount of logic in the redundant system divided by the amount of logic in the individual or simplex system, is slightly larger than three.

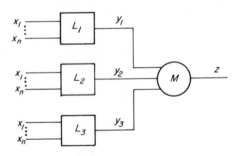

Figure 5.20   Basic TMR System

If we assume that the majority element in the TMR system does not fail, then the system fails only if any two or more subsystems L_i fail. If we assume that each of the subsystems has probability $R(t)$ of surviving to time t, then the triplicated system probability of survival is defined by

$$R'(t) = \underbrace{e^{-\lambda t}\, e^{-\lambda t}\, e^{-\lambda t}}_{} + \underbrace{3e^{-2\lambda t}\,(1 - e^{-\lambda t})}_{}$$

| Probability of all three of the subsystems surviving | Probability of any two of the subsystems surviving |

$$= 3e^{-2\lambda t} - 2e^{-3\lambda t}$$

If the probability of survival of the majority element is actually $e^{-\lambda' t}$, then the system survival probability must be multiplied by this factor. However, if L_i is significantly more complex than the majority element, then $\lambda' \ll \lambda$ and the overall effect on system survival is negligible. The preceding analysis is also conservative in the sense that it assumes the system will fail if any two subsystems fail. In fact, the system will continue to function properly unless the two subsystems fail for *the same input excitation*.

The functions $R(t)$ and $R'(t)$ are plotted in Figure 5.21. Note that for $t > t_0$, $R'(t) < R(t)$, indicating that the TMR system is more likely to have

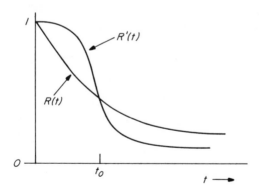

Figure 5.21   Graph of Functions $R(t)$ and $R'(t)$

failed than the irredundant circuit. This is due to the fact that the increased hardware in the TMR system causes the probability of two faults in that system at time t to exceed the probability of one fault in the simplex system at time t, for large t. For $t < t_0$, $R'(t) > R(t)$, indicating that the TMR system has a smaller probability of failure than the simplex system. The value of t_0, which depends on λ, is determined from the equation

$$3e^{-2\lambda t_0} - 2e^{-3\lambda t_0} - e^{-\lambda t_0} = 0$$

which has a solution $t_0 \cong \dfrac{.7}{\lambda}$. The *MTBF* of R' is equal to $5/6\lambda$ which is less than that of the simplex system. Thus the TMR system is useful for increased reliability (i.e., higher probability of system survival) over a relatively short period of time.

The concept of triplicated modular redundancy can also be applied on the subsystem level, as illustrated in Figure 5.22. In this case a single error in any subsystem (including the subsystem majority gates) will be cor-

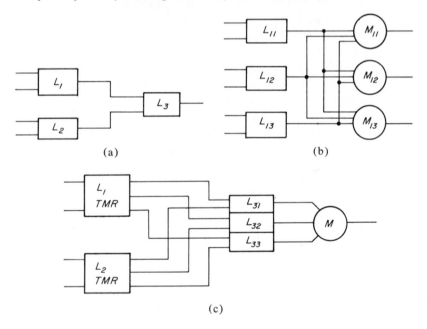

(a)   (b)

(c)

Figure 5.22   (a) A System Containing Three Modules (b) A TMR Subsystem for L_1 (c) System Designed from TMR Subsystems

rected at the system output. In addition, multiple errors which occur in different subsystems will be corrected. This scheme has been referred to as *multiplexing*.

5.2.2   N Modular Redundancy and Hybrid Redundancy

The concept of TMR can be generalized to N Modular Redundancy (NMR) in which there are N copies of the basic system, where $N \geq 3$ and N is odd. Assuming ideal majority elements, such a system would fail when S modules failed, where $S \geq (N + 1)/2$. In such a system all modules are active, and errors in a minority of the modules are masked. The basic system configuration never changes and hence this type of scheme is referred to as *static redundancy*. In a system which utilizes static redundancy, system reliability tends to decrease with age.

In another type of redundancy scheme a failed module could be repaired or replaced by a spare module. In a system which utilized such a *dynamic* redundancy scheme, where the system reconfigures after each fault, the system reliability remains relatively constant over a long period of time (i.e., no substantial aging effect).

A *hybrid redundant* system is an example of dynamic redundancy where reconfiguration occurs automatically after detection of a fault. Such a system is depicted in Figure 5.23(a). The switching network gates the outputs of 3 of the n modules $L_1, L_2, \ldots, L_n$ to the correction circuit. This circuit generates the correct output $Z = M(z_1, z_2, z_3)$ and another output C. This is a correction signal which specifies the faulty module in case one of the three inputs to the correction unit is different than the other two. The switching network then replaces (switches out) the faulty module L_i and switches in a module L_j which has not previously been gated to the correction circuit. If the switching network and correction circuit do not fail, the system will survive until $n - 1$ modules fail as compared to $(n + 1)/2$ for the static redundancy scheme, in which there is no reconfiguration by switching.

In a hybrid redundant system the design of the circuit to perform the module switching is of great importance since the reliability of the switch has a great effect on the overall system reliability. An efficient switch design for a hybrid redundant system with three active units and two spares is shown in Figure 5.23(b).

Corresponding to each of the five modules there is an exclusive-OR element which is used to set a flip-flop M_i to record disagreement between the module and the voter output. The delay element is used to prevent a flip-flop from being set due to a transient signal. The logic circuits, A_i, $1 \leq i \leq 5$, constitute an iterative array which is used to determine the first three modules which have not previously failed (Problem 5.11). The ouputs of this array are used to connect these first three unfailed modules through

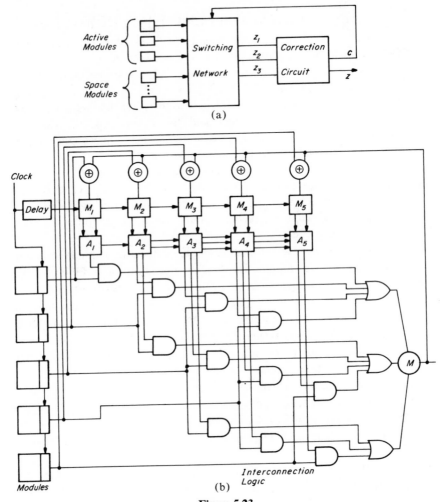

Figure 5.23

the interconnection logic to the voter M, the ith such module being connected to the ith voter input, $1 \leq i \leq 3$.

If the switching network of a hybrid redundant system does fail, there are two distinct modes of failure: (1) some good module cannot be switched in, or (2) some faulty module cannot be switched out.

In (1), the error can be determined by the correction circuit, which then causes the switching network to switch in another module. This case corresponds to a hybrid system with $(n - 1)$ good modules. However, (2) corresponds to a system with one permanently faulty module and hence a duplicated rather than a triplicated system. In such a system error detection remains possible but error correction is impossible. Hence one type of failure is much more serious than the other. It is possible to design a system so that no single gate input failure prevents the system from switching out a module as depicted in Figure 5.24(a). Here C_1 and C_2 are assumed independent. Note that with a single gating control signal C, the fault C s-a-1

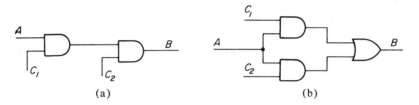

(a)   (b)

Figure 5.24   (a) Fail safe switching out circuit and
(b) fail safe switching in circuit

would result in $B = A$ and hence would prevent a module from being switched out. In the circuit of Figure 5.24(b), no single gate input fault prevents setting B equal to A, i.e., switching in a unit. Such designs are said to be fail safe with respect to switching out or switching in respectively.*

5.2.3   Fail Safe Design

Fail safe design is important in systems in which one type of failure is much worse than the other. Examples of such systems include a traffic control system (two red lights preferable to two green lights at an intersection) and an airplane landing system (preferable to be stuck in open position than in closed position). A circuit is *0(1) fail safe* if no single fault can produce an incorrect 1(0) (or more realistically if the probability of an incorrect 1(0) is very small). The output value 0(1) is called the *safeside* output. If an incorrect 1 output is disastrous, 0 fail safe design is used while 1 fail safe design protects against a disastrous 0 output. Fail safe systems can be designed using an error detecting code concept as illustrated in Figure 5.25. Upon receipt of a non-code word the correction circuit generates the "safe" output and, if in an environment in which repair is possible, an error signal is generated. Such a system is fail safe except for faults in the correction circuit.

---

*Note that the system is not fail safe with respect to a fault on the output B.

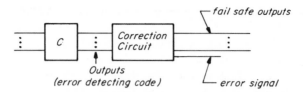

Figure 5.25   Fail Safe System

Example 5.7:   Consider the design of a fail safe circuit to realize the functions z_1, z_2, specified in the truth table of Figure 5.26(a). The output z_1 is to be 0 fail safe and z_2 is to be 1 fail safe. We define an even parity check bit z_3, as shown in Figure 5.26(a), and specify a correction circuit truth table, as shown in Figure 5.26(b), with inputs z_1, z_2, z_3 and output Q_1 which is equal to z_1 for all code words and equal to 0 for all non-code words,

x_1	x_2	x_3	z_1	z_2	z_3
0	0	0	0	1	1
0	0	1	0	0	0
0	1	0	1	0	1
0	1	1	1	0	1
1	0	0	0	1	1
1	0	1	1	1	0
1	1	0	0	0	0
1	1	1	1	0	1

(a)

z_1	z_2	z_3	Q_1	Q_2	Q_3
0	0	0	0	0	0
0	0	1	0	1	1
0	1	0	0	1	1
0	1	1	0	1	0
1	0	0	0	1	1
1	0	1	1	0	0
1	1	0	1	1	0
1	1	1	0	1	1

(b)

Figure 5.26

Q_2 which is equal to z_2 for all code words and equal to 1 for all non-code words, and an error signal Q_3 which is equal to 0 for all code words and equal to 1 for all non-code words. The fail safe circuit is then realized as shown in Figure 5.25 with the design of C constrained so that for any input, any fault affects only one output.   □

Fail safe sequential circuits can be designed using state assignments corresponding to k/n codes in a manner similar to the design of self checking sequential circuits (Section 5.1.3). However, in this application the generation of the outputs must be modified as follows:

(1) For any fault internal to C and for any input x_i the output is either correct or safeside and the next state is either correct or a non-code word (i.e., not k/n).

(2) For any state q_e corresponding to a non-code word which results from a fault α in C, and for any input x_i, the output generated by C with fault α is safeside and the next state generated is a non-code word.

Several procedures for the design of such circuits have been developed [10, 30, 36].

Fault Tolerant Systems

Several fault tolerant computing systems have been designed and are described in the literature [6, 7, 20]. Typically these systems utilize many of the design procedures described in the preceding sections. Some common features include: (1) the use of error detecting or correcting codes and self checking in conjunction with rollback, and (2) the use of massive redundancy techniques (such as TMR) for critical párts of the system.

One of the more widely utilized maintenance techniques involves the extensive use of codes and automatic hardware checkers, in conjunction with *rollback* or *retry*. In such systems the system status is periodically stored. Upon detection of an error, the system is reconfigured (rolled-back) to its most recently stored status and the subsequent instructions are repeated (retried). This strategy is effective for intermittent faults which constitute a substantial percentage of all faults in many systems. The implementation of this maintenance technique requires additional hardware including snapshot register and scratchpad memories as well as special software.

In a comparative study Wensley et al [39] evaluate various combinations of fault redundancy techniques such as error detection, error correction, duplication, and triplication in the design of a computer to support a time-sharing system. Important attributes such as percentage of redundancy, probability of error, single fault system degradation, and mean-time to system unavailability are evaluated. The study concludes that adequate fault tolerant design techniques exist for applications with high reliability requirements.

5.2.4   Coverage in Redundant Systems

In our previous analysis of system reliability we assumed that the system always successfully reconfigured until no more fault-free modules were available. However, in practice the system may be unable to successfully reconfigure from certain faults. Such faults are said to be *uncovered*. The percentage of covered faults (i.e., those from which the system can successfully reconfigure) is called the *coverage* of the system. As we shall see, the concept of coverage is very important in the computation of system reliability.

We shall consider a system in which all modules are duplicated and fault detection is obtained by comparison (matching) of the outputs of the duplicated subsystems. An example of such a system is the electronic telephone switching system, ESS 1 [11, 21]. The basic system is duplicated. Both modules process the same data simultaneously and continuously. However, one module (active) is controlling the switching network while the other module (standby) is being used to check the results of the active unit. These results are compared by a match circuit (Figure 5.27). In this manner, errors are automatically detected but not located. Upon occurrence of an error, indicated by a mismatch, the active unit and standby unit run diagnostic programs to determine which module is faulty, the active, the standby, or the match circuit. If it is determined that the active unit is faulty, the standby unit is switched to active. Otherwise, the active unit remains on-line, and repair is initiated for the faulty unit. Note that some faults in the

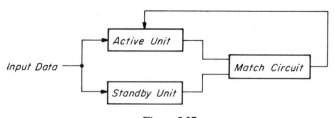

Figure 5.27

active unit may be improperly diagnosed, since the unit is diagnosing itself. For such faults, the incorrect unit may stay on-line.

System failure in such an idealized model of a duplicated repairable system can be represented as a Markov process consisting of three states, S_1 representing the condition that both units are operational, S_2 representing the condition that one module is inoperative and S_3 representing the condition that both modules are inoperative (i.e., the system is down). Assuming that the MTBF of a module is $1/\lambda_1$ and the mean time to repair is $1/\lambda_2$, the idealized system (before system failure) can be represented by the graph of Figure 5.28(a), where the value on an arc from S_i to S_j represents the incremental probability that a system in state S_i at time t will be in S_j at time $t + \Delta t$.

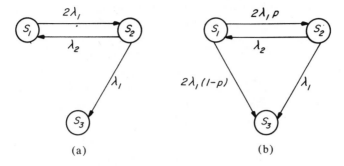

Figure 5.28 (a) Idealized Model of System (b) Model of System with Coverage p

Note that the system fails if the second unit fails before the first unit is repaired. Let $P_i(t)$ be the probability that the system is in state S_i at time t, assuming at $t = 0$ it is in state S_1. Then

$$\frac{dP_1(t)}{dt} = \underbrace{-2\lambda_1 P_1(t)}_{\substack{\text{Probability} \\ \text{of going} \\ \text{from } S_1 \text{ to} \\ S_2}} + \underbrace{\lambda_2(t)P_2(t)}_{\substack{\text{Probability} \\ \text{of going} \\ \text{from } S_2 \text{ to} \\ S_1}}$$

$$\frac{dP_2(t)}{dt} = \underbrace{2\lambda_1 P_1(t)}_{\substack{\text{Probability} \\ \text{of going} \\ \text{from } S_1 \text{ to} \\ S_2}} \underbrace{-(\lambda_1 + \lambda_2)P_2(t)}_{\substack{\text{Probability} \\ \text{of going} \\ \text{from } S_1 \text{ or} \\ S_3 \text{ to } S_2}}$$

$$\frac{dP_3(t)}{dt} = \underbrace{\lambda_1 P_2(t)}_{\substack{\text{Probability} \\ \text{of going} \\ \text{from } S_2 \text{ to} \\ S_3}}$$

$$P_1(0) = 1$$

$$P_1(t) + P_2(t) + P_3(t) = 1.$$

Using standard calculus techniques, these equations can be solved and the MTBF is found to be approximately $\lambda_2/2\lambda_1^2$. Assuming $1/\lambda_1 = 3$ months and $1/\lambda_2 = 2$ hours, the MTBF is about 100 years. However, as previously mentioned, the system may also fail due to an inability to recover from some single faults. The Markov process defined by a duplex system with coverage p is represented by the graph of Figure 5.28(b). Note that the graph of Figure 5.28(a) corresponds to the special case $p = 1$. Analysis of this case leads to the result

$$MTBF \approx \frac{\lambda_2}{2\lambda_1^2}\bigg/\left(1 + \frac{\lambda_2}{\lambda_1}(1 - p)\right).$$

The following table shows the value of the system MTBF for various values of p where $1/\lambda_1 = 3$ months and $1/\lambda_2 = 2$ hours.

p	MTBF (years)
1.0	100
.995	20
.99	10
.95	2.5
.9	1

Note that when $1 - p > \lambda_1/\lambda_2$, the imperfect coverage becomes the dominant factor in the failure rate of the system. This illustrates the importance of accurate modeling in reliability evaluation. A further refinement of this model, in which different classes of uncovered faults have different mean repair times, has been utilized in evaluating expected down time of a duplex system over a period of years [5].

5.3 A MATHEMATICAL MODEL OF SYSTEM DIAGNOSIS

System diagnosis is often performed using one subsystem to diagnose another subsystem. The ESS system employs this technique. However, a faulty module M_i may indicate that a good module M_j is faulty. Given a system of interconnected modules which diagnose each other it is interesting to determine which classes of faulty modules can be accurately diagnosed. Two measures of system diagnosability have been proposed corresponding to: (1) the simultaneous repair of all faulty modules, and (2) the repair of one faulty module at a time. A system is *one-step t-fault diagnosable* if any set of at most *t* faulty units can be correctly diagnosed. A system is *sequentially t-fault diagnosable* if, for any set of at most *t* faulty units, at least one of the faulty units can be identified. This unit can then be replaced, the diagnosis repeated, and another faulty unit identified. In at most *t* iterations the system is completely repaired.

A system may be represented by a *diagnostic graph* with a node for each subsystem and an arc from node *i* to node *j* if the subsystem represented by node *i* diagnoses the subsystem represented by node *j*. The outcome of this diagnosis is represented by a Boolean variable a_{ij} where $a_{ij} = 1$ if module *i* indicates module *j* is faulty, and $a_{ij} = 0$ if module *i* indicates module *j* is not faulty. The graph of Figure 5.29(a) represents a system of two modules which diagnose each other. If module 1 is faulty and module 2 is good, then $a_{21} = 1$, but a_{12} may be either 0 or 1. Since the value of a_{12} is indeterminate in this case it is left unspecified and the outcome of this diagnosis is represented as shown in the first line of the table of Figure 5.29(b). Similarily,

Faulty Module	a_{12}	a_{21}
1	—	1
2	1	—

(a)   (b)

Figure 5.29   Graph and Table Representation of System Diagnosis

the outcome of the diagnosis if module 2 is faulty is as represented in the second line of the table. Note that $a_{12} = a_{21} = 1$ can occur in either circumstance and hence this system cannot accurately diagnose single faulty modules. A specific set of faulty modules, *F*, is called a *fault condition* and the values of $\{a_{ij}\}$ produced by the fault condition *F* is called the *test outcome* of *F*. In general, a system is one step *t*-fault diagnosable if and only if, for any pair of fault conditions F_1, F_2 involving at most *t* modules, there is some variable a_{ij} which takes the value of 0 in the test outcome of F_1 and 1 in the test outcome of F_2 or vice-versa. For the system of Figure 5.30(a) all single fault conditions and the associated test outcomes are listed in the first three lines of the table of Figure 5.30(b). Since the test outcomes for each pair of these conditions satisfies the aforementioned property, the system is one-step, 1-fault diagnosable. The table of Figure 5.30(c) indicates the faulty module (assuming at most one such module exists) for all possible values of the variable set (a_{12}, a_{23}, a_{31}). The system is not one-step, 2-fault diagnosable since lines 3 and 4 of the table of Figure 5.30(b) do not have the aforementioned property. Hence, the fault sets {1,2} and {3} are indistinguishable.

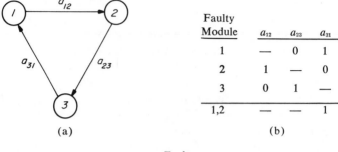

Faulty Module	a_{12}	a_{23}	a_{31}
1	—	0	1
2	1	—	0
3	0	1	—
1,2	—	—	1

(a)   (b)

a_{12}	a_{23}	a_{31}	Faulty Module
0	0	0	0
0	0	1	1
0	1	0	3
0	1	1	3
1	0	0	2
1	0	1	1
1	1	0	2
1	1	1	impossible with 1 fault

(c)

Figure 5.30   (a) A System Graph (b) Its Diagnostic Table
(c) Faulty Modules Associated with Symptoms

The following theorem presents some general necessary properties of the diagnostic graph required for 1-step diagnosability.

Theorem 5.3:   In a one-step t-fault diagnosable system:
(a) There must be at least $2t + 1$ subsystems (nodes).
(b) Each subsystem must be diagnosed by at least t other subsystems.

Proof: (a) Suppose there are $n \leq 2t$ nodes. Partition these nodes into two disjoint sets A and B each with at most t members. Then the diagnostic graph can be represented as shown in Figure 5.31, where a_{AA} is the set of

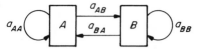

Figure 5.31   Partition of System Into Two Subsystems

connections within A, a_{BB} is the set of connections within B, a_{AB} is the set of connections from A to B, and a_{BA} is the set of connections from B to A. The following table shows the value of these variables if all units in A or all units in B are faulty.

faulty modules	a_{AA}	a_{AB}	a_{BA}	a_{BB}
all units in A	–	–	1	0
all units in B	0	1	–	–

Since no variable has the value 1 and 0 (or 0 and 1) respectively for these two fault conditions they are indistinguishable and hence the system is not one step t-fault diagnosable.

(b) Suppose some module i is tested by $k < t$ other modules $1, 2, \ldots, k$. Consider the following two sets of faulty modules.

$$A = \{1, 2, \ldots, k\}$$
$$B = \{1, 2, \ldots, k, i\}.$$

These fault conditions are indistinguishable and since neither contains more than t faults, the system is not one step t-fault diagnosable.   □

The conditions expressed in Theorem 5.3 are necessary but not sufficient for one-step t-fault diagnosability (see Problem 5.12).

In order for a system to be sequentially t-fault diagnosable for any set of fault conditions $(F_1, F_2, \ldots, F_r)$ which do not satisfy the conditions of 1-step diagnosability, all fault conditions in this set must have a common element (i.e., $F_1 \cap F_2 \cap \ldots \cap F_r \neq \phi$). Since the system in the proof of Theorem 5.3(a) does not satisfy this condition, any system with fewer than $2t + 1$ subsystems is not sequentially t-fault diagnosable.

Example 5.8:   We will examine the diagnostic capabilities of the system of Figure 5.32. Since $n = 5$, from Theorem 5.3(a) we know that the system

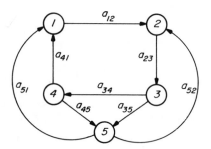

Figure 5.32   A Diagnostic System Graph

is at most 2-fault diagnosable (either one step or sequentially). Furthermore, since node 3 is only tested by node 2, it follows from Theorem 5.3(b) that the system is at most one step 1-fault diagnosable. The following table shows the test outcomes for all single fault conditions.

faulty modules	a_{12}	a_{23}	a_{34}	a_{35}	a_{41}	a_{45}	a_{51}	a_{52}
1	–	0	0	0	1	0	1	0
2	1	–	0	0	0	0	0	1
3	0	1	–	–	0	0	0	0
4	0	0	1	0	–	–	0	0
5	0	0	0	1	0	1	–	–

Since each pair of test outcomes satisfy the condition for one step diagnosability this system is one step 1-fault diagnosable. In order to determine if the system is sequentially 2-fault diagnosable we must examine the test outcomes for all fault conditions with two faulty modules and compare them among themselves. (It is not necessary to compare them with single fault patterns since the sequential fault condition between a double fault pattern and a single fault pattern will automatically be satisfied if the condition is satisfied between all pairs of double fault patterns). The following table shows the set of all double fault patterns. The sets of patterns which do not satisfy the one step diagnosable condition are {(2,3), (2,4)}, {(3,4), (3,5)}, each of which have a common element. Therefore, the system is sequentially 2-fault diagnosable since for any test outcome at least one module can definitely be determined as faulty and replaced.   □

faulty modules	a_{12}	a_{23}	a_{34}	a_{35}	a_{41}	a_{45}	a_{51}	a_{52}
(1,2)	–	–	0	0	1	0	1	1
(1,3)	–	1	–	–	1	0	1	0
(1,4)	–	0	1	0	–	–	1	0
(1,5)	–	0	0	1	1	1	–	–
(2,3)	1	–	–	–	0	0	0	1
(2,4)	1	–	1	0	–	–	0	1
(2,5)	1	–	0	1	0	1	–	–
(3,4)	0	1	–	–	–	–	0	0
(3,5)	0	1	–	–	0	1	–	–
(4,5)	0	0	1	1	–	–	–	–

This model of diagnosable systems is restricted to systems in which an individual module is capable of testing another module. The measures of diagnosability are restricted to worst case measures and to repair strategies in which only faulty modules are replaced. A more realistic model must consider systems in which more than one module may be required to test another module, as well as more realistic measures of diagnosability such as t/s *(t out of s) diagnosable,* where t $\leq$ s, in which at most s modules must be replaced in order to repair any set of at most t faulty modules.

In the two measures of diagnosis considered so far an upper bound on the number of faulty modules is assumed. Without this upper bound one step system repair or sequential system repair would, in general, be impossible. Thus, for the simple diagnostic graph consisting of a single loop, the test outcome $(a_{12}, a_{23}, \ldots, a_{(n-1)n}, a_{n1}) = (1,1,0,0,0, \ldots, 0)$ could be produced by any of the fault conditions shown in Figure 5.33. It is obvious that

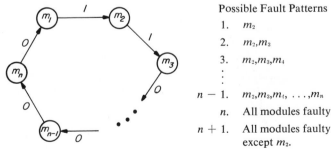

Possible Fault Patterns
1. m_2
2. m_2, m_3
3. m_2, m_3, m_4
  $\vdots$
$n-1$. $m_2, m_3, m_4, \ldots, m_n$
n. All modules faulty
$n+1$. All modules faulty except m_2.

Figure 5.33

repair of such a system is "probabilistic" in the sense that it depends on the relative probabilities of different fault patterns. Furthermore, if the upper bound on the number of possible faulty modules exceeds 1, one-step repair is not possible without the possible replacement of non-faulty modules. Because of these factors another measure has been proposed to incorporate this possibility. A system is one-step t/s (t out of s) diagnosable if any fault condition consisting of $f \leq t$ faulty modules can be diagnosed and repaired in one-step by replacement of at most s modules.

The value of $(s - f)$ as a function of t, the (probabilistic) upper bound on the number of faulty modules, is a measure of system diagnosability. For the simple system of Figure 5.33 it can be shown that in the worst case

$$s = \max_{f \leq t} \left(f \cdot (t - f + 2) - 1 \right).$$

The graph of Figure 5.34 shows s as a function of f for several values of t. Note that for a fixed value of f, small increases in t (the upper bound on the number of faulty modules) result in larger increases in s. This indicates that the more realistic the upper bound is for t, the easier repair will be. The choice of t thus involves a classical engineering tradeoff of cost vs. confidence of repair. It is also possible to let the value of t be determined by the

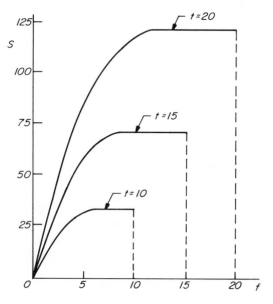

Figure 5.34

actual error pattern observed. This leads to the problem of determining from an error pattern, the minimal set (or sets) of faulty modules which could produce that pattern. Adham [1] has developed an efficient procedure for solving this problem.

In the model we have considered so far each test t_i is applied by a single module m_j to a single module m_k. Thus the test t_i is invalidated (i.e., does not provide useful diagnostic information) if and only if m_j is faulty. In an effort to handle more realistic systems this model has been extended to the case where a test t_i may be applied by a set of modules (collectively) to a single module [28]. In this case it is assumed that the outcome of t_i is invalidated if any one of the modules in the set applying the test is faulty. We can thus associate an invalidation expression consisting of a sum of literals with each test. This model has been further generalized to the case where the invalidation expression associated with a test can be any Boolean function [1]. For example, an invalidation expression of $m_i m_j + m_j m_k$ would indicate that the associated test was invalidated if and only if m_j was faulty and m_i or m_k was also faulty.

In addition to being applicable to the problems of testing and diagnosing digital systems, models such as those considered in this section are also intended to provide insight into the properties of easily diagnosable and easily testable systems and hence lead to the development of design procedures for easily maintainable systems, a topic we will now consider.

5.4 DESIGN TO SIMPLIFY TESTING

Several relatively simple concepts have been proposed which if incorporated in digital system design would greatly facilitate the problem of test generation. Some of the most significant of these concepts are as follows:

(1) *Test points:* Reserve some card pins for use as test points to increase testability. Use test points to break up long chains of logic. Some other suggested heuristics for test point placement include points of substantial fanin or fanout, outputs of memory elements, outputs of counters, etc.

(2) *Initialization:* Connect some flip-flop inputs, such as direct set or reset inputs, directly to input pins to facilitate initializaion.

(3) *Redundancy:* Remove redundancy by the use of test points with respect to which the circuit is irredundant, or model the redundant circuit as an irredundant circuit for test generation simplification.

(4) *Disabling logic:* Use additional logic in the form of interrupt circuitry on feedback loops to simplify sequential circuit testing.

(5) *Enabling logic:* Use additional enabling logic to provide individual access to modules in complex systems such as ROM's.

(6) *Internal clocks:* Allow internal clocks to be easily disabled and their clocking function replaced via an external clock. The same concept applies to one-shots.

We shall now consider in more detail some aspects of these rules as well as design procedures of more theoretical interest which minimize the number of tests required for fault detection and/or simplify the generation of such tests. Different realizations of the same function may require different numbers of excitation inputs as tests. Perhaps the best example of this is the n-variable parity check function which has the value 1 if and only if an odd number of the n variables are 1. A two level sum of products or product of sums realization of this function requires all 2^n possible excitations as tests to detect all single stuck type faults. However, this function can also be realized as a multi-level tree or cascade of two-bit parity check circuits and these realizations only require 4 tests, independent of n, to detect all single stuck type faults. This follows from the fact that for a fanout free linear circuit, any single error always propagates to the output, independent of the input vector.

5.4.1 Parity Cascade Realizations of Combinational Functions

In general, two-level circuit realizations usually require more tests than multi-level realizations of the same function. Because of the relative simplicity of testing systems consisting of modules of two bit parity check circuits, attempts have been made to realize arbitrary functions by factoring out such modules. It has been shown that any combinational function of n variables can be expressed in the form

$$f(x_1, \ldots, x_n) = C_0 \oplus C_1 x_1 \oplus C_2 x_2 \oplus \ldots \oplus C_n x_n \oplus C_{n+1} x_1 x_2 \oplus C_{n+2} x_1 x_3$$

$$\oplus \ldots \oplus C_{2^n-1} x_1 x_2 \ldots x_n.$$

where $C_i = 0,1$. This is called the Reed-Muller representation. There is one product term for each subset of the variables $x_1, x_2, \ldots, x_n$ plus a constant term C_0. Thus any function can be realized by the canonical circuit of Figure 5.35 which contains a linear cascade of two bit parity check circuits fed by AND gates, one corresponding to each *non-zero* C_i.

The constant C_0 has been replaced by a variable x_0 which has the value C_0 during normal operation. In order for the circuit to be irredundant x_0

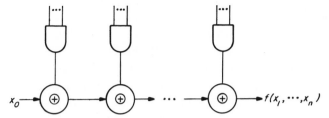

Figure 5.35 Canonical Realization of Combinational Functions

must be able to assume the value $\overline{C}_0$ during testing. If $C_0 = 0$, x_0 may be eliminated and the leftmost module replaced by a direct transmission of the AND gate output. Note that the AND gates corresponding to the non-zero coefficients C_i, $1 \leq i \leq n$, will be degenerate one input gates and hence can be eliminated.

Theorem 5.4: [29] In the Reed-Muller realization of an arbitrary combinational function $f(x_1, x_2, \ldots, x_n)$,

(a) at most $n + 4$ tests are required to detect all single stuck type faults, excluding input faults, and

(b) at most $3n + 4$ tests are required to detect all single stuck type faults including input faults.

Proof: (a) Consider the set T_1 consisting of the four tests defined in the following table.

x_0	x_1	x_2	x_3	$\ldots$	x_n
0	0	0	0	$\ldots$	0
0	1	1	1	$\ldots$	1
1	0	0	0	$\ldots$	0
1	1	1	1	$\ldots$	1

T_1 can be shown to detect all single stuck faults in the cascade of parity check circuits. The first test of T_1 results in applying the inputs $(0,0)$ to each cell in this cascade. The third test results in applying the inputs $(1,0)$ to each cell in the cascade. The second (fourth) test results in applying the input $(0,1)$ to all odd (even) cells and the input $(1,1)$ to all even (odd) cells. Hence the four tests apply all four combinations to each cell and hence completely test each cell. The fourth test of T_1 also detects all AND gate s-a-0 faults.

To test for s-a-1 faults on the AND gates we define a set of n tests, $T_2 = \{T_{21}, T_{22}, \ldots, T_{2n}\}$, where test T_{2i} has $x_i = 0$ and $x_j = 1$ for all $j \neq i$. The set of tests $T = T_1 \cup T_2$ detects all internal single stuck type faults.

(b) Consider a fault on a primary input x_i. In order to sensitize a single path from x_i to the output, consider all AND gates with an x_i input. Select such a gate G_i with the minimal number of other inputs. Define two tests, T_{i1} which specifies $x_i = 0$, all other inputs to G_i are 1 and all other inputs are 0, and T_{i0} which specifies $x_i = 1$, all other inputs to G_i are 1, and all other inputs are 0. Then T_{i1} detects x_i s-a-1 and T_{i0} detects x_i s-a-0. Repeating for all n inputs, we obtain a set of $2n$ tests for input faults. Combining these with the test set specified in the proof of part (a) of this theorem we obtain a set of $3n + 4$ tests which detect all single stuck type faults including primary input faults.   □

Theorem 5.4 thus provides us with an upper bound on the number of tests required for an n-input combinational function. (However, recall that this realization may be redundant.) As stated in Section 2.10.1, the number of tests $|T|$ required to detect all single (and multiple) stuck type faults in fanout-free combinational circuits is bounded by $2\sqrt{n} \leq |T| \leq n + 1$. Since fanout-free circuits are in general much easier to test than comparably sized circuits with fanout, this is probably a useful lower bound on the number of tests required for an n-input combinational function.

5.4.2   Placement of Observation and Control Points

Another design technique which has been proposed to simplify testing is to add observation points (outputs) and control points (inputs) to the circuit. (Observation points and control points are often referred to as *test points*.) This increases the pin and logic requirements of the circuit. Hence, it is desirable to limit this concept to the addition of a relatively few points.

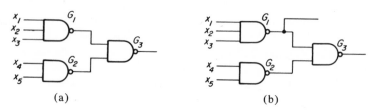

(a)   (b)

Figure 5.36   (a) A Combinational Circuit (b) The Same Circuit with Observation Point Added

Consider the circuit of Figure 5.36(a). It is easily shown that for this circuit, five tests are required to detect all single stuck type faults. However, if an observation point is added at the output of G_1, the set of four tests $T = \{0,1,1,1,0), (1,0,1,1,1), (1,1,0,0,1), (1,1,1,0,0)\}$ is sufficient to test for all stuck type faults. Note that T fails to detect the fault x_2 s-a-1 in the original circuit. This is because the only test that has $x_2 = 0$ does not propagate the effect of the fault through G_3. However, when the observation point is added, to detect the fault it is only necessary to propagate the error to the output of G_1. Adding an observation point at the output of G_2 instead of G_1 would not reduce the number of tests required.

The circuit of Figure 5.37(a) can be used to illustrate the benefit of control points which enable the value of a signal to be determined by an (external) control input. This circuit requires four tests to detect all single stuck type faults. If an observation point is added at the output of G_1 (the only possible useful position for one), four tests are still required. However, if a control point C is added at the output of G_1, with two observation points as shown in Figure 5.37(b), the set of three tests $T = \{(0,1,1,0),$ $(1,0,0,1), (1,1,1,0)\}$ detects all single stuck type faults. If $C = 0$, the two circuits are equivalent. Hence C is always 0 during normal operation, but may have the value 1 during testing. For the original circuit C is in effect

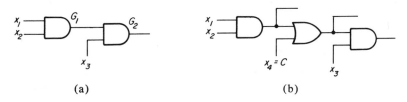

(a)   (b)

Figure 5.37   (a) A Combinational Circuit (b) The Same Circuit with
a Control Point and Observation Points

always 0, and any set of three tests which detect all faults on G produce only a single 1 output from G_1. To test G_2 we require at least two tests with G_1 outputs equal to 1. This is accomplished in the revised circuit in conjunction with testing of G_1, by the use of the control input.

Example 5.9:   [17] A three bit decoder requires eight tests to detect all single stuck type faults. Using three control points (with a common control signal x) as shown in Figure 5.38, the six tests specified in Figure 5.38 are sufficient to detect all such faults.   □

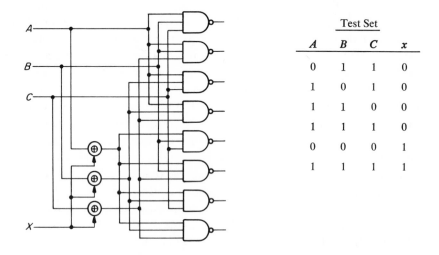

Test Set			
A	B	C	x
0	1	1	0
1	0	1	0
1	1	0	0
1	1	1	0
0	0	0	1
1	1	1	1

Figure 5.38   An easily testible decoder

For fanout free combinational circuits realized with all NAND gates (or all NOR gates), if each gate output is an observation point, $N_{max} + 1$ tests are sufficient to detect all single stuck faults where N_{max} is the maximum number of inputs on any gate. If all gate outputs of the original circuit are observation points and all gate inputs of the original circuit are control points, then this result is also valid for circuits with fanout. Since a circuit can be designed for any function using only 2-input NAND gates, three tests are sufficient to test any function.

Most circuits are severely limited as to the use of additional pins which are required for control and observation points. Therefore, an interesting problem is how would a limited number of pins be best utilized (i.e., where to place control and observation points). This problem has been considered by Hayes and Friedman [19] and they have obtained some results for the placement of observation points in fanout free combinational circuits. A useful heuristic seems to be to place k observation points so as to partition the circuit into $(k + 1)$ segments of approximately equal size. The problem of test point placement for more general classes of circuits is still open.

Controllability and Observability

The use of test points and observation points also has important applications to system level diagnosis. The concepts of *controllability* and *observability* are important in this application. Control refers to the ability to apply a complete set of tests to a subsystem via external inputs (i.e., control points) or previously verified subunits. Observation refers to the ability to observe the outputs of a subsystem via external outputs (i.e., observation points) or previously verified subunits. The property of direct access to subsystem inputs and outputs is referred to as *scan-in* and *scan-out* respectively. Consider the simple system of Figure 5.39, which consists of a linear cascade of modules.

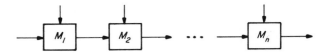

Figure 5.39   A Linear Cascade of Modules

If all intermodule connections were observable and controllable, tests could be applied directly to all subunits, and faulty subunits easily determined through direct observation of their outputs. However, this may be very expensive, especially with respect to pin requirements, and may not be necessary. An alternative diagnostic procedure is called *bootstrapping*. It is assumed that a small part of the system can be verified independent of the other parts of the system. This implies test design and/or system design so that tests detect faults in only one system segment (*isolation*). This verified part can then be used to check another subsystem. If that is normal, it can be used to check still another part of the system. At any time all subsystems which have already been verified can be used to test additional subsystems. There are no systematic techniques for system design and/or test design so as to diagnose a system in this manner. However, for a given system the placement of observation and control points to enable systematic bootstrap testing can be readily determined as illustrated in the following example.

Example 5.10:   Consider the system represented by the graph of Figure 5.40. The observability and controllability relationships between modules are expressed by the arcs of the graph.

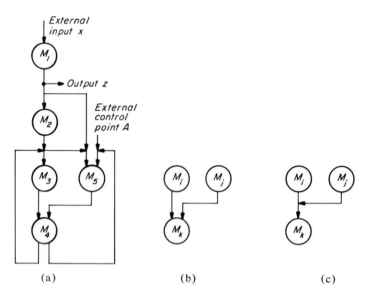

Figure 5.40

An arc from M_i to M_j indicates that M_i controls M_j. Separate arcs from M_i and M_j to M_k indicate that M_i and M_j collectively control M_k (Figure 5.40(b)). Arcs from M_i and M_j to M_k which combine (Figure 5.40(c)) indicate that M_k can be controlled by either M_i or M_j individually. Thus M_4 is controlled by the combined effects of M_3 and M_5 and is observed partially by M_3 and partially by M_5. Logic associated with the test point A, the input x and the output z, is assumed to be previously verified or hardcore. M_1 can be diagnosed since it is controlled by x and observed by z, both of which are assumed verified. For each of the remaining unverified modules (M_2, M_3, M_4, M_5) it is not possible to both control and observe it through previously verified modules or hardcore. Hence additional test points are needed. By placing an external observation point B at the output of M_5 this module can be verified since it can be controlled by M_1 and A which have been previously verified. At this stage M_2 can be controlled by M_1 and observed by M_5, both of which are previously verified modules and thus M_2 can be verified. By placing an observation point C at the output of M_3, M_3 can then be verified, following which M_4 can be verified since it can be controlled and observed by M_3 and M_5, both of which have been previously verified.   □

5.4.3 Design of Sequential Circuits with Imbedded Shift Registers

In sequential circuits the problem of fault detection is complicated due to the inability to control and observe memory elements. By adding observation and control points to these signals, as shown in Figure 5.41, the problem essentially reduces to the case of combinational circuits. However, for systems with k memory elements, this requires $2k$ pins. Williams and Angell [40] have proposed a design procedure which accomplishes this objective and only requires two pins.

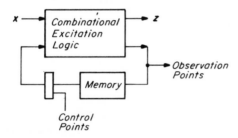

Figure 5.41 Sequential Circuit with Observable and Controllable Feedback Paths

The basic idea is to use a control signal c, and to design the memory element excitation logic so that when $c = 0$, the circuit behaves in its normal manner, but when $c = 1$, the circuit enters a mode in which the memory elements are connected to form a (synchronous) shift register, with the first flip-flop of the register connected directly to an input, and the last flip-flop connected directly to two outputs (or an output and an observation point if the circuit has only one output). For instance, assume the normally designed circuit has n SR flip-flops, defined by state variables $y_1, y_2, \ldots, y_n$, and excitation logic defined by the following equations:

$$\left. \begin{array}{l} S_i = f_i(\mathbf{x,y}) \\ R_i = g_i(\mathbf{x,y}) \end{array} \right\} \quad 1 \le i \le n$$

$$z_j = h_j(\mathbf{x,y}) \qquad 1 \le j \le m \text{ (output lines)}.$$

The shift register realization uses the control signal c and the modified excitation functions

$$S_1 = \bar{c}f_1(x,y) + cx_1$$

$$R_1 = \bar{c}g_1(x,y) + c\bar{x}_1$$

$$S_i = \bar{c}f_i(x,y) + cy_{i-1}$$

$$R_i = \bar{c}g_i(x,y) + c\bar{y}_{i-1} \qquad \Big\} \quad \text{for all } i, 2 \le i \le n$$

$$z_1 = \bar{c}h_1(x,y) + cy_n$$

$$z_2 = \bar{c}h_2(x,y) + c\bar{y}_n$$

where z_2 is an observation point if the circuit has only one output. A common control signal is used for all flip-flops so that either all are in normal mode or all are in testing (shift register) mode. Designed in this manner, the circuit behaves as a shift register when $c = 1$ and normal operation ensues when $c = 0$. Such a circuit has the following desirable properties: (1) it is easily initializable to any desired internal state, and (2) the state of the circuit is easily observable. For a given fault, a test pattern consists of an initial state and an input (not sequence) which, from that initial state, produces an incorrect state or output. Such test patterns can be derived using the procedures considered for combinational circuits. These test patterns can then be used to test the sequential circuit by the following procedure.

Procedure 5.1 *(Testing embedded shift register circuit):*
(1) Set $c = 1$ to switch circuit to shift register mode.
(2) Check operation of shift register.
(3) Select a test pattern and set shift register to desired initial state by sequentially shifting in appropriate inputs.
(4) Set $c = 0$ to return to normal mode.
(5) Apply test pattern input to generate incorrect state (or output) by clocking the flip-flops.
(6) Set $c = 1$ to return to shift register mode.
(7) Shift out final state to detect fault.
(8) Repeat (3)-(7) for all other test patterns.   □

The testing of certain faults in the shift register may present some difficulties but the sequences consisting of n consecutive 0's, n consecutive 1's, and n alternating 0's and 1's will probably detect most such faults.

Procedure 5.1 assumes that each feedback loop contains a memory element. Otherwise, some modifications of the design are necessary to enable the use of combinational test generation procedures. However, in general, a circuit designed in this manner is considerably simpler to test. Steps (3) and (7) of Procedure 5.1 each require n units of time. If the circuit has k inputs and at least $2k$ outputs, it may be modified to have k shift registers of length n/k instead of one shift register of length n. This can be used to speed up the testing procedure, but is limited by the number of circuit inputs and outputs which are available.

REFERENCES

[1] Adham, M., "Diagnosis of Digital Systems," Ph.D. Dissertation, University of Southern California, July 1975.

[2] Anderson, D. A., "Design of Self-Checking Digital Networks Using Coding Technique," University of Illinois Coordinated Science Laboratory, Report R-527, September 1971.

[3] Anderson, D. A. and G. Metze, "Design of Totally Self-Checking Check Circuits for m-out-of-n Codes," *IEEE Transactions on Computers*, Vol. C-22, pp. 263–269, March 1973.

[4] Armstrong, D. B., Friedman, A. D. and P. R. Menon, "Design of Asynchronous Circuits Assuming Unbounded Gate Delays," *IEEE Transactions on Computers*, Vol. C-18, pp. 1110–1120, 1969.

[5] Arnold, T. F., "The Concept of Coverage and Its Effect on the Reliability Model of a Repairable System," *IEEE Transactions on Computers*, Vol. C-22, pp. 251–254, March 1973.

[6] Avizienis, A. et al., "The STAR (Self-Testing and Repairing) Computer: An Investigation of the Theory and Practice of Fault-Tolerant Computer Design," *IEEE Transactions on Computers*, Vol. C-20, pp. 1312-1321, November 1971.

[7] Borgerson, B. R., "A Fail-Softly System for Time-Sharing Use," *Proceedings Fault Tolerant Computing Symposium*, pp. 89–93, 1972.

[8] Bouricius, W. G., Carter, W. C., Jessup, D. C., Schneider, P. R. and A. B. Wadia, "Reliability Modeling for Fault-Tolerant Computers," *IEEE Transactions on Computers*, Vol. C-20, pp. 1306–1311, November 1971.

[9] Carter, W. C. and P. R. Schneider, "Design of Dynamically Checked Computers," *IFIP Proceedings*, Vol. 2, pp. 873–883, 1968.

[10] Diaz, M., Geffory, J. C. and M. Courvoisier, "On-Set Realization of Fail-Safe Sequential Machines," *Proceedings Fault Tolerant Computing Symposium*, pp. 145–149, 1973.

[11] Downing, R. W., Nowak, J. S. and L. S. Tuomenoksa, "No. 1 ESS Maintenance Plan," *Bell System Technical Journal*, Vol. 43, pp. 1961–2019, 1964.

[12] Friedman, A. D., "A New Measure of Digital System Diagnosis," *Proceedings Fault Tolerant Computing Symposium*, pp. 167–170, 1975.

[13] Gaddess, T. G., "Improving the Diagnosability of Modular Combinational Logic by Test Point Insertion," Coordinated Science Lab, University of Illinois, Urbana, Illinois, Report R-409, March 1969.

[14] Gogineni, B., private communication.

[15] Goldberg, J., Levitt, K. N. and R. A. Short, "Techniques for the Realization of Ultra-Reliable Spaceborne Computers," Final Report — Phase I, Project 5580, Stanford Research Institute, Menlo Park, California, September 1966.

[16] Hamming, R. W., "Error Detecting and Error Correcting Codes," *Bell System Technical Journal*, Vol. 29, pp. 147–160, 1950.

[17] Hayes, J. P., "On Modifying Logic Networks to Improve Their Diagnosability," *IEEE Transactions on Computers*, Vol. C-23, pp. 56–63, January 1975.

[18] Hayes, J. P., "On Realizations of Boolean Functions Requiring a Minimal or Near-Minimal Number of Tests," *IEEE Transactions on Computers, Vol.* C-20, pp. 1506–1513, December 1971.

[19] Hayes, J. P. and A. D. Friedman, "Test Point Placement to Simplify Fault Detection," *Proceedings Fault Tolerant Computing Symposium*, pp. 73–78, 1974.

[20] Hopkins, A. L., Jr., and T. B. Smith III, "The Architectural Elements of a Symmetric Fault-Tolerant Multiprocessor," *Proceedings Fault Tolerant Computing Symposium*, pp. 4.2–4.6, 1974.

[21] Keister, W., Ketchledge, R. W., and H. E. Vaughan, "No. 1. ESS: System Organization and Objectives," *Bell System Technical Journal,* Vol. 43, pp. 1831–1844, 1964.

[22] Ko, D., "Self-Checking of Multi-Output Combinational Circuits Using Forced-Parity Technique," USCEE Report 451, Univ. of Southern California, June 1973.

[23] Kolupaev, S. G., "Self-Testing Residue Trees," Stanford Electronics Lab, Stanford University, Technical Report No. 49, August 1973.

[24] Mathur, F. P. and A. Avizienis, "Reliability Analysis and Architecture of a Hybrid Redundant Digital System: Generalized Triple Modular Redundancy with Self-Repair," Spring Joint Computer Conference, *AFIPS Conference Proceedings,* Vol. 36, pp. 375–383, 1970.

[25] Mine, H. and Y. Koga, "Basic Properties and a Construction Method for Fail-Safe Logical Systems," *IEEE Transactions on Electronic Computers,* Vol. EC-16, pp. 282–289, 1967.

[26] Preparata, F. P., Metze, G. and R. T. Chien, "On the Connection Assignment Problem of Diagnosable Systems," *IEEE Transactions on Electronic Computers,* Vol. EC-16. pp. 848–854, 1967.

[27] Reddy, S. M., "Easily Testable Realizations for Logic Functions," *IEEE Transactions on Computers,* Vol. C-21, pp. 1183–1188, November 1972.

[28] Russell, J. D. and C. R. Kime, "System Fault Diagnosis: Closure and Diagnosability with Repair," *IEEE Transactions on Computers,* Vol. C-24, pp. 1078–1089, November 1975.

[29] Saluja, K. K. and S. M. Reddy, "On Minimally Testable Logic Networks," *IEEE Transactions on Computers*, Vol. C-23, pp. 552–554, May 1974.

[30] Sawin, D. H., "Fail-Safe Asynchronous Sequential Machines Using Modified On-Set Realizations," *Proceedings Fault Tolerant Computing Symposium*, pp. 3.7–3.12, 1974.

[31] Sawin, D. W., Makin, G. W., and S. R. Groenig, "Design of Asynchronous Sequential Machines for Fault Detection," *Proceedings Fault Tolerant Computing Symposium*, pp. 170–175, 1972.

[32] Sellers, F. F., Hsiao, M. Y. and L. W. Bearnson, *Error Detecting Logic for Digital Computers*, McGraw-Hill, New York, N. Y., 1968.

[33] Shedletsky, J. J. and E. J. McCluskey, "The Error Latency of a Fault in a Combinational Digital Circuit," *Proceedings Fault Tolerant Computing Symposium*, pp. 210–214, 1975.

[34] Siewiorek, D. P. and E. J. McCluskey, "Switch Complexity in Systems with Hybrid Redundancy," *IEEE Transactions on Computers*, Vol. C-22, pp. 276–282, March 1973.

[35] Siewiorek, D. P. and E. J. McCluskey, "An Iterative Cell Switch Design for Hybrid Redundancy," *IEEE Transactions on Computers*, Vol. C-22, pp. 290–297, March 1973.

[36] Tohma, Y., Ohyama, Y. and R. Zakai, "Realization of Fail-Safe Sequential Machines by Using a k-out-of-n Code," *IEEE Transactions on Computers*, Vol. C-20, pp. 1270–1275, November 1971.

[37] Von Neumann, J., "Probabilistic Logics and the Synthesis of Reliable Organisms from Unrealiable Components," *Automata Studies*, Annals of Math. Studies No. 34, C. E. Shannon and J. McCarthy, eds., Princeton University Press, Princeton, New Jersey, pp. 43–98, 1956.

[38] Wakerly, J. F., "Partially Self-Checking Circuits and Their Use in Performing Logical Operations," Stanford Electronics Lab., Stanford University, Technical Report No. 50, August 1973.

[39] Wensley, J. H., Levitt, K. N. and P. G. Neumann, "A Comparable Study of Architectures for Fault-Tolerance," *Proceedings Fault Tolerant Computing Symposium*, pp. 4.16–4.21, 1974.

[40] Williams, M. J. Y. and J. B. Angell, "Enhancing Testability of Large-Scale Integrated Circuits Via Test Points and Additional Logic," *IEEE Transactions on Computers*, Vol. C-22, pp. 46–60, January 1973.

PROBLEMS

5.1 a) Consider a 6-bit residue code with $m = 3$ with the rightmost two bits being check bits. For each of the following, assuming at most a single bit error, determine if such an error is present and if so which bits might be erroneous.

$$0\ 1\ 0\ 1\ 1\ 0,\ 0\ 1\ 1\ 1\ 1\ 0,\ 0\ 1\ 1\ 0\ 0\ 1$$

b) Consider a 7-bit Hamming single error correction code. For each of the following, assuming at most a single bit error, determine the erroneous bit if any.

$$0\ 1\ 0\ 1\ 1\ 0\ 0,\ 0\ 1\ 0\ 1\ 1\ 0\ 1,\ 0\ 1\ 1\ 1\ 1\ 0\ 1$$

5.2 Consider a residue code and an error which results in the interchange of two successive bits. Prove that all such errors are detected or present a counterexample to this conjecture.

5.3 Prove that the $k/2k$ checker of Figure 5.15 is totally self-checking.

5.4 Consider a residue code and a burst error which results in unidirectional errors in a sequence of k successive bits. Will all such errors be detected?

5.5 Consider a diagnostic graph consisting of a loop of n modules.

a) Prove that such a system is one step t-fault diagnosable only for $t < 2$.

b) Prove that such a system is one step 2/3 fault diagnosable if $n > 6$ by showing that for any fault pattern produced by 2 or fewer faults, at least $n - 3$ modules can be ascertained to be properly functioning under the assumption that at most 2 modules can be faulty.

5.6 Consider a system whose diagnostic graph has 5 nodes $\{0,1,2,3,4\}$ and a branch from i to $(i + 1)$ mod 5 and from i to $(i + 2)$ mod 5 for all i.

a) Prove that such a system is one step 2-fault diagnosable and sequentially 2-fault diagnosable.

b) What is the maximum number of arcs which can be removed from this graph so that it is still one step 2-fault diagnosable, or so that it is still sequentially 2-fault diagnosable?

5.7 a) Derive a Reed-Muller canonical realization of the combinational function $f = x_1 x_2 + \bar{x}_1 x_3 + \bar{x}_2 \bar{x}_3 x_4$.

b) Derive a set of tests to detect all single stuck faults.

c) Compare the actual number of tests required with the bounds of Theorem 5.4.

d) Consider the problem of fault location in such a realization. Specify a procedure to derive a set of tests so as to locate the fault as closely as possible.

5.8 a) For the circuit of Figure 5.42 place a single observation point at the output of G_1, derive a set of tests to detect all single stuck faults and compare with the number of tests required in the original circuit.

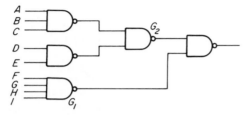

Figure 5.42

b) Repeat if the observation point is placed at the output of G_2 instead of G_1.

5.9 Realize the state table of Figure 5.43 with a control input c so as to act as a shift register when $c = 1$, assuming SR-flip-flops. Derive a diagnostic test for such a circuit.

	x	
	0	1
1	2,0	4,1
2	3,1	1,0
3	3,1	2,0
4	1,1	4,0

Figure 5.43

5.10 Consider the following design of a k-bit equality checker $(k \geq 3)$ to determine the equivalence of two words $(a_1, a_2, \ldots, a_k)$ and $(a'_1, a'_2, \ldots, a'_k)$. The circuit has two outputs f_k and g_k defined by the recursive equations

$$f_k = f_{k-1}b_k + g_{k-1}a_k$$

$$g_k = f_{k-1}a_k + g_{k-1}b_k$$

where $b_k = \bar{a}'_k$ and f_2 and g_2 are as defined in Figure 5.17. Verify that this circuit is totally self checking for all single stuck faults.

5.11 a) For the hybrid redundant switching network of Figure 5.23, specify logical realizations for the circuits A_1, A_2, A_3, A_4, A_5.

b) Show that the module M_i is connected to the jth voter input if and only if M_i is fault free and exactly $j - 1$ of the modules $M_1, M_2, \ldots, M_{i-1}$ are fault free. Thus the occurrence of a fault in a module M_p may cause a module M_k, $k > p$, to be switched from the jth voter input to the $(j - 1)$st voter input.

5.12 Prove that the conditions of Theorem 5.3 are not sufficient for one-step t-fault diagnosability.

INDEX